Feng Shui That Rocks the House

Shake Up the Energy and Get the Life You Want

Master Denise Liotta Dennis

Ω

Moon Gate Press

The Woodlands, Texas USA

This book is dedicated to Linda Dennis, my beloved sister, best friend and talented writer.

Feng Shui That Rocks the House
Shake Up the Energy and Get the Life You Want

First Edition, First Printing

Photography & Illustrations
Illustrations and charts created by Denise Liotta Dennis. Clipart and stock photos are from Microsoft Word. Photos provided by Unsplash Pixabay. Credit and thanks to the following photographers featured throughout the book: Alesia Kazantceva, Alexander Pemberton, Andrew Neel, Anne Edgar, Anne Edgar, Arunas Naujokas, Benjamin Child, Brooke Cagle, Carly Rae-Hobbins, Chi N Ph M, DC Lovensky, Gul Kurtaran, Jacob Culp, Joanna Nix, Jon Tyson, Amanda Weightman, Lee Campbell, Logan Nolin, Marc A. Sporys, Meghan Holmes, Linda Dennis, Mia Baker, Nathan Fertig, Neonbrand, Cristian Logan, Justyn Warner, Mubariz Mehdizadeh, Oskar Wimmerman, Rishab Lamichane, Taylor Grote, Pablo Heimplatz, Pavel Badrtdinov, Robert Nyman, Seth Reese, Sefan Stefancik, Sweet Ice Cream Photography, Tanja Heffner, John Salvino, Tina Gabes, Toa Heftiba, Jamie Street, and William Stitt.

Cover/Book Designer: Denise Liotta Dennis; front cover photo by Yann Maignan (Unsplash) and back cover photo by Kari Shea (Unsplash).

Published by Moon Gate Press (713-897-1719) and Create Space (www.createspace.com)

ISBN-13: 978-1986762892

Published in the United States of America
April 2018

CONTENTS

Introduction

Feng Shui is an ancient Chinese science that was used to secure prosperity, health, relationships, and life in general. Home sites and villages were selected so people would, not just survive, but thrive.

The media often creates a lot of buzz around Feng Shui. Particularly when, movies stars, Oprah, famous business people like Bill Gates, Sir Richard Branson and even President Trump are said to be long-time fans. But what is it exactly, and how does it work? Is it moving things around in your home or business? Is it painting walls red or placing crystals in the window? Is it a religion? Is Feng Shui all about clearing your clutter? Or is it interior design that looks and feels Zen.

All of these questions and more will be answered about this ancient art/science. A Chinese invention to improve the quality of life, Feng Shui certainly has staying power. Dating back about 4,000 years, it still has applications for modern-day living.

Like many ancients, the Chinese were sky-watchers. They observed the cycles of, not only nature, but the cosmos. While it may seem odd to us, they came to understand that our entire universe is comprised of energy. In our present day, there are numerous studies on quantum physics and this idea of 'everything is energy' is more widely accepted. Human beings are, in fact, pure energy. As it turns out, so is *everything* in our universe including planet Earth. This idea is a fundamental and driving force behind the principles of Feng Shui.

After a rather long history, the practice of Feng Shui developed many systems and methods. All had a simple goal in mind, create superior living where people could thrive. The focus of this book is regarding one of those systems.
The Eight Mansions method is people-oriented. There are other systems whose focus is on the time dimension aspect, the exterior environment or the building itself.

In Eight Mansions you will find a simple system, yet one that can produce profound results and really rock the house! In order to accomplish this, get comfortable with the idea that direction is one of the biggest secrets to Feng Shui. You'll need to take a compass direction of your home. This information is vital in order to shake up the energy and get the life you want. A personal 'magic number' or Life-Gua number is assigned to you in the Eight Mansions method. That number reveals all sorts of important clues as how to set up your home. Eight Mansions can also be used to gain support in the workplace and help boost your career.

Feng Shui can help improve every area of life that is essential to happiness; prosperity, health and relationships. By making some simple adjustments, you can turn the tides of fortune and opportunities.

Chapter One
Feng Shui Concepts

"A book that is tightly shut is but a block of paper." ~**Chinese Proverb**

Feng Shui is not a religion, Zen design, coin-chocked frogs, bamboo flutes, picture frames, crystals hanging in the window, mirrors, popular tchotkies or part of the New-Age movement.

What Feng Shui Is and Is Not

The origins of Feng Shui are exceptionally ancient and its concepts of 'better living' can be traced to the Tang Dynasty. However, oral tradition places it much earlier. This secret knowledge, once obscure to Westerners, is more popular than ever. Even after being in practice for thousands of years, Feng Shui is still viable. In fact, the principles and concepts of Feng Shui are needed as never before. The uncertain and often unstable times in which we live could benefit greatly from its wisdom.

The story of how it came to be, is entrenched in ancient philosophies and acute observations that formed the great Chinese culture. The translation of Feng Shui is 'wind' and 'water'. In literal terms, this refers to the topography of the land, the mountains, valleys, and natural water features whose flow, direction, and size, are influenced by the constant interaction of these two powerful forces on earth. To the Chinese people, Feng Shui is a mystical practice that blends ancient wisdom with a body of knowledge that provide guidelines for life's different situations.

It is best to experiment when applying Feng Shui to your home or office. Pay attention to the transformations in personal prosperity, opportunities, relationships and other areas of your life. Is your health improving? Are you attracting better relationships or improving the ones you have? Are opportunities for more wealth or career luck showing up? In short, are things getting better in your life?

Sadly, Feng Shui has fallen in and out of favor throughout its long history. General Mao was the last Chinese leader to forbid its use. As a result, Feng Shui masters were forced to flee to Hong Kong *(then ruled by the British)*, Malaysia, Singapore and Taiwan. It is in these locations that the most sophisticated forms of Feng Shui are practiced today. Americans have rarely heard of Classical Feng Shui, even though high profile billionaires and major institutions such as Oprah, Steve Wynn, Donald Trump, Bill Gates, Wells Fargo and Chase Banks use it. Some of these illustrious people and institutions got their first introduction in Hong Kong, which is often called the 'unofficial capital of Classical Feng Shui', while doing business there.

Being born Chinese, either in China, America or elsewhere does not guarantee knowledge of this ancient science. An extremely water-down version of Feng Shui arrived in America during the 1970's. The Asian masters refer to this as faux Feng Shui. This false Feng Shui is featured in 90% of the books and at least 50% on the internet. Therefore, it is difficult to find clear information about Feng Shui's valuable principles. Added to the mix of confusion, is Chinese cultural superstitions which have nothing to do with Feng Shui at all.

Further, just to be clear, Feng Shui is not a religious practice or derived from a religion. It is not a charming Eastern philosophy. It is not magic or rooted in the New Age movement. It has nothing to do with your cat, dog, car, Zen design, phone number, house number, chandeliers, or food arrangement. Westernized Feng Shui was simply the successful commercialization of an ancient, geomantic science. Real Feng Shui considers:

- The exact orientation of the building
- The birthdates of the occupants
- The design layout or floor plan
- Shape of the house or building
- The surrounding environment (natural or man-made) such roads, canals, mountains, swimming pools, electrical towers, lakes, highways, slopping land, high-rise structures, streams, graveyards, alleys, and nearby parks.

There is so much confusion surrounding Feng Shui, it's hard to keep it all straight. Once it was introduced to the non-Asian world, it was either embraced or dished. No matter the sentiment, Feng Shui is either authentic or faux/commercial.

Authentic, traditional Feng Shui will NOT have any of following ideas or with a commercial bent to sell tchotkies:

Westernized Feng Shui is often linked to the Eight Life Aspirations or Black Sect (aka Black Hat Sect Tantric Buddhist or BHTB), brought over to America in the 1970's.

They divide the home into eight 'life stations/aspirations' such as career, wealth, knowledge, family, marriage, children and helpful people.

The location of the front door is always north, even if it isn't. This is how they allocate the eight aspirations of life.

They are heavy on cures such as mirrors, crystals, bamboo flutes, red ribbons, fu dogs, coin-chocked frog, fish tanks, lighting, paintings/pictures, bells, and plants. These types of Feng Shui cures were created in order to sell 'things'.

Feng Shui's Core Principles

Feng Shui's basic core theories are how the ancients viewed the universe and energy. Virtually, every book on Feng Shui introduces the famous precepts of the Ba Gua, five elements, yin-yang theory, Luo Shu and He Tu. This often leaves the reader confused as how to apply them.

These tools are *principles* and not stand alone formulas or techniques. If you have several books on Feng Shui, you've already been introduced to the basic concepts. However, you may want to skim over these basic building blocks of Feng Shui even if you are somewhat familiar. If this is your very first Feng Shui book, take a few minutes to peruse these important ideas. This chapter of the book is *not for implementation*, rather to deepen your appreciation of Feng Shui and its roots.

There continues to be a certain mysticism surrounding the practice of Feng Shui. Understanding its many principles and canons requires the acceptance of fundamental theories about the universe. This may, at first glance, seem alien in the context of how the modern world works.

At any rate, Feng Shui is part of Chinese metaphysics which is a huge body of knowledge that is comprised of five major categories of study. All five categories (aka the 'five arts') have their foundation in the same energy tools [the two Ba Guas, five elements, yin-yang and so forth] and then develop into different branches of study. We'll start with the five arts and then briefly discuss them, one by one.

The Five Metaphysical Arts (Wu Shu)

Classical Feng Shui is just one of the five (5) main art-sciences of Chinese metaphysics. Deeply rooted in the I Ching and the Tao, these philosophical tenets—mountain, medicine, divination, destiny, and physiognomy—are the origins of the Chinese culture developed over 5,000 years. It is said that if you are able to master just one of these studies it would be a significant life-accomplishment.

Mountain (Shan or Xian Xue): This category encompasses philosophy (e.g. the teachings of the fourth-century B.C. philosophers Lao Tzu and Zhuang Zi), Taoism, martial arts, Qi Gong, Tai Chi Chuan, meditation, healing, and diet. It also includes the study of Alchemy—the science of prolonging life through specific rituals and exercises, which are deeply rooted in Taoism.

Medicine (Yi): The Chinese follow an integrated, holistic, and curative approach to medicine and healing such as acupuncture, herbal prescriptions, and massage.

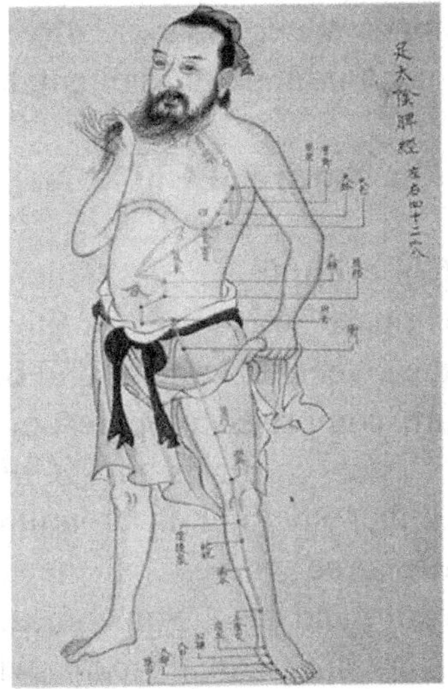

Divination (Po): The Chinese are acknowledged for their intuitive skills and abilities to read and interpret symbols. The divination techniques of Da Liu Ren, Tai Yi Mystical Numbers, Qi Men, Mei Hua Xin Yi (Plum Blossom oracle) employ numbers to predict everything from wars or missing persons, to the details of one's past and future.

Destiny (Ming): Most forms of Chinese augury seek to interpret fate and determine the timing of life events. The ancient sages devoted much time and research to this study. The most popular methods of Chinese fortune-telling include Zi Wei Dou Shu (Purple Star Astrology) and BaZi (literally means 'eight characters' but is also commonly known as the Four Pillars of Destiny), both of which examine a person's destiny and potential based on their date and time of birth. A complimentary form of Ming is the Science of Divination (Bu Shi), which is analogous to the mathematics of probability.

Physiognomy (Xiang Xue): Grandmaster Yap Cheng Hai refers to this category as *Sow,* and it involves making predictions based on the image, form, and features of the landscape, the human face and palms, architecture, and gravesites. Feng Shui is the fortune-telling of a building by rendering an accurate observation of the structure's appearance, shape, direction, and other surrounding environmental features.

The Nature of Chi

Chi simply means energy. The ancient Chinese was one of the first cultures to discover that humans and our entire universe are comprised of pure energy. Modern-day science confirms this. Chi also spelled *qi*, (either spelling is pronounced *chee*) is the life-force energy of the universe, heaven, earth, and man. Sometimes it is also referred to as the *cosmic breath,* which is present in every living and non-living entity. It can be auspicious, inauspicious, or benign. Chi is the life-force energy that pervades mankind's existence. It is the unseen force that moves through the human body and the environment. Feng Shui's main objective is to attract and harness auspicious energy to support people. It is energy that determines the shape and form of the landscape as well as the vitality of all living things. The famous Tai Chi symbol, which resembles two interlocking fish demonstrates the polarity of energy which is either yin (female) or yang (male).

The Eight Guas or Trigrams

The Guas, also known as Trigrams, date back to Chinese antiquity. These important symbols give a macro, inclusive perspective of our universe, energy and direction. Each of the eight Guas is comprised of three lines either solid or broken. The broken lines indicate yin/female energy while the solid lines represent yang/male energy. The three lines also represent the cosmology of heaven, earth and man. The famous Ba Gua includes all eight trigrams; "Ba" means *eight*, and "Gua" means the *result of divination.*

The eight Guas, in addition to representing the eight directions, have several layers of information that becomes useful in assessing the energy of land, homes or buildings. The Chinese related this information to everyday life, resulting in each Gua representing the father, mother, eldest son, eldest daughter and so forth. In the end, each Gua represents yin or yang energy, relates to a family member, an element, a body part, a possible illness, a season, a number, human personality types, and direction. Additionally, they have numerous interpretations and slight distinctions that can be overwhelming for a novice of Feng Shui. All the same, these implications and interpretations have great significance in Feng Shui and other Chinese metaphysical studies. The eight Guas are Kan, Gen, Chen, Xun, Li, Kun, Dui, and Chien representing North, Northeast, East, Southeast, South, Southwest, West and Northwest respectively.

In modern-day language, the trigrams are the eight binary numbers of 111, 110, 101, 100, 011, 010, 001 and 000. The *solid lines* represent the 1 digit, while the *broken lines* represent the digit 0; they are read from the bottom up. It's been said that the Chinese were the first to use binary arithmetic. Binary codes are the 'language' of computers.

The Eight Trigrams (Guas)
And Binary Codes

111 The "Creative" and Heaven Family Member: The Father Element: *Big* Metal Represents the Northwest Color: Gold, Silver, White Body Part: Head & Lungs Luo Shu Number: 6	000 The "Receptive" Family Member: Mother Element: Earth Represents the Southwest Color: Brown and Yellow Body Part: Stomach, Abdomen Luo Shu Number: 2
100 "Arousing" and Thunder Family Member: Oldest Son Element: Big Wood Represents the East Color: Jade Green Body Part: Liver, Feet Luo Shu Number: 3	011 "Gentle" and the Wind Family Member: Oldest Daughter Element: *Small* Wood Represents the Southeast Color: Green Body Part: Liver, Thighs, Buttocks Luo Shu Number: 4
010 The "Abysmal" and Water Family Member: Middle Son Element: Water Represents the North Color: Black, Blue Body Part: Kidneys, Blood Luo Shu Number: 1	101 "Clinging" and Fire Family Member: Middle Daughter Element: Fire Represents the South Color: Red, Purple, Orange, Pink Body Part: Heart, Eyes Luo Shu Number: 9
001 "Stillness" and Earth Family Member: Youngest Son Element: *Mountain* Earth Represents the Northeast Color: Brown, Yellow Body Part: Bones, Hands/Fingers Luo Shu Number: 8	110 "Joyful" and the Marsh Family Member: Youngest Daughter Element: *Small* Metal Represents the West Color: Gold, Silver, White Body Part: Mouth, Throat, Lungs Luo Shu Number: 7

Tien Di Ren

*"**Heaven Luck** is the boat given to you by God. **Earth Luck** is the wind that fills the sails and the currents of the ocean. **Man Luck** is the way in which you use the wind and the currents to steer your boat."*
–Grandmaster Yap Cheng Hai

The three types of luck (opportunities), known as Tien Di Ren, are heaven luck, Earth Luck and Man Luck. Each one of these categories will champion you in a very different way. This aspect of Feng Shui is called the Cosmic Trinity. In other words all three areas will influence your life and living space.

Heaven Luck (Tien)
This category of luck is often referred to as destiny or karma. The Chinese believe that what goes around comes around; that past deeds, for good or evil, will visit you again in this life. They also contend that this area of luck is fixed and may not be influenced; it counts as 1/3 of your overall luck and opportunities in life.

Earth Luck (Di)
This category is the dominion of Feng Shui. If your home site and living space has auspicious and harmonious energy, you will reap the rewards. Additionally, life will support your efforts, goals, relationships, health and prosperity if this aspect is taken care of. In Earth-luck, you have total control and it can exceed the normal 1/3 associated with it if you have superior energy at home and work. Grandmaster Yap purports that it can be raised to 2/3.

Man Luck (Ren)
This category of luck is another area you have total control over. This is created by you own efforts and the choices you make in life. This may include your education, morals, hard work, beliefs and your ability to seize and exploit good opportunities.

Chapter Two
Feng Shui Origins

"Better to light a candle than to curse the darkness." **~Chinese Proverb**

Feng Shui dates back more than 4,000 years. It is deeply rooted in the I Ching which was authored by Confucius, King Wen, Duke of Chou and the sage, Fu Xi.

The He Tu and Luo Shu

These two very distinct mathematical diagrams representing universal energy are so ancient and intrinsic in the Chinese culture that its people are often referred to as the He-Luo culture. Together they form the foundation of Chinese philosophy and are the genesis of Classical Feng Shui. These famous diagrams are frequently mentioned in ancient Chinese literature and are shrouded by legend and mystery. There are a series of lines connected with black and white dots in both diagrams. Most scholars believe the He Tu chronicles the cycle of birth, while the Luo Shu represents the process of death: yin and yang.

Ancient lore surrounding the He Tu began with the reign of the shaman king Fu Xi, who was born in the 29th century B.C. witnessed a mythical dragon-horse bearing strange, unusually patterned markings on its back emerging from the mighty Yellow River. This design became known as the He Tu (pronounced *hur too*). As Fu Xi examined these markings (see illustration), valuable information pertaining to cosmic laws of the universe was revealed. The dots (black are yin and white are yang) of the He Tu illustrate several concepts; including direction, the five elements of Feng Shui and the flow of chi.

Following Fu Xi's life, succeeding scholars meticulously preserved and passed down the mysteries of the He Tu. Even today, it is found in written texts and ancient scrolls which pervade Eastern ideologies, including traditional Chinese medicine and some of the initial principles of Feng Shui. The five element theory (water, wood, fire, earth, and metal) have its basis in the He Tu. These elements indentify, interpret and predict natural phenomena. Later to arrive on the scene would be the Guas or trigrams. Therefore, the theories and principles of the He Tu gave birth to the first Ba Gua, known as the Early Heaven Ba Gua (Xien Tien Ba Gua).

The Luo Shu is also surrounded by legend and myth. Emperor Yu of the Xia Dynasty, while sitting next the River Lo saw a giant turtle emerge in or around 2100 B.C. It too, had a pattern and series of black and white dots on its back. The Luo Shu is a nine square grid containing nine numbers. Each of the nine numbers represents a trigram, body organ, family member, direction, or element and it is either male or female energy. Interestingly, no matter which way you add the numbers in the grid they total 15. The Luo Shu is often referred to as the Magic Square of 15. This arrangement of numbers became part of the Later Heaven Ba Gua (LHB). The Luo Shu is used extensively in all methods and applications of Classical Feng Shui.

The Luo Shu and He Tu are coded maps that represent the cosmology of heaven and earth; they are energy tools which are used to assess buildings, living spaces and land sites. These ancient oracles are considered the backbone of Chinese metaphysics. Unlocking their mysteries takes many years of study, contemplation and a learned teacher. Please note that South is placed at the top, not North in the He Tu and Luo Shu images. This may take some getting used to.

The Five Elements (Wu Xing)

All categories of Chinese metaphysics explain the world and the universe, in terms of the five elements. As with most brilliant discoveries made by humans, nature served as the inspiration. In ancient China, they paid close attention to the predicable cycles of energy—fire burns wood, and metal comes from the Earth. By associating this information in everyday life and events, the Five Element theory was created.

The Chinese knew that energy was part of everything. Therefore, by placing energy into five different categories offered a viable solution in which to assess their interaction. These five categories, or five phases of energy are known as Wu Xing. The five elements are metal (jin-literally the word for gold), wood (mu), water (shui), fire (ho), and earth (tu). Each element is a representation of matter and energy as it coalesces from one form to the next. The Five Element theory simply elucidates the relationship among different types of energy. It is understood as both figurative and literal in Feng Shui applications.

The premise of the Five Elements is used in every study of Chinese metaphysics, Feng Shui, astrology, traditional Chinese medicine, and martial arts. If you wish to master Feng Shui, you must master the Five Elements. The Five Elements have three cycles—productive, weakening, and controlling.

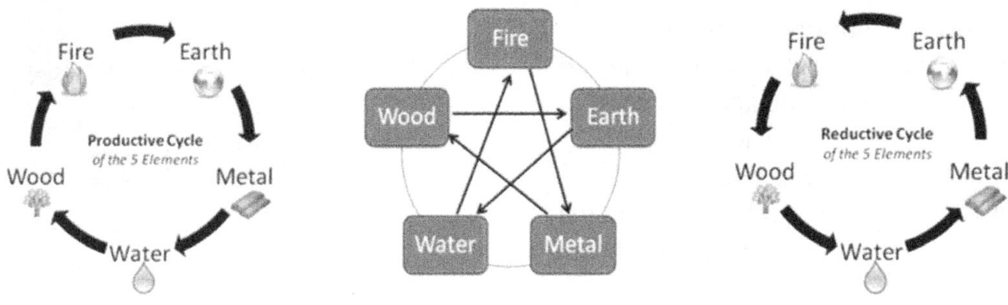

Productive Cycle: It represents the productive force that drives the smooth flow of events in their natural order. This important cycle produces or gives birth to something. Wood feeds fire. Fire produces ash and creates earth. Earth gives birth to metal. Metal melts into a fluid and becomes water, which in turn produces wood.

The Weakening/Reductive Cycle: This cycle represents the retarding force that inhibits and reverses the natural flow of events. This process is the reverse of the productive cycle, because what we give birth to weakens us. Wood stokes fire, therefore, fire weakens wood. Fire generates ash and creates earth, therefore, earth weakens fire. Earth produces metal, therefore, metal weakens earth. Metal melts to a fluid and produces water, therefore, water weakens metal. Water produces wood, therefore, wood weakens water.

The Controlling Cycle: This cycle describes conflict. Constructive conflict is referred to as controlling, while destructive conflict is called killing energy. This process can conquer, control or destroy. Water extinguishes fire, fire melts metal, and metal cuts wood. Wood, in the form of plants or tree roots, controls the Earth by breaking it apart or keeping it together. Earth is big enough to hold water—without earth water would have no boundary.

The Two Ba Guas

Likely the second most recognized image after the Tai Chi symbol is the Ba Gua; however most are not aware that there are two. The Ba Gua literally appears in all Feng Shui books; it is an octagonal map that depicts the eight trigrams. The two Ba Guas are the Early Heaven Ba Gua—Fu Xi or Xien Tien Ba Gua and Later Heaven Ba Gua (Ho Tien or Wen Wang Ba Gua). Both are used in the practice of Classical Feng Shui as all formulas, methods, and techniques are born from the two arrangements of the Guas.

The Early Heaven Ba Gua (EHB), which dates back approximately 6,000 years, depicts the polarities in nature. It reflects an ideal world of harmony in which chi is in a constant, perfect state of polarization. The eight Guas, or trigrams, create a conceptual model that marks the changes in energy. The Early Heaven Ba Gua, representing a 'perfect' world, can be commonly seen over doorways to repel negative energy. It is used extensively in Westernized styles of Feng Shui. It has more profound implications and uses in Classical Feng Shui as it is the basis of complex formulas.

The Later Heaven Ba Gua (*Ho Tien* or *Wen Wang Ba Gua),* was the brilliant work of King Wen, a Chou Dynasty ruler who elaborated on Fu Xi's earlier diagrams. This

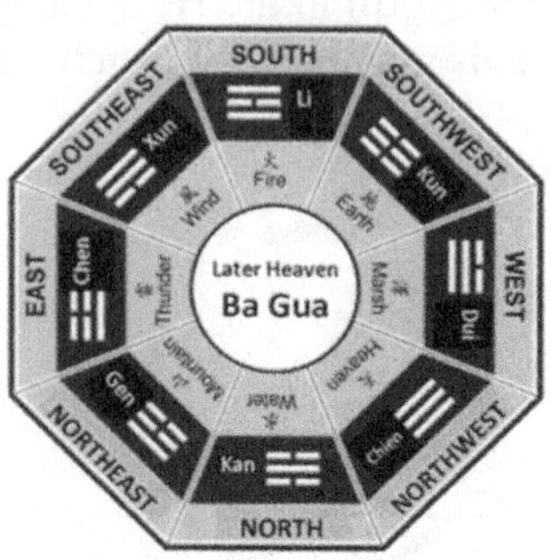

arrangement was done to represent the cyclical forces of nature. The Later Heaven Ba Gua (LHB) describes the patterns of environmental changes. Unlike Earlier Heaven Ba Gua, the LHB is dynamic, not static. It represents the ever-changing structure of the universe and the circular nature of life.

Many Feng Shui applications
stem from the understanding of the Later Heaven Ba Gua. For instance, the Luo Shu is the numerical representation of the Later Heaven Ba Gua. Note that South is placed at the top of the images, not North.

The Chinese Luo Pan

Hundreds of years before the Europeans, the ancient Chinese discovered the magnetic compass. There is an intriguing legend about how they acquired this enormous gift as part of their culture—it's the ancient legend of the *Warrior-Goddess of the Nine Heavens*. When China's first ruler, the Yellow Emperor Huangdi (2698 to 2598 BC), was asleep one night, there appeared a bright light from heaven in which the goddess emerged.

She held in her hand a 9 by 8 inch jade box. The Yellow Emperor received the jade box from the goddess and found that it contained a magic scroll written on dragon skin. It is said that by following the secrets written on the 'dragon scroll', the Emperor defeated the evil wizard (Chi You) in the famous Battle of Zhuolu.

Thus began the start of the great Han Chinese civilization. Other stories tell about Huangdi's unique invention, a compass cart which leads to victory. Either way, the compass/Luo Pan soon became the quintessential tool of the Feng Shui master.

Throughout its illustrious and long history, the Luo Pan has been redesigned and refined many times over so that it would align with the latest discoveries relating to landforms, techniques, and directional energy. There are two standard types of Luo Pans—San He and San Yuan—designed to include formulas of these two main disciplines of Classical Feng Shui.

The third standard Luo Pan is the Chung He, which combines the most important information of the San He and San Yuan Luo Pans. The purpose of the Luo Pan is the same as a conventional compass—to precisely locate direction. However, the Luo Pan contains some very important differences.

A typical compass may display four or eight directions. A Luo Pan divides up the 360° into 24 sectors. This is derived by dividing the forty-five degrees of the eight directions into three, fifteen degree increments (3x 8=24).

This is very fundamental in Classical Feng Shui, and this ring on the Luo Pan is known as the 24 Mountain ring (not actual mountains, it's just a term).

The Luo Pan is an impressive and beautiful instrument, truly a work of art, and well worth the several hundred dollars it commands. Here are the three types of Luo Pans:

San Yuan Luo Pan*:* Used in the Flying Stars and the Xuan Kong systems, the San Yuan Luo Pan is readily indentified by the 64 hexagrams of the I Ching ring. It has only one 24 Mountain ring. The first ring of this Luo Pan is always the Later Heaven Ba Gua arrangement of trigrams.

San He Luo Pan: The San He Luo Pan, used for San He (aka San Hup) formulas and schools, is easily identified by its *three* 24 Mountain rings. These rings are used to measure direction, mountains, and water as each of these elements has distinctly different energy. However, these rings also relate to the three harmonies associated with this branch of Classical Feng Shui.

Chung He Luo Pan: Also spelled, or referred to as Zong He, Zhung He, or Chong He. This Luo Pan is an amalgamation of the San He and San Yuan compasses. This is a great instrument for practitioners who employ both systems. Though some rings have been eliminated for size considerations, all essential rings are intact.

This extraordinary instrument is often called the 'universe on a plate' by Feng Shui masters and practitioners.

For more information on the Luo Pan and its history, refer to Dr. Stephen Skinner's book entitled *Guide to the Feng Shui Compass*. Thus far, it is the most comprehensive book ever written on the subject.

Chapter Three
Eight Mansions' History and Famous Manuals

"To the mind that is still, the whole world surrenders."~**Lao Tzu**

The Eight Mansions system dates back to the Tang Dynasty. While there were several popular styles back in the day, there were two that survived to present. They are the Eight House Bright Mirror and the Golden Star Classic.

The two most popular styles of Feng Shui for the interiors of homes/buildings, is Eight Mansions and Flying Stars. While Eight Mansions is not as complex as Flying Stars, it is amazing[1]. The Eight Mansions system's focus is on the *people* aspect, while Flying Stars' on the *structure*.

When the Eight Mansions formula is applied correctly, it can bring dazzling prospects for love and romance, business opportunities, health, promotions at work, flourishing investments and money-luck. It can help identify negative energy, which will be apparent when people suffer from disease, poor health, a crippling divorce, bad relationships, accidents, disastrous events and bankruptcy. In addition, it is the *only* system which has a 'personality type' aspect which is extremely useful for home and working relationships.

Classical Feng Shui systems, including Eight Mansions, are all compass-based methods. Which means you'll need to take a compass direction of certain things in your space. This is why compass-based methods are more powerful than the one-size-fits-all types—they are accurate and specific to you and your unique space. Although Eight Mansions concerns itself with both direction and location, direction is the most important.

In order to really shake up the chi and get the life you want, you must be open minded to the fact that direction will influence your luck and opportunities. It may not sound logical, but by nature, Feng Shui is a metaphysical science. So, if you want to change things for the better, relax into the idea that you'll be arranging your space using specific degrees and directions.

ജ്ജ

Eight Mansions has five aspects: The Magic Life-Gua Number; East and West Groups; 4 Good and 4 Bad Directions; Advanced Eight Mansions; and 8 Personality types.

ജ്ജ

[1] Refer to *The Secrets of Mastering Flying Stars Feng Shui*, also by the author.

History and Famous Eight Mansions Manuals

Interestingly enough, the first book to introduce Eight Mansions to the public was *Applied Pa-Kua and Lo Shu Feng Shui* by Lillian Too in collaboration with Grandmaster Yap Cheng Hai (my teacher); this was in 1993. In this book, the author retells the story of how Master Yap spent three years unlocking the secrets from a tattered, antique manual. This book was copied from a volume originally written during the Chien Lung period of the Chin Dynasty by a Feng Shui Master from Southern China. While studying with Master Yap, he told his students many times, how fortunate he was to have received several, handwritten original texts from his four teachers and he treasured them greatly.

Master Yap used the *Golden Star Classic* (Jin Guang Dou Lin Jing) style of Eight Mansions and was a huge fan of this system. However, he practiced it much differently than other masters. It was the first formula he taught in his world-famous classes (Eight Mansions in Chinese is *Pa Chai* also spelled *Ba Zhai*).

He would humorously demonstrate the power of the formula and bring the point home by saying:

"How are you going to help the homeless person on the street, change his bed or door? He doesn't have a door! But if you have him sleep to his best direction, maybe someone will come along and offer him a job."

This is why he loved this system, *everyone* can benefit with just a little information, even someone in dire straits. While the system is wildly popular in Southeast Asia, Western societies around the world weren't really familiar with it. In the early 90's, books on Feng Shui, of any kind in English were rare indeed. While Eight Mansions is more widespread now, many still shrug it off as too simplistic to have any real impact on your Feng Shui. Not so. While the system *is* simple, it's capable of delivering profound results. There are many layers and applications that make it rich and viable. If you wish to get a full experience of Classical Feng Shui, you must factor-in the Eight Mansions system.

Remember, the primary objective of Feng Shui is to determine whether the energy will support people in their homes and workplace or not. Classical Feng Shui is traditionally practiced by combining several systems at once, however Eight Mansions can be implemented as a stand-alone application. This is the precise focus of this book. At some other time, you can implement all systems together for a more comprehensive review of your home or office. Without a doubt, you will be delighted at how a few simple changes can change your life.

Eight Mansions dates back hundreds of years but is not part of the *Eight Life Aspirations* of Western Feng Shui. You will see very soon, there is no 'universal' wealth corner, marriage corner, or fame area that fits everyone. You'll have your own *personal directions* to activate these life areas.

Famous Works on Eight Mansions Feng Shui

This amazing system dates back to the Tang Dynasty (960-1279 AD). Three representative books on Eight Mansion were mentioned in the *History of the Song Dynasty*:

1. **The Yellow Emperor's Classic of BaZhai** (Huang-Di BaZhai Jing)
2. **The Classic of BaZhai According to the King of Southern Huai (**Huai-Nan-Wang Jianji BaZhai Jing**)**
3. **The BaZhai of Old Man Yellow Stone (**Huang-Shi-Gong BaZhai

After the Song Dynasty, more Eight Mansions schools continued to prosper. Eventually, eight styles were developed and the books describing the system and formulas are:

1. **An Abstract on Yang Houses** (Yang Zhai Cuo-Yao)
2. **The Great Achievements of Yang Houses** (Yang Zhai Da Cheng)
3. **The Golden Star Classic** aka The Big Dipper Casting Golden Light Classic (Jin-Guang Dou Lin Jing also spelled Kam Kwong Dou Lam King
4. **The Ten Books of Yang Houses** (Yang Zhai Shi Shu)
5. **The Complete Anthology of Yang Houses** (Yang Zhai Ji Cheng)
6. **The Three Requirements of Yang Houses** (Yang Zhai San Yao)
7. **Eight House Bright Mirror** (Pa Chai Ming Jing)
8. **A Comparison of Yang Houses** (Yang Zhai Ai Yiang Pian)

The two that immerged as the most popular are The Golden Star Classic and Eight House Bright Mirror. The very popular book The Complete Idiot's Guide to Feng Shui features the style of Eight House Bright Mirror. This book is based on The *Golden Star Classic* which I learned directly from Grandmaster Yap Cheng Hai (GMY). In order to really rock your house using Eight Mansions, you will need to start by getting your Life-Gua number. Let's see how that is achieved in the next chapter.

Chapter Four
Your Magic Life-Gua Number

"Better a diamond with a flaw than a pebble without."~**Confucius**

Calculating Your Magic Life-Gua Number
Using the Chart

According to this Feng Shui system, you will be influenced in positive and negative ways by the eight directions: four will support you and four won't. The lucky directions will augment wealth and money luck, health, good relationships, and stability. The other four can set into motion divorce, bankruptcy, betrayals, lawsuits, cancer, and so forth. The idea is to use and activate your good directions and diminish the negative ones. Before you can begin using this great system, you will need to determine your personal Life-Gua number.

To find your personal Life-Gua number, refer to Eight Mansions chart on page 20. Make sure you are in the right column as there is one for males and one for females. There is a specific calculation to arrive at this number, but I've included the quick reference chart for ease. If you were born prior to February 4th in any given year, use the previous year to get your Life-Gua number.[2] For example, if you were born January 28, 1970, use the previous year 1969 to find the correct Life Gua number.

Calculating Your Personal Life Gua Number
Using the Formulas

If you wish to calculate the Life-Guas using the formulas, they are as follows. The formulas differ for males and females. Check the chart for accuracy.

I. Eight Mansions Formula for MALES

(Males will subtract from either 10 or 9)

Formula for those born *before* 2000: Add the last two digits of your birth year until you reach a single digit. Subtract that number from 10. If you end up with 5, you will take the 2 Gua number. If you were born before February 4th in any given year, use the previous year. Zero always takes the energy of the 9.

Male example 1: Born *January 2, 1980* will use the previous year, 1979. Add 7 + 9 = 16.

1+6= 7 Now subtract 7 - 10 = 3. This man is a 3 Gua.

Male example 2: Born *June 21, 1962*. Add 6 + 2 = 8. Now subtract 10 - 8 =2. This man is an 2 Gua.

Formula for those born in 2000 and *after*: Add the last two digits of your birth year and add them together until you reach a single digit. Subtract that number from 9. If you end up with 5, you will take the 2 Gua number. If you were born before February 4 in any given year, use the previous year.

Male example 3: Born *September 27, 2000.* Add 0 + 0= 0. The zero takes the 9. This boy is a 9 Gua.

Male example 4: Born *October 12, 2004.* Add 0 + 4 = 4. Now subtract 9- 4= 5. This boy is a 2 Gua; there is no 5 Gua in this system, a male 5 takes the 2 Gua.

[2] In Feng Shui, the Chinese solar calendar is used exclusively. Additionally, the New Year usually begins on February 4th. On rare occasions, it starts on the 3rd or 5th.

II. Eight Mansions Formula for FEMALES

(Females will add either 5 or 6)

Formula for those born *before* 2000: Add the last two digits of your birth year until you reach a single digit. Add 5 to that number. If you end up with 5, you will take the 8 Gua number. If you were born before February 4 in any given year, use the previous year. Zero always takes the energy of the 9.

Female example 1: Born *September 10, 1954.* Add 5 + 4 = 9. Now add 9 + 5 = 14. Keep adding until you reach a single digit: 1 + 4 = 5. There is no 5 in this system; females will take the 8 number. This woman is an 8 Gua.

Female example 2: Born *March 15, 1962.* Add 6 + 2 = 8. Now add 8 + 5 = 13. Keep adding until you reach a single digit: 1 + 3 = 4. This woman is a 4 Gua.

Formula for those born in 2000 and *after:* Add the last two digits of your birth year until you reach a single digit. Add 6 to that number. If you end up with 5, you will take the 8 Gua number. If you were born before February 4 in any given year, use the previous year.

Female example 3: Born *February 28, 2000.* 0 + 0=0. The zero takes the 9. Now add 9+6=15. Add 1+5=6. This girl is a 6 Gua.

Female example 4: Born *December 12, 2010.* Add 1+0=1. Now add 6 + 1=7. This girl is a 7 Gua.

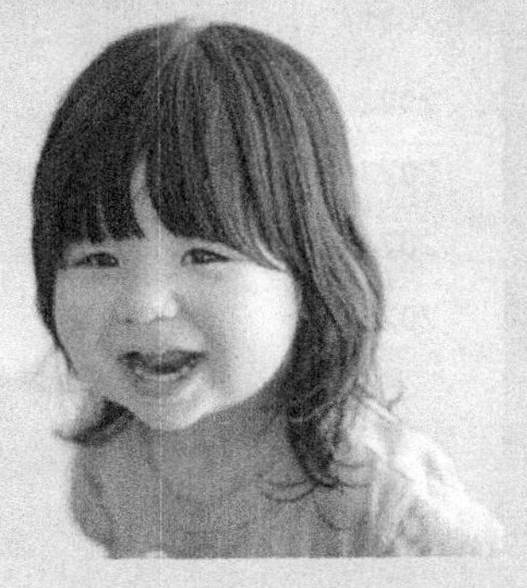

Life Gua Determination for Feb 3, 4 or 5th

For those born on Feb 3, 4 or 5th in any give year, please refer to Appendix I.

Life Groups and GMY Codes

Now that you have your personal Life-Gua number, let's examine the chart on page 21, as it contains a good deal of information. First, based on your Life Gua number, you will be part of the *East Life Group* or the *West Life Group*. Those who are a 1, 3, 4 or 9 Guas are part of the East group, and those who are a 2, 6, 7, or 8 belong to the West group. As opposites attract, it's not unusual for couples to belong to a different group.

Next, notice the GMY Code column; this is the clever creation of my teacher Grandmaster Yap Cheng Hai to refer to your good and bad directions without using the Chinese words associated with them. For example your best direction will be +90 which indicate prosperity or wealth luck. The +80 will help you to secure vital health. The +70 direction is your personal direction to enhance romance, relationships and harmony and so forth. We will use the GMY code from now on throughout the book. Once you have located your personal Life Gua number on the chart, just follow down that column to see all good and bad directions and a brief description of what they'll indicate if you use them. On page 22-23, you'll see the full descriptions and indications.

The Life-Gua number is highly significant, not only can you derive the directions that support you, but get important clues about your personality. It's also used to determine the capability of spouses, the relationship between parents and children, the dynamic between siblings, work mates and business partners. In Chapter Five, we will explore these exciting aspects.

Locate your Magic Life-Gua Number below; there is a column for males and females.

1933-1963

Animal	Year	Male ♂	Female ♀
Rooster	1933	4	2
Dog	1934	3	3
Pig	1935	2	4
Rat	1936	1	8
Ox	1937	9	6
Tiger	1938	8	7
Rabbit	1939	7	8
Dragon	1940	6	9
Snake	1941	2	1
Horse	1942	4	2
Goat	1943	3	3
Monkey	1944	2	4
Rooster	1945	1	8
Dog	1946	9	6
Pig	1947	8	7
Rat	1948	7	8
Ox	1949	6	9
Tiger	1950	2	1
Rabbit	1951	4	2
Dragon	1952	3	3
Snake	1953	2	4
Horse	1954	1	8
Goat	1955	9	6
Monkey	1956	8	7
Rooster	1957	7	8
Dog	1958	6	9
Pig	1959	2	1
Rat	1960	4	2
Ox	1961	3	3
Tiger	1962	2	4
Rabbit	1963	1	8

1964-1994

Animal	Year	Male ♂	Female ♀
Dragon	1964	9	6
Snake	1965	8	7
Horse	1966	7	8
Goat	1967	6	9
Monkey	1968	2	1
Rooster	1969	4	2
Dog	1970	3	3
Pig	1971	2	4
Rat	1972	1	8
Ox	1973	9	6
Tiger	1974	8	7
Rabbit	1975	7	8
Dragon	1976	6	9
Snake	1977	2	1
Horse	1978	4	2
Goat	1979	3	3
Monkey	1980	2	4
Rooster	1981	1	8
Dog	1982	9	6
Pig	1983	8	7
Rat	1984	7	8
Ox	1985	6	9
Tiger	1986	2	1
Rabbit	1987	4	2
Dragon	1988	3	3
Snake	1989	2	4
Horse	1990	1	8
Goat	1991	9	6
Monkey	1992	8	7
Rooster	1993	7	8
Dog	1994	6	9

1995-2025

Animal	Year	Male ♂	Female ♀
Pig	1995	2	1
Rat	1996	4	2
Ox	1997	3	3
Tiger	1998	2	4
Rabbit	1999	1	8
Dragon	2000	9	6
Snake	2001	8	7
Horse	2002	7	8
Goat	2003	6	9
Monkey	2004	2	1
Rooster	2005	4	2
Dog	2006	3	3
Pig	2007	2	4
Rat	2008	1	8
Ox	2009	9	6
Tiger	2010	8	7
Rabbit	2011	7	8
Dragon	2012	6	9
Snake	2013	2	1
Horse	2014	4	2
Goat	2015	3	3
Monkey	2016	2	4
Rooster	2017	1	8
Dog	2018	9	6
Pig	2019	8	7
Rat	2020	7	8
Ox	2021	6	9
Tiger	2022	2	1
Rabbit	2023	4	2
Dragon	2024	3	3
Snake	2025	2	4

This chart has the good and bad directions for all eight (8) Life-Guas.
Go to Appendix IV for **Gua Cards** that you can place in your purse or wallet.

Eight Mansions Chart: The Magic Life-Gua Numbers

	East Life Group				West Life Group			
	Kan Water	Chen Big Wood	Xun Small Wood	Li Fire	Kun Mother Earth	Chien Big Metal	Dui Small Metal	Gen Mt. Earth
Good Directions:	1	3	4	9	2	6	7	8
+90 Best for Money (Sheng Chi)	SE	S	N	E	NE	W	NW	SW
+80 Best for Health (Tien Yi)	E	N	S	SE	W	NE	SW	NW
+70 Relationships (Yen Nien)	S	SE	E	N	NW	SW	NE	W
+60 Stability (Fu Wie)	N	E	SE	S	SW	NW	W	NE
Bad Directions:								
-60 Nothing Goes Smooth (Wo Hai)	W	SW	NW	NE	E	SE	N	S
-70 Lawsuits & Bad Romance (Wu Gwei)	NE	NW	SW	W	SE	E	S	N
-80 Bad Health/Betrayals (Liu Sha)	NW	NE	W	SW	S	N	SE	E
-90 Divorce & Failures (Chueh Ming)	SW	W	NE	NW	N	S	E	SE

SE +90	S +70	SW -90
E +80	1	W -60
NE -70	N +60	NW -80

SE +70	S +90	SW -60
E +60	3	W -90
NE -80	N +80	NW -70

SE +60	S +80	SW -70
E +70	4	W -80
NE -90	N +90	NW -60

SE +80	S +60	SW -80
E +90	9	W -70
NE -60	N +70	NW -90

SE -70	S -80	SW +60
E -60	2	W +80
NE +90	N -90	NW +70

SE -60	S -90	SW +70
E -70	6	W +90
NE +80	N -80	NW +60

SE -80	S -70	SW +80
E -90	7	W +60
NE +70	N -60	NW +90

SE -90	S -60	SW +90
E -80	8	W +70
NE +60	N -70	NW +80

Work and Health for 3 and 4 Life Gua	Work and Health for 1 Life Guas	Work and Health for 9 Life Guas	Work and Health for 6 and 7 Life Guas	Work and Health for 2 and 8 Life Guas
Education, philosophy, medicine, pharmaceuticals, print media, publishing, farming, agriculture, Textiles, Fashion, technicians, musicians, broadcast announcers. Gua 3—Feet Gua 4—Liver	Sales, finance, banking, freight, shipping, spa, communications, pub/bar, tourism, fishing, firefighting, water produce, police, sex industry, diplomat, painters and artists. Gua 1 —Kidneys	Acting, show business, public speaking, fuel/oil, chemicals, optical, cosmetics, advertising, restaurants, lighting, writers, war correspondence, soldiers, barbers, and hairdressers. Gua 9—Eyes & Heart	Engineering, computers, goldsmith, machinery, metal mining, excavation, hi-tech goods, internet, lawyer, judging, white goods, metal jewelry, government service, sports equipment, clocks, & lecturers Gua 6—Head Gua 7—Lung, Throat & Mouth	Property, real estate, construction, earthenware, consultancy, hotel, insurance, architecture, interior design. pottery, recruitment, quarry, HR, handyman, farmer, OB-GYN, monks, & clergyman Gua 2—Stomach Gua 8—Hands & Bones

The following are the Eight Mansions descriptions. They include Grandmaster Yap's code along with a one or two word summary of what they indicate if you activate or use these directions.

Your Four GOOD Directions:

+90 MONEY! Sheng Chi: Life-giving chi, growing chi and generating breath. Great wealth, great success and millionaire chi. This is the best direction to use for money-luck; also good for timing and opportunities. The Sheng Chi direction is good for the managing director, promotion, wealth, health, and children. Use this direction to set up a high position of power/politics. For wealth-luck set doors, stove knobs, bed direction, and face this direction! Activating this direction with the stove or bed may produce fives sons or lots of children who are very successful and good. ***Stove:*** If you suppress your Sheng Chi with the stove placement, the women in the household cannot conceive. If you do succeed in having children they will be foolish, and there will be no money. If the ***firemouth*** (stove knobs, button or controls) or the ***bed*** is to this direction, it will bring great success and harmony!

+80 HEALTH! Tien Yi: Good for wealth and health; the *Heavenly Doctor* protects you. Using this direction brings good friends, the power of speech, social standing and a long life. By activating this direction, a VIP and the government support you. For health-luck set doors, stove knobs, bed direction, and face this direction! You will have gentle and good children, expect three sons when this direction is activated. ***Stove:*** If you suppress this direction with a stove, you will encounter sickness, disease and there will be no harmony in the household. If the *firemouth* (stove knobs, buttons or controls) activates this direction, it will brings riches very quickly, a high position of authority and less illness.

+70 RELATIONSHIPS! Yen Nien: The *Yen Nien* direction supports relationships, longevity, health, family, harmonious families, love, romance and networking. While this direction may indicate a slighter lower income than the +90 or +80, you will have wealthy descendants, conceive children quickly, or children who become specialized, rich and famous; four sons are possible. Place children or young adults in the father's Yen Nien for harmony. Using this direction indicates a very successful, middle class life. This direction may indicate a life less than 70 years, or if exceeding 70 years, the death is celebrated with a party. ***Stove:*** If you suppress this direction there will be quarrels and a short life. If the ***firemouth*** (stove knobs, button or controls) or ***bed*** face this direction it indicates lots of harmony, being upper middle class, almost a millionaire, having powerful connections, good relationships and love.

+60 STABILITY! Fu Wei: Using the *Fu Wei* direction brings stability and peace that can mirror your own energy, moderate happiness/wealth, a middle class family-life, and can protect you from bad luck. Use this direction for adult children living at home so that they may 'move on'. You'll have less children, perhaps only one daughter and one son. For stability-luck set doors, stove knobs, bed direction, and face this direction. ***Stove:*** If you suppress this direction a short life is indicated. If the ***firemouth*** (stove knobs, buttons or controls) or ***bed*** face this direction brings less sons, living under 70 years, but a good middle class life.

Your Four BAD Directions:

-90 BANKRUPTCY! Cheuh Ming: By activating the *Chueh Ming* direction, you will attract the worst things to you! It indicates bankruptcy, divorce, extremely bad health, fatality, business failures, loss of wealth, no harmony, family break-ups, accidents, and no descendants. Using this direction can bring the worst events ever, including death in the family. This is a good location for a toilet or stove. Marriages that are of the –90, the second wife can have two sons. ***Stove:*** Burning up this area with a stove will bring a long life, lots of money and kids.

-80 BAD HEALTH & BETRAYALS!
Lui Sha: The *Six Killings* brings back-stabbing, thievery, injury, loss of wealth, ill health, bad money-luck, accidents, the wife leaves the family, lawsuits by the government, gossip, lingering/ongoing problems, legal issues, couples divorce or separate, no children, bad romance, grievous harm to the family, self-inducing disabilities, being unrecognized in the world, unfortunate accidents (even death), and betrayals. This location is good for a stove or toilet. Old age can be ok or pleasant. ***Stove:*** Burning up this area with a stove can bring money, children, no lawsuits, and no disasters or sickness.

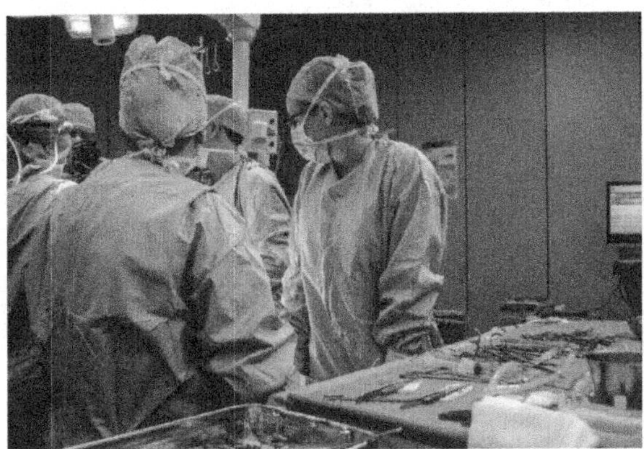

-70 **LAWSUITS & BAD ROMANCE**! Wu Gwei: The *Five Ghosts* direction will activate lawsuits, bad romance, difficulty in conceiving, disobedient/rebellious children, fighting, gambling, drug use, petty people, robbery, bad health, fire hazards, career failures, betrayals, bad tempers, annoyances, undermining, no employee support, gossip, hot arguments, no harmony or peace. This is a good location for a stove or toilet. The son is not supporting the family. ***Stove:*** No fires, no sickness, no money problems, good employers and support.

-60 SETBACKS! Wo Hai: Activating this direction will indicate that *nothing* goes smooth, things turns out badly, irritating events, obstructions, accidents, afflictions, loss of investments, constant set-backs, and mild disasters. You can win a court case but lose money or lose the court case altogether if you use this direction for doors, beds, stove knobs or by facing it. ***Stove:*** Suppress or 'burn' this sector with a stove and there will be very little sickness in the household.

The 24 Mountains

Take a compass direction of your home; see the Appendix. In Classical Feng Shui and in Eight Mansions, the 360 degrees of the compass is divided into 24 sections/directions (each comprised of 15 degrees). This famous division is referred to as the *24 Mountains.* According to this understanding, all abodes, buildings/homes can only face one of these 24 directions. The 24 Mountains are not literal mountains, it's just a term. These 24, 15-degree increments are also referred to as subsectors of a main direction. For example, terms such a South 1, South 2 and South 3 indicate the entire 45 degrees of South, but for Feng Shui purposes, are divided neatly into three subsectors.

General Direction	Exact Direction	Compass Degrees	Energy or Animal
SOUTH	**S1**	**157.6--172.5**	Yang Fire
	S2	**172.6--187.5**	**HORSE**
	S3	**187.6—202.5**	Yin Fire
SOUTHWEST	**SW1**	**202.6—217.5**	**GOAT**
	SW2	**217.6—232.5**	Earth
	SW3	**232.6—247.5**	**MONKEY**
WEST	**W1**	**247.6—262.5**	Yang Metal
	W2	**262.6—277.5**	**ROOSTER**
	W3	**277.6—292.5**	Yin Metal
NORTHWEST	**NW1**	**292.6—307.5**	**DOG**
	NW2	**307.6—322.5**	Metal
	NW3	**322.6—337.5**	**PIG**
NORTH	**N1**	**337.6—352.5**	Yang Water
	N2	**352.6—7.5**	**RAT**
	N3	**7.6—22.5**	Yin Water
NORTHEAST	**NE1**	**22.6—37.5**	**OX**
	NE2	**37.6—52.5**	Earth
	NE3	**52.6—67.5**	**TIGER**
EAST	**E1**	**67.6—82.5**	Yang Wood
	E2	**82.6—97.5**	**RABBIT**
	E3	**97.6—112.5**	Yin Wood
SOUTHEAST	**SE1**	**112.6—127.5**	**DRAGON**
	SE2	**127.6—142.5**	Wood
	SE3	**142.6—157.5**	**SNAKE**

Advanced Eight Mansions for Fine-Tuning Auspicious Directions

Some Good Stuff for Couples of Different Life Groups

What happens if my partner and I belong to different Life Groups? Actually, this happens all the time; opposites attract. However, there is a solution. The Eight Mansions system has another level, *Advanced Eight Mansions* (AEM), which is used to assist couples belonging to opposite groups. Basic Eight Mansions is used to determine your Life-Gua Number, good/bad directions, and personality type.

In order to have the Feng Shui support both people, you'll have to use Advanced Eight Mansions for fine-tuning a desirable direction. This is really important in the 'shared space' (the bed). AEM allows certain 15 degree increments of your 'bad' directions to be used. This is how it works: the South is a bad direction for anyone who is West Life Group (2, 6, 7 or 8), but in AEM the first and third 15 degree of South can be used. Which means you can face your bed direction, desk or use doors facing these increments.

If you are East Life Group (1, 3, 4 or 9), the West is one of your bad directions. However, in AEM you can use the first and third 15 degree increments. Now having said that, the entire 45 degrees of North cannot be used by anyone who is part of the West Life Group (2, 6, 7 or 8), unfortunately, not one single degree.

You may also use Advanced Eight Mansions if you want to use a direction because you have a great view, but it's one of you bad directions. In this case, use AEM to fine tune the desired direction. For example, I want to face East while sitting at my desk to see the lake, but I'm an 8 Life-Gua and East is my -80. I simply angle my desk between 67.6° to 82.5° OR between 97.6° to 112.5° whichever is practical and looks the best. Now, I have a great direction that supports me and I have my lake view!

Advanced Eight Mansions for Fine-Tuning			
East Life Group (1, 3, 4 & 9) North, South, East and SE **plus:**		**West Life Group (2, 6, 7, & 8)** SW, West, NW and NE **plus:**	
Direction	**Degrees**	**Direction**	**Degrees**
Southwest 1	202.6° to 217.5°	South 1	157.6° to 172.5°
Southwest 3	232.6° to 247.5°	South 3	187.6° to 202.5°
West 1	247.6° to 262.5°	North	none
West 3	277.6° to 292.5°	East 1	67.6° to 82.5°
Northwest 1	292.6° to 307.5°	East 3	97.6° to 112.5°
Northwest 3	322.6° to 337.5°	Southeast 3	142.6° to 157.5°
Northeast 3	52.6° to 67.5°		

Chapter Five
Eight Mansions Applications

"When luck visits you, everyone will know where you live".
–Chinese Proverb

Eight Mansions has several practical applications. In this chapter we'll learn how to apply it to your home.

Now that you know your Life-Gua number, you'll be able to improve the Feng Shui of your home and business environments considerably, thereby maximizing the potential of the rooms in which you live and work. You will need to either locate or draw a simple floor plan of your home or office to make changes. Go to Appendix II on page 141 and see *How to Take a Compass Direction*. Refer to the *24 Mountain Chart* on page 24 to see the exact facing direction. Later in this chapter, you will see examples of how to divide up your floor plan and superimpose the Eight Mansions values (+90, -70, +60 and so forth) plus the directions.

On the next page, you'll see how Eight Mansions is actually applied. All of these principles are discussed one by one and in detail in this chapter.

OVERVIEW of Eight Mansions Applications

The Doors Always use a door that faces one of best directions (+60, +70, +80, and +90). In Feng Shui, doors are considered a major feature. If your front door is 'bad', use it only 10% of the time while using your good door 90% of the time.	
The Beds The headboard should be towards one of your good directions. Select a direction that supports what you want, romance, wealth or good health (+60, +70, +80, and +90). For example, place the bed on your wealth direction (+90) for money or career opportunities.	
The Kitchen and Stove Stoves are best located in one of your bad/negative direction (-90, -80, -70, or -60). Stoves 'burn up' bad luck.	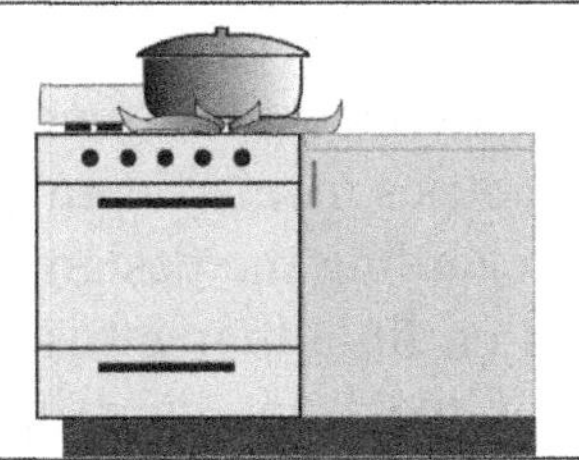
Sit or Face While sitting at your desk working, giving a presentation, negotiating a deal, making a sale over the phone, giving a speech or meeting someone at Starbucks for an important meeting-- face one of your good directions to support you (+60, +70, +80, and +90).	
The Toilets The toilets in the house should be located on your bad directions (-60, -70, -80 and -90).	

The Doors

There is an ancient saying *"If your door is worth a thousand pieces of gold, your house is worth four"* emphasizing the importance of a great door. The main door rates #1 in importance and one of the most significant ways to instantly change your luck. Therefore, the main door must be attended to, and it should ideally face one of your four auspicious directions (+60, +70, +80 or +90). While there are other things to consider regarding a main door, for our purposes here, we are examining it via direction. For clarification, the main door is usually the front door. However, we often have a choice to enter and leave from our front door *or* an interior garage door.

Builders and architects in America and other western countries could learn much from Feng Shui regarding the design and location of doors. Often little thought is given to the placement of the front door in new home building. When the main door of your home, shop, or office enjoys good Feng Shui, then the forces are well-balanced and auspicious energy moves into the home, bringing good fortune.

On the other hand, when the main door is afflicted with inferior Feng Shui, then the residents will suffer from harmful energy and events in their lives. Therefore, you must have a good door in order to energize prosperity, vibrant health, and great relationships.

At this point, you should grab your smart phone (use the compass app) or hiking compass and put your back to the door and make note of the degree. It will give you a digital read, for example 158° South. Measure the degree of the front door, back door, interior garage door, or apartment or condo door.

Master Yap loved telling the story of how his client, Mr. Chen (not his real name), stopped using his front door and entered the back door and became a millionaire. Why? He stopped using a -90 door (disasters, money loss) and started using a +90 door (wealth, power). I've had clients use a back patio slider door as the 'main' door and totally change their prosperity, attracted better relationships and lost unwanted pounds.

You may totally change the events in your life by using a good door! Do not miss this opportunity to activate excellent luck by using a different door if needed. If you must use a 'bad' door, use it only 20% of the time and the 'good' one 80% of the time. See the charts on the next page to see which doors will support your life.

The Indications for Door-Facings

If your Gua Number is...	......and your main door is facing:
1	South, you should have excellent relationships. East, great health and Southeast superior money-luck.
2	Northwest, harmonious household. Northeast or West, get high position and riches.
3	Southeast lots of children, and promotions. South or North, you get riches and vitality.
4	East, your family will produce brilliant scholars. South or North, fame and riches that last.
6	Southwest, you'll be prosperous and good family life. Northeast or West, you and children will be wildly successful.
7	Northeast, good and successful family life. Northwest or Southwest, good stability, and wealth grows.
8	West, good relationships and children. Southwest or Northwest, the house is filled with riches.
9	North, plenty of gold and silver for the family. East or Southeast, you will good children and intelligent children.

Good and bad doors for East Life Groups. Please note that all 45 degrees of North, South, East and Southeast are excellent for those in the East Life Group!

East Life Group (1, 3, 4 and 9 Guas)			
Good Doors to Use:	**Exact Degrees**	**Bad Doors to Use:**	**Exact Degrees**
North	337° to 22°	**Southwest** 2	217° to 232°
South	157° to 202°	**West** 2	262° to 277°
East	67° to 112°	**Northwest** 2	307° to 322°
Southeast	112° to 157°	**Northeast 1**	22° to 37°
Northeast 3	52° to 67°	**Northeast** 2	37° to 52°
Southwest 1	202° to 217°		
Southwest 3	232° to 247°		
West 1	247° to 262°		
West 3	277° to 292°		
Northwest 1	292° to 307°		
Northwest 3	322° to 337°		

Good and bad doors for West Life Groups. Please note that all 45 degrees of Southwest, West, Northwest and Northeast are excellent for those in the West Life Group!

West Life Group (2, 6, 7 and 8 Guas)			
Good Doors to Use:	**Exact Degrees**	**Bad Doors to Use:**	**Exact Degrees**
Southwest	202° to 247°	**North** 1, 2 & 3	337° to 22°
West	247° to 292°	**East** 2	82° to 97°
Northwest	292° to 337°	**Southeast** 1	112° to 127°
Northeast	22° to 67°	**Southeast** 2	127° to 142°
East 1	67° to 82°	**South** 2	172° to 187°
East 3	97° to 112°		
Southeast 3	142° to 157°		
South 1	157° to 172°		
South 3	187° to 202°		

The Bedrooms

Bedrooms are such an important part of our life as we spend 1/3 of our lives in the sleep state. Therefore, the energy should be conducive to harmonious living. Since the master bedroom is crucial, particular attention should be paid to this room as it will determine the luck of the patriarch, head of household or breadwinner (male or female).

This room governs the finances, harmony and well-being of the family. It will determine the relationship luck, personal and business. The woman of the house's luck is also affected by the master bedroom location and arrangement. Feng Shui places great emphasis on, not only the location of the bedroom, but the bed direction as well. The sleeping direction is of vital significance for both married and single people. This area of the house is an opportunity not to be missed to enhance your life.

The head acts as an antenna, when it receives energy from the wrong direction, you can't see anything. Good directions mean good vibrations. When good energy comes through the top of the head, it supports the entire body. If it's bad energy the same applies.

While it would be ideal to have your bedroom located in the part of the house that is one of your four good sectors, this is usually not so. It is impractical and not necessary to move out of your master bedroom into another part of the house for the sake of 'location'. Direction rules in Feng Shui, and this is much easier to manage. If you were doing a new home design, you could feasibly get both. So no need to fret over the bedroom location, make sure however, that your bed and everyone else in the house are well-placed by situating the headboard in a great direction.

If you are a mixed Life Group, the shared space is the bed. You will need to use *Advanced Eight Mansions* to make it work for both parties. Remember, this is where you are allowed to use 15-degree increments in your 'bad' directions. For example, you want to place or the bed is already on the South wall. The East Life Group person (1, 3, 4 or 9) is already well placed as South is one of their great directions. The West Life Group person (2, 6, 7 or 8) will need to have the headboard angled to either 157.6° to 172.5° OR 187.6° to 202.5° on that South wall.

I choose whatever is more visually pleasing and practical in the room. Again use your smart phone or compass to get the degree right. Refer to the *Advance Eight Mansions* chart to find the acceptable degrees for all eight directions.

Bedrooms for Wealth

To improve wealth, select a wall direction that is your +90. If the bed must be placed on a wall with windows, use a tall, solid headboard. All types of disasters will ensue if your bed is placed in the -90 direction. The bed should not be placed in the direction of the -90 as it will cause bankruptcy and several other negative events such as divorce, fatality, and failure in business.

Bedrooms for Improving Health

Your heavenly doctor (Tien Yi) position can be activated in the bedroom by sleeping and having your headboard to that direction. To improve health *(also the second wealth direction),* place the bed in the +80 direction. This will indicate long life and good social standing in the world with support from VIPs and the government. You'll be blessed by the heavens and the 'heavenly doctor' protects you. Beds placed on the -80 direction will indicate bad health, all sorts of betrayals and bad romance. You could lose a partner through an affair. Disabilities are also indicated when this direction is activated by sleep.

Bedrooms for Improving Romance and Relationships

To attract a partner or improve all relationships such as romantic, employee, children, relatives and clients, place the bed to the +70 (Yen Nien) direction. This direction is excellent for networking and children and also indicates a unique, specialized business that makes you rich and famous. This is also the direction you'll need to place the bed if you want to conceive children; it is best placed in the father-to-be +70 direction. If the bed is placed on your -70, it will bring lawsuits, bad romance, gossiping, quarrels and no harmony. It will be very difficult to attract or keep a partner by activating this direction as well as problems with conceiving and childbirth.

Bed Directions for Children

For children, use one of their good directions to place their headboards. If you have a grown child that you would like to see 'move on', then place him/her in her father's +70 (*Yen Nien*). For example, the grown child's father is a 1 Gua, place the headboard to the South.

Place young children to one of their good directions, but masters agree that the best is their +60 or +70 directions. Don't place your children 'better' (e.g. +90) than yourself, they tend to act-out or question their parents' authority.

Mirrors in the Bedroom

The rule for mirrors in a master bedroom is, while lying on the bed, you should not be able to see yourself. This means mirrors on the ceiling, while very sexy, are taboo in Feng Shui. The ever-popular mirrored-closet doors are also very bad. Improperly placed mirrors can bring extra-marital affairs, fighting, conflict, love triangles, and divorce. Mirrors placed behind the bed are not as serious or harmful, but are not ideal either.

Dressing mirrors that do not reflect the martial bed or full-length ones behind a door are fine. Mirrors hung high so that you cannot see yourself while lying in bed are fine too. While mirrors located in master bedrooms can cause strife and affairs, if located in other bedrooms can disturb the chi and thus sleep patterns. It may cause conflict with family members a well.

Cover closet doors that have mirrors. These are usually floor to ceiling and at least eight feet wide. Use drapes, wall paper or better yet, replace them with wooden doors if you own the home. If you use drapes to cover the mirrors, you only need to close them at night. Remove or cover mirrors on the ceiling, and re-hang mirrors in the bedroom in locations where you cannot see the bed. Nowadays, there are other ways to cover the mirror with film that can be purchased at the Home Depot and stores online.

Exposed Overhead Beams

If the overhead beams run horizontal, which will cut across the heart, reproductive organs, or the stomach, they can cause heart issues, lung/breathing problems, serious digestive problems such as Crohn's disease, and sexual or reproductive problems.

Beams that are located over the bed and run vertical can cause the couple to split, however depending where you sleep they may cause health issues as well. The lower the ceiling and the closer they are, the more serious the negative results may be.

The only real remedy for this is to completely cover the beams with plaster or sheetrock. Classical Feng Shui does not rely on bamboo flutes in these scenarios as a 'cure'. The beams are still there and can cause great harm. Make them disappear by covering them up *if,* no matter where you place the bed, you are under them. If you do not own the home, then try covering the area where you bed is located, with fabric using thumb tacks.

Televisions and Computers in the Bedroom

Televisions can reflect objects just like a mirror, and should not be placed directly across from the martial bed. It can cause couples to fight and argue over petty things. Your love life will also improve if you do not have a television in the master bedroom. In addition to having a reflective quality like mirrors, a television emits electromagnetic energy that is disturbing to human chi.

The closer you are to televisions, and the bigger they are—you can experience negative results. This can cause restlessness and insomnia. Computers also have the same affect on our energy fields and are best left out of the master bedroom. Leave the work and careers out of the bedroom and focus on each other. Master bedrooms should be reserved for sleeping and love-making only—find other areas for your home office and exercise equipment.

Actually, it is best to remove televisions and computers from the master bedroom for a deeper rest and more physical enjoyment with your partner. If you house the television in an armoire with doors to close it off from view and unplug it before sleeping, you will not be affected negatively. Flat screen televisions that hang on the wall are not as bad as the old analogue one.

Water Features in the Marital Bedroom

Water features should not be placed in a master bedroom as it will disturb your energy and may cause affairs. Water is primarily used to enhance wealth and harmony in a home, but when water is improperly placed it can ignite sex scandals, affairs, incest, alcoholism, drug abuse and other undesirable results. Aquariums, wall fountains, desk fountains, or waterfalls in the bedroom can generally bring scandals and affairs and should be avoided. Remove all water features from the master bedroom.

General Stuff

Beds should not be placed against a wall sharing a toilet or fireplace, while not detrimental, it is not ideal. Do not place your bed directly under a toilet from the floor above.

Newly married couples should purchase a new mattress to begin the marriage. The furniture in the master bedroom should be proportional to the size, and the room should be free of excess clutter. Make sure that you have a solid headboard; the open type design is not as auspicious. The lack of headboard can harm your relationships and they will not be as stable. Children need a solid headboard to make them feel more secure. The lack of one may cause them to misbehave or act out.

It's important to create a peaceful environment. Bedrooms should have a nice balance of yin and yang energy. For example, windows should have blinds or drapes (or both) so that at night the room can become yin. During the day, the yang energy of the sun can infiltrate the room. But exposed windows at night are too yang for restorative sleep. If the room is not yin enough *(dark, quite, soothing, and cool temperature)*, it is difficult to get into the deep REM sleep stage that helps us stay young-looking and healthy. Loud wall patterns or yang colors (reds, oranges, and purples) should be used sparingly.

The Stove & Kitchen

According to the old texts on the Eight Mansion formula, the placement and orientation of the stove and kitchen is one of the most potent of all. This formula requires that kitchens be assigned to your negative or unlucky sectors. The premise behind this important idea is that the fire will *'burn up'* your bad luck thus attracting auspicious, good luck and events. This also applies to stove locations—they should be placed in one of your negative sectors/directions (-90, -80, -70, or -60).

The Bad, Bad, Good Principle

This principle in Eight Mansions states that the kitchen **location** (1st bad) should be in a negative sector of the house (-90, -80, -70 or -60). However, the stove **location** (2nd bad) is more important and should also be located in one of your negative sectors *within* the kitchen! Also, having the stove knobs (aka firemouth) correct is essential and they should face one of your good **directions** (+90, +80, +70 or +60). Here's a recap:

1. The kitchen should be in a BAD *location* (-90, -80, -70, or -60)
2. The stove should be in a BAD *location within* the kitchen (-90, -80, -70, or -60)
3. The stove's knob direction should be in a GOOD *direction* (+90, +80, +70, or +60)

The last two are the most practical to implement as the kitchen in existing homes cannot be moved unless you're undertaking a massive remodel. See several floor plan analysis at the end of this chapter.

Finding a good location for the stove is one of the most powerful ways to use the Eight Mansions system. After all, fire can burn up a bad luck sector. The stove should be placed in any of your negative areas, especially on your -90 if you want to increase wealth. This is also known as *burning up* or *depleting* your bad luck. A gas stove brings the best wealth-luck when well-placed.

The Indications for Kitchen and Stove Locations

Eight Mansions Kitchen and Stove Locations	
If the Kitchen, but especially if the STOVE is located in your:	***This will result in:***
+90 Money (Sheng Chi)	Women can't conceive, miscarriages, unpopularity, foolish children if conceived, no livelihood/career or money.
+80 Health (Tien Yi)	Much sickness in the household, contracting a serious disease, difficulty in getting well and no harmony in the house.
+70 Relationships (Yen Nein)	Lots of quarrels, difficulty in getting married or finding a life partner, bad affairs, and a short life.
+60 Stability (Gu Wei)	A short life, no money-luck, and always being poor.
-60 Set-Backs (Wo Hai)	Suppress this sector with a stove and there will be very little sickness in the household.
-70 Lawsuits and Affairs (Wu Gwei)	There will be no fires, sickness, and no money problems. Good employer and support. No affairs or lawsuits.
-80 Bad Health and Betrayals (Lui Sha)	Can have money, children, and no lawsuits. No disasters and excellent health.
-90 Divorce and Bankruptcy (Cheuh Ming)	Long life, good health, lots of money and children.

Substitute Cooking Areas

If you are not remodeling your kitchen and cannot move the stove, place a two-burner, portable stove and set up a new cooking area. Use the bad, bad, good rule to locate it.

Since rice is a daily staple for those of Chinese decent, face the knobs of the rice-cooker to one of your good directions. To improve the health of someone in the household, place a second rice cooker to their +80. There have been times when I have flipped the stove and refrigerator locations; this is not always possible but when it does, it saves lots of remodeling cost.

The Desk & Home Office

Today, more and more people work from home. The more hours you are working at your desk, the more important the facing direction is. Ideally you should face your +90 if you have a home-based business.

Equally important would be to face good directions (+90, +80, +70 or +60) while negotiating, giving a presentation, or making a speech—all of these actions affect our luck and energy. So make sure that your desk and chair are positioned to capture one of your most auspicious directions.

If, in addition to working from a home office, you also go to an office everyday read Chapter 6 on using Eight Mansions for career and business. This chapter addresses issues that are common to most corporate settings.

The Toilets

This is for examination purposes; you can't move a toilet once the home is built. You do have a choice if you are building or selecting a new one. Toilets should be located in negative areas of the house (-90, -80, -70, or -60). If your master bathroom/toilet is located in one of your good areas, find another toilet to frequent. The bath/shower sinks and closets are not a problem, but a toilet is if it is located in one of your auspicious locations (+90, +80, +70, or +60). Having and using toilets in your good locations can destroy specific types of luck represented by the location, they are as follows:

- Toilets located in your +90 will cause struggles with money
- Toilets located in your +80 will harm your health
- Toilets located in your +70 may lead to 'crappy' romance-luck and relationships

The Student Placement

The Chinese culture has always placed great emphasis on education. In olden times, this was the only way for someone lowly to raise their fortunes and prospects. If you could pass the court/imperial exams, you were assured a living the rest of your life and catapult your way to a higher social status. Not only would this secure your future, but your family's as well. Even today, the Chinese have come to understand that success rests on a superior education and taking advantage of opportunities.

If your children have a study area, have them face their +70 or +90 direction while sitting at the desk or work table. If they are doing poorly in school, check the door in which they enter the house and change if necessary. Make sure their headboard is to the +60, +70 or +80. Stoves are not placed for children. This is reserved for the head of household, breadwinner or the parents.

The Family

In almost every culture in the world, a good family life is pivotal to happiness and meaningful experiences. Feng Shui addresses this important aspect of life and is designed to support the overall harmony within a family unit.

Feng Shui and Eight Mansions is used to:

- Increase love between partners
- Produce children for childless couples
- Reduce friction in the family
- Improve the health of family members
- Help an adult child to 'move on'
- Bring about a marriage
- Reduce conflict between relatives
- Bring harmony between siblings

If wish to improve any of the above mentioned areas, use the Yen Nien (+70, +80 or +90) positions. Depending on which member of the family, you can activate this via direction. The bed and desk orientation is generally the best. However, if the breadwinner is affected, then you can use the stove placement as well. For example, if the couple is out of harmony and the stove is burning up their +70 (relationship-luck), this needs to be changed. Stop using the stove and place it on a negative sector to mitigate the bickering.

If children are being rebellious or disobedient, make sure their bed direction is either on the +60 or +70. They should not be more powerfully placed than the parents. For example, they should not be activating their +90 position, while the parents are activating their -80 direction. This will throw things out of balance. You should notice an immediate change, if not the entire house's Feng Shui should be further examined. Now let's look at some practical examples of how to implement Eight Mansions.

Floor Plan #1: HOUSE

In our first example floor plan, the house faces Northwest and is for an 8 Life-Gua. The following is how the eight directions are allocated when a home faces northwest. Refer to the Appendix to find out how all the other are distributed. First note that the door faces Northwest and this person's +80 direction. This indicates good fortune in health and this is the second wealth direction. The interior garage door also faces Northwest and this will be a well-used door. Next, while the master bedroom is located in the East sector of the house, the bed is well-placed and located on the Northeast wall. This placement is excellent and bed direction is more important than the location of the bedroom. The stove is located on the +60 and while not ideal, it's not detrimental. The stove knobs are facing to the Southwest which is a +90 for this person. The kitchen itself is located in the East and Southeast areas of the home. Overall, the 'fire' in this house is excellent for the 8 Life-Gua. There is one toilet in the Northeast and one in the Southwest. This person should use the Northeast one and not frequent the Southwest one since it is located in the +90 area and may hurt prosperity. The bedroom located in the West would make a good home office; face the desk to the front of the house (Northwest). While sitting in the living room, face Southwest (the big sofa) and not the small sofa which faces Southeast.

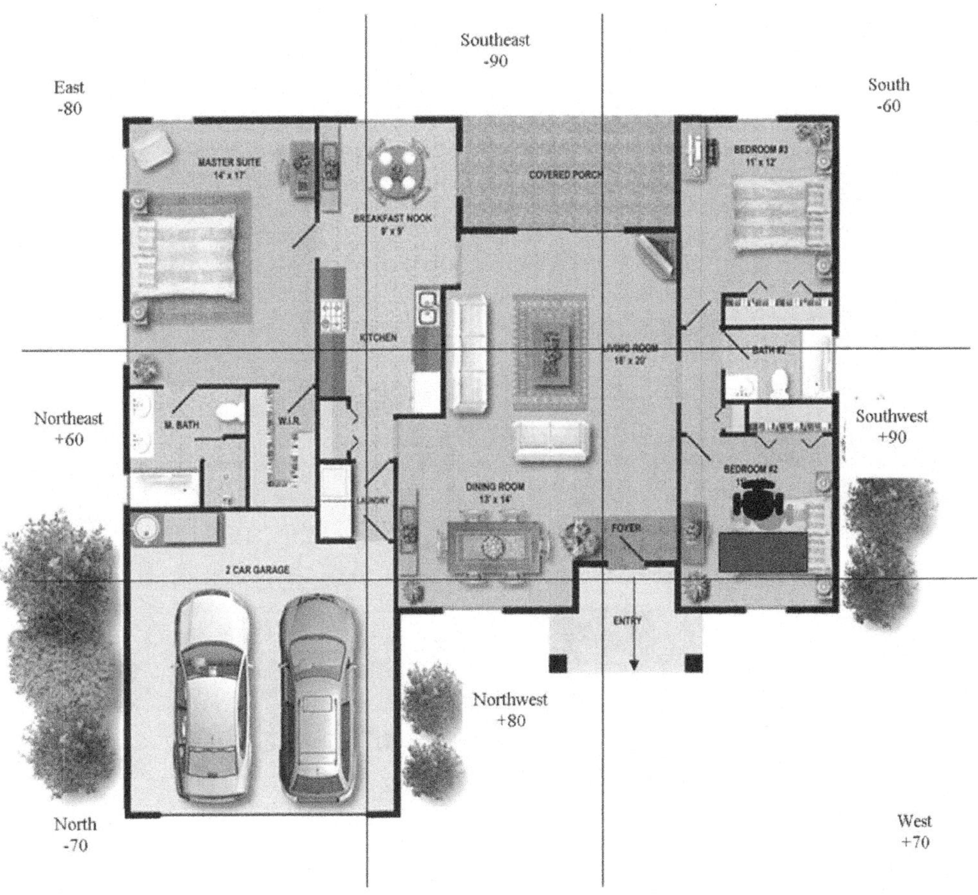

Floor Plan #2: HOUSE

This house faces south; the husband is a 3 Life Gua and the wife is a 6 Life-Gua. The home faces South which is excellent for the husband. The wife should park in the single garage and enter from the West-facing door. The master bed placement, which is located on the West wall is good for the wife, but it will need to be between 247° to 262° OR 277° to 292° to work for him. The bed will still be west but fine-tuned to work for the East Life Group person, the husband. The kitchen is located in the Northeast of the house, better for him than her.

However, the stove is located North within the kitchen which burns up his good health luck (+80). The stove facing is good for him, which faces his wealth direction (+90). The stove burns up her bad luck (-80), which makes it good for her. The stove should be left as is, there is some mixed luck for them both, but overall a good stove.

The master bathroom toilet is located in the Northwest, and this is only in her +60. The toilet is well-placed for him and will enhance good relationships. In the home office, he should face South (+90) instead of east (only a +60).

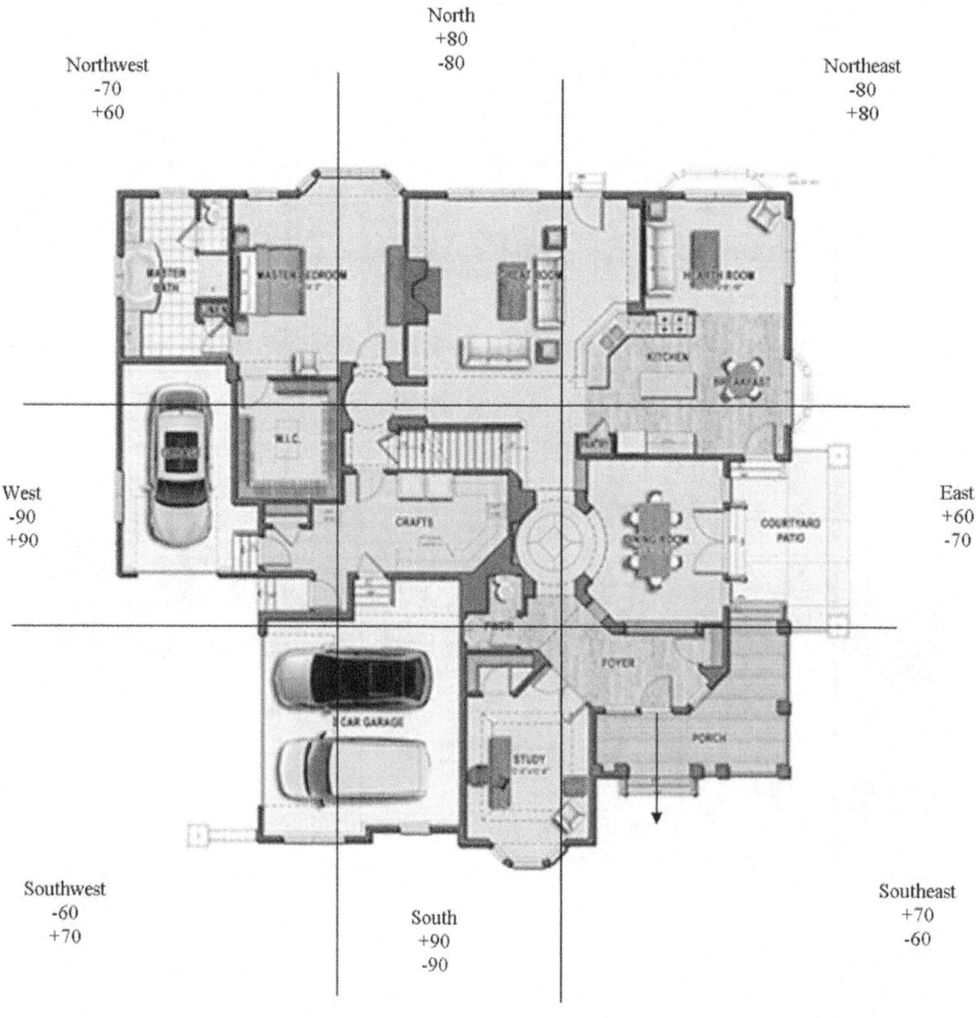

Floor Plan #3: CONDO or APARTMENT This floor plan is of an apartment and the person is a 7 Life-Gua. The door to enter the unit is excellent. Since there is only one way in and one way out, this door must be good! This door will constantly activate good health and wealth. Although the bedroom is located in the North, the bed is placed on the Northwest wall, also excellent. This placement will enhance prosperity. The toilet located in the master while, not ideal (+60) is not totally harmful. For better luck, use the toilet located in the south area. If the other bedroom is used for a home office, the desk should face northwest. While sitting in the living use the sofa, it faces Northwest. The stove is not well-placed and can hurt health. The stove knobs do face the relationship direction. If this person was young, I would leave the stove. If this person was older and not in good health, a two-burner stove could be placed in the north with knobs to the West. See ideas on the next page.

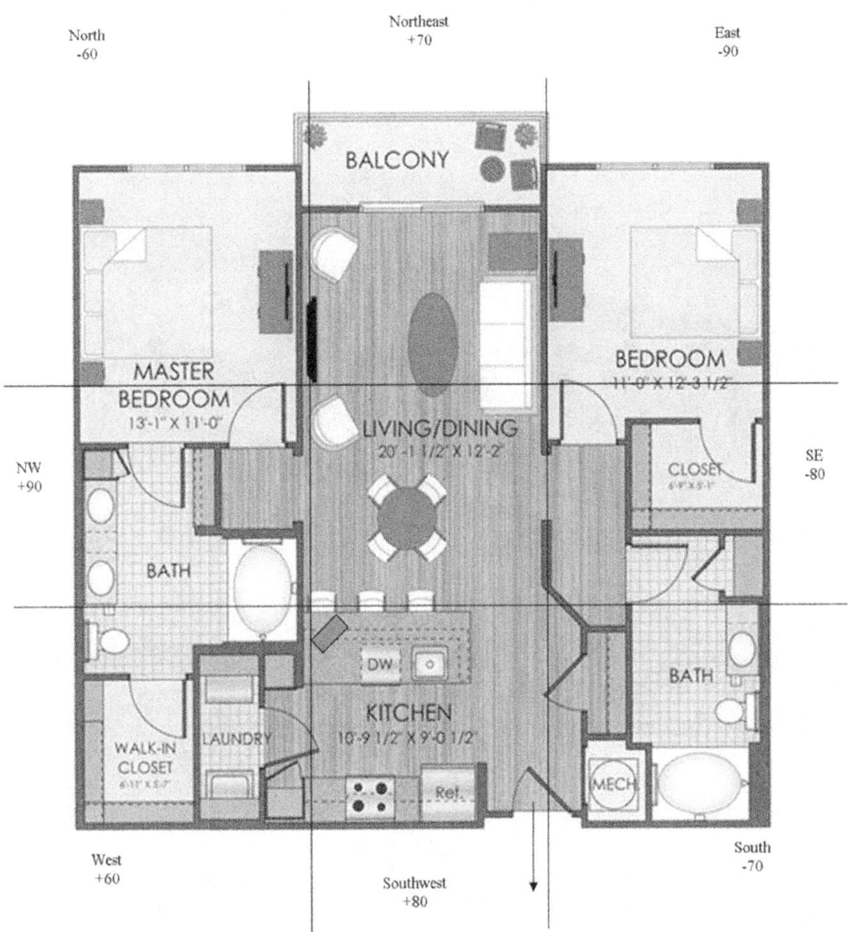

Setting Up a New Cooking Area

Here are some ideas for setting up a new cooking area with a two-burner stove. Remember it should be located on a negative area (-90, -80, -70 or -60). While the knobs/controls should face a good direction (+90, +80, +70 or +60). For rice cookers, face the controls to a good direction. Microwave and toaster oven doors should face a good direction.

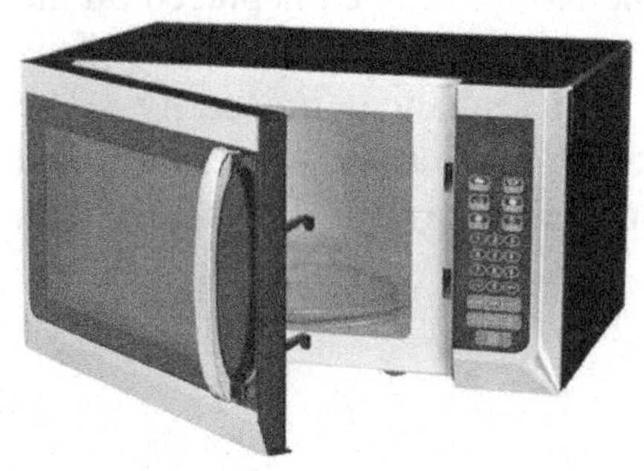

Chapter Six
Using Eight Mansions for Career and Business

"Choose a job you love, and you'll never have to work a day in your life". ~**Confucius**

The Emperor's Position is to secure success and power for the CEO or President of a business. He or she should be placed in the far, upper left-hand corner of the office layout or floor plan. If another person is placed there, it may invite fierce rivalry and competition.

By now you are aware of, not only of your Life-Gua number, but whether you are East Life Group or West Life Group. Remember, according to the Eight Mansions formula, every person in the world is born with four auspicious directions and four harmful directions. These directions will attract a slightly different kind of luck to you. To enhance career and money, the best directions to use are your +90 (*Sheng Chi*), +80 (*Tien Yi*), and the +70 (*Yen Nien).* They represent your wealth/power, unexpected wealth from heaven, and great connections/relationships respectively.

Career-luck is slightly different from wealth luck, although money luck is part of having a good, successful career. Wealth luck is for building and creating assets, whereas career luck deals with gaining positions of power, being recognized and acknowledged, receiving accolades, and earning promotions or partnerships.

So career luck will bring you opportunities for advancement within the world of corporate politics. Some people jokingly refer to this as the 'food chain'. A large corporation, which is similar to a small village, has a defined bureaucratic system. Career luck is all about playing and winning this game using Feng Shui to your clear advantage.

Corporations that wish to possess this distinctive edge should have good Feng Shui. The ideal place to begin is the corporate headquarters. Due to the fact that this building drives the rest of the business, it must have excellent Feng Shui. This is particularly true for the main entrance. If it is aligned correctly to capture the chi/energy, then abundant good fortune will definitely flow into the company. Consider the following design concepts for your individual office and immediate environment.

The Emperor's Position

Every person within an organization can benefit from Feng Shui to improve their personal career-luck by simply re-orientating the sitting direction alone. However, it is the CEO's office and sitting direction which will have the greatest impact on the success or failure of the business. For executives, the office located furthest from the entrance is the most commanding space; it is the position of power. This is known as the *Emperor's Position* because it offers the most protection from unwelcomed intruders and should be reserved for the head of the company. If this office is held by a female, it is known as the Empresses' Position. In ancient times, the Emperor was placed some distance from the main entrance, and visitors would have to go through an army of soldiers to reach him.

If another member of the management team resides in this location, there will be fierce competition with the CEO causing rivalry and discord. I consulted with a cutting-edge software firm in Houston, Texas who had this scenario. Once I reminded them to switch the CEO/President to the 'Emperor's Position', everything calmed down. Not only that, this start-up company received numerous, rich investors for their projects. When Feng Shui is implemented considering the entire chain of command within the organizational structure, then the potential for good fortune is considerably enhanced.

For extra luck, always enter the office building via one of your four auspicious directions (+90, +80, +70 or +60). That way even before you even begin work, you'll be energizing good fortunes.

The Importance of Backing

Protecting your back is a basic human instinct. Look at all the expressions that relate to the back: "He's a back stabber," "They went behind my back," "I need some backup," "I've been backed into a corner," and "You better watch your back, buddy." The real reason for this is the spinal column is one of the most vulnerable areas of the body. If it is compromised, the result could be devastating. So we tend to be protective of it, especially when we can't see who is approaching from behind. If climbing the corporate ladder is your goal, never leave your back exposed. Rather, protect it by adhering to the following ideas.

Backing an internal T-juncture via a hallway. An internal T-juncture, just like its outdoor cousin, is a head-on collision waiting to happen. This layout is the most detrimental to your success and it may indicate a direct attack on you. Just think of yourself as the sitting-duck house at the top and center of the *T*.

Backing a busy hallway. The energy of a busy hallway is active and therefore distracting to your concentration. You will constantly be looking over your shoulder every time you hear footsteps, a sound that doesn't register, or you feel someone approaching. While you stay on guard, your energy will be scattered and divided.

Backing a large window or set of windows. Energy streaming through a large window is intense, like virtual water. Without a solid wall of protection, you are energetically *flapping in the breeze*. Energy needs stable footing to be powerful; windows at your back do not provide this. This configuration indicates a lack of support from your employees, a possible uprising from subordinates, or a power struggle. Tall, pointed buildings outside the window will exacerbate negative outcomes.

Backing a large mirror. A mirror is disconcerting to your energy field. It is like virtual water and offers no support. This type of setup will cause confusion and a lack of concentration as energy is deflected away from you.

Backing a water feature such as a fish tank. Real water at your back is inauspicious and will indicate danger in the workplace or unpredictable events. If you are a key person, such as a manager or an executive, your back most definitely should be against a wall in order to receive 'support' within the company. Also, make sure you face the door so you can see who is entering.

Distance your desk from the entrance of your office—the extra space will give you an imposing and commanding stance while instantly establishing a position of authority.

Office Location

If you are not a manager or an executive of a firm, you probably won't have much control over the location of your office. In many businesses, large and small, cubicles, created by partitions, are the norm. Don't expose your back to a busy pathway. If you have a choice, select a cubicle with some type of backing.

Make all your important phone calls facing the hallway or the pathway. If you are not able to do that, place a mirror so you can see who is behind you at all times. Though this countermeasure is not ideal, it can help. If you spend a great deal of time at your workspace, either on the phone or at the computer, you may find your sales numbers off or your work unrecognized. Pay close attention to the best producers and performers in your company and where they are located. Also, be cognizant of where the troublemakers and bad employees sit—and take note of their surroundings.

When it comes to business meetings, give yourself an edge. First and foremost, make sure you are well placed, then allow your opposition to choose their seats, and let the chips fall where they may. As the head of a company, you should have the best seat in the house in a boardroom setting, the head of the table with your back to a solid wall. If the president of the company is not as well placed as the vice president, for example, a battle for power could ensue.

Do not position yourself near the doorway a the conference room or boardroom. If you wish to empower someone else, place him or her on your right side.

When I consult with large firms, this is an area we discuss in some detail. I identified the ideal location for each counselor of a law firm whose corporate office building I designed in Las Vegas, Nevada. We also had alternate positions for the lead counsel on any given case, providing each attorney the maximum amount of empowerment possible.

Face Your Power Direction

In Feng Shui, direction is everything, this is how energy comes to you and supports you. So if you haven't discovered your Life-Gua number using the Eight Mansions chart in Chapter Four, do so now. Remember, in this system you have four good directions relating to different areas of your life—one for money, one for health luck, another for relationship luck, and finally a direction for stability.

Sheng Chi (+90) is your power direction and specifically applies to money-luck, power, and authority. You will want to face this direction while sitting at your desk to experience the best wealth and career-luck possible. If you are unable to activate this direction, use your +80 direction, supporting health and wealth, as an alternate.

If you work at your computer a great deal, place your monitor and keyboard so that you may face towards your Sheng Chi. Same goes if the phone is your mainstay, always face your Sheng Chi while you're doing business on it to enjoy maximum influence over your clients, customers, employees, and so forth. If you spend an equal amount of time on the computer and on the phone, face your +90 and +80 directions. This is what is meant by activating a direction—using it, facing it. If you are permitted to install a gorgeous wall fountain, you will have a great office space.

When consulting directly with a company, I generally reserve the +90 (Sheng Chi) direction for top executives, and I will situate subordinates in good directions that do not compete with upper management.

Generally, I place them in their +70 (Yen Nien) direction, which is auspicious for relationships and harmony in the workplace. If you are lucky enough to have this information, you definitely have an advantage. Use Eight Mansions to place yourself well in your office environment, and take a compass reading to determine the correct orientations. This system may sound simple, but try it. You may be pleasantly surprised with the results.

Other Office Considerations

Clutter-free. Organize your office and clear away the clutter, especially around doors and pathways. This will improve money-luck, mental clarity, and work efficiency.

Doors. Do not sit too close to a door or have your back to it. It will weaken your position in the workplace and make you vulnerable. Generally, less than three feet is *too* close.

Opposing desk positions and opposing doors. In Feng Shui, when doors oppose or are in direct alignment with each other, it is considered confrontational. The same principle applies to desks. This type of layout can cause bickering and power plays. Old-fashioned *partner's desk*, when two workers face each other, is never recommended. Partners tend to break up.

Desk shape. Kidney-shaped desks are considered auspicious in Feng Shui and will bring good money luck. I had a client who was a psychologist and quite the local celebrity, appearing frequently on radio and television. She had a kidney-shaped desk. Square, rectangular, or u-shaped desks are also good. If you select a u-shaped desk, align your computer on the work surface with your power direction.

Avoid desks and office setups that force you to face a wall. This is like confronting a mountain; it won't bring you good career-luck.

Desk proportion. The desk should be in exact proportion to your position in the company. If you are an executive, your desk should be suited to your position. You can't command employees with a small desk intended for a juvenile. If you operate a home-based business, and you are the president of it, sit behind a desk that represents your authority and where you want to go in the world.

Lighting. Lots of research has been conducted on the effects of fluorescent lighting and how it influences the energy field. Fluorescent lighting weakens your energy field; it emits a subtle hum that encourages negativity. Instead, use good incandescent lighting, especially for performing tasks. This will reduce stress, eyestrain, and headaches.

Overhead beams. Support beams are necessary in large office buildings. But if they are exposed do not sit directly under them. They will cloud your thinking and cause headaches.

Protruding columns. The sharp edges of square columns are considered sha chi (negative energy). Do not place yourself in the trajectory of one of these poison arrows. If you cannot move your desk, soften or disguise the offending corner by incorporating a screen, plant, or drape.

Large windows. If your personal office has a wall of windows that goes from the floor to the ceiling, energy could escape if there are no boundaries. To protect the chi, you must secure these windows with some simple drapery panels on the ends.

Life Guas and Working Relationships

The Eight Mansions system provides lots of information regarding the relationships you have with co-workers and management. If you wish to understand these bonds better, learn their Life-Gua number and then refer to the Eight Mansion chart in Chapter Four. You must know their full birthday—month, day, and year. Based primarily on the five-element theory, the following information offers some guidelines and suggestions. Each Gua has a particular energy that influences a person's propensities and personality traits, which are listed below.

WATER Energy: 1 Guas

If you are a 1 Gua, the best employees for you to hire, to work with or have as a business partner are 9, 3, 4, 6, 7, and another 1 like yourself. You may feel as if you've found a kindred spirit in a 1 Gua. You will have a great deal of control and influence over a 9 Gua. This person will also make a good business partner if you want the lead position or controlling interest. 3 and 4 Guas are highly compatible with you but may weaken your energy at times, while 6 and 7 Guas have an energy that will support of you. The 2 and 8 Guas can control your energy and this may be your boss's Gua number.

EARTH Energy: 2 and 8 Guas

If you are a 2 or 8 Gua, the best employees for you to hire, to work with or have as a business partner are 1, 2, 9, 6, 7, or an 8. You may become friends with an 8 or a 2 Gua. You will have a great deal of influence over a 1 Gua, so if you want controlling interest in a partnership, this is the person with whom to team up with. A 6 or a 7 Gua will slightly deplete your energy. Meanwhile, a 3 or a 4 Gua will try to control you and this may be your boss's Gua number. A 9 Gua will invigorate you and support your ideas and position.

WOOD Energy: 3 and 4 Guas

If you are a 3 or 4 Gua, the best employees for you to hire, to work with or have as a business partner are 1, 3, 4, 2, and 8. You may be close friends with 3 and 4 Gua employees. You will have a great deal of control over a 2 or an 8 Gua, these people are also the best to team up with if you want to run the show. A 1 Gua will best support you. A 9 Gua will try to control you. They may also drain your energy altogether, leaving you feeling exhausted most of the time—this may also be your boss's Gua number.

METAL Energy: 6 and 7 Guas

If you are a 6 or 7 Gua, the best employees for you to hire, to work with or have as a business partner are 2, 8, 3, 4, and 1. Don't be surprised if you bond or collaborate with another 6 or 7. You will wield a good amount of control and influence over a 3 or a 4, so choose this type of person if you want the upper hand in business. A 1 Gua is extremely compatible and supportive and will help you turn ideas into reality. 9 Guas can melt you down and totally wipe out your energy; he or she is probably your superior at work.

FIRE Energy: 9 Guas

If you are a 9 Gua, the best employees for you to hire, to work with or have as a business partner are 3, 4, 6, 7, and 9. You may enjoy the company of other 9 Guas, especially on an intellectual level. You will have control over 6 and 7 Guas and can stop them cold in their tracks! Choose either Gua if you want supremacy in a business relationship. You are compatible with 3 and 4 Guas, who can be your greatest champions. But 8 and 2 Guas will deplete your energy. A 1 Gua will totally wash you out, try to control you, and dampen your spirits and ideas; this may be your boss.

For those of you who spend a great deal of time in an office environment, this information can be invaluable. Most managers have no choice; they must be present to help run the company and deal with employees. So, hiring supervisory staff with this knowledge in mind will create energy that works for you. It's much better than spending tortuous days at the office, navigating conflicting personalities.

So in summary, enter the building through a good door. The office space/headquarters' main entrance, within the building, should also face a good direction. If possible, select a personal office space that has a good door. And lastly, secure your backing and face a good direction while sitting at your desk.

Chapter Seven
Life-Gua Personalities

"When I let go of who I am, I become of what I might be." ~**Lao Tzu**

The Life-Gua gives important clues as how to arrange your home or office. It also gives insights into the personality.

The Eight Life-Gua Personality Types
As I mentioned earlier, in addition to having good and bad directions, you're assigned particular personality traits based on your Life-Gua number. In this chapter you'll find general descriptions of the eight Life Guas *(Life Gua Personalities)*, then more detailed ones matched with the 12 Animals of the Chinese Zodiac (*Life-Gua Zodiac Personalities*) and finally comparing all the Life-Guas with each other (*Life-Gua Compatibility*) in Chapter Nine.

Although the Life-Gua Personalities cannot be found in the ancient classic texts, the information on the Guas can. The idea started when Master Yap gave us quick, verbal description of each of the Life Guas' propensities in class one day in Cologne, Germany (2000). We were greatly entertained by this and I began sharing the descriptions when consulting with my clients giving them key information about their spouses, children, co-workers, business partners, bosses and family members. I also started including it in my training classes and public lectures; people loved it! It gives some very interesting insights into personalities, and clients have confirmed their accuracy. After many years of doing this verbally and informally, I decided to expand on Master Yap's three-word description of the Life-Guas and pen it. This was based on the extensive information available on the Guas, the five element theory, and the Tan Lang Stars (the 9 Stars) which share roots with this system.

In the descriptions you will see the good and bad. Please keep in mind that everyone is capable of exhibiting their negative aspects. We all have times we are not 'on'. Don't focus on the negative, you may already have evolved past most of it. The following are the *general* personality traits of the eight Guas. It is much like astrology when we refer to people as being a Gemini, Aries, Scorpio and so forth. *The Complete Idiot's Guide to Feng Shui* also features this personality aspect of Eight Mansions, albeit not as detailed as the descriptions you'll find in *Feng Shui That Rocks the House*.

1 Life-Gua

Gua Name: KAN "The Abysmal"
Element: WATER
LIFE GROUP: East

Secretive, Emotional, Scholarly

Personality: The 1 Gua's are highly intellectual and can be studious or even scholarly. To the outside world, they appear calm and cool, however inside they have a rich emotional makeup. As a result, at times they can be overly emotional, moody, anxious and high strung. They are full of brilliant ideas and concepts, and are usually very good at making and holding onto money. The 1 Gua's are skilled at sizing up people using their natural, intuitive abilities. Since their element is water, they can be hard to pin down. They are sensual and can be highly sexual. The 1 Guas are known to have secret lives.

The Best Occupations: The philosopher, irrigation, finance, freight, shipping, spa and pool industry, communications, bars/pubs, tourism, firefighting, law enforcement, maritime, sex industry (therapist or tantric sex), diplomacy, counselors, consultants, sales, teachers, wine-maker, scholars, and designers.

Health Issues: Kidney, blood disease, blood pressure, blocked blood vessels, heart/stomach vessel blockage, kidney stress, water retention, dehydration, food poisoning, ovarian problems, nerve sickness, circulation problems, , incontinence, weak sperm, premature ejaculation, alcoholism, sickness related to childbirth, problems associated with sex organs, tinnitus, dry throat, and problems with childbirth.

2 Life-Gua

Gua Name: KUN "The Receptive"
Element: EARTH
LIFE GROUP: West

Persistent, Reclusive, Dependable

Personality: The 2 Gua's exhibit persistence, dependability, and a calm demeanour. They can also be nurturing and supportive to their inner circle. With their calm, relaxed demeanors, 2 Guas are dependable and tend to have developed psychic abilities. They make excellent doctors or practitioners of alternate healing arts such as *chiropractry,* massage therapy, and acupuncture. Since the 2 Guas have the most yin energy of the Guas, they enjoy and feel comfortable in dark spaces, but have a tendency to depression or dark moodiness. Good spelunkers, these grounded people relish activities that focus on the earth—gardening, farming, construction, and agriculture.

The Best Occupations: Property, real estate, construction, earthenware, consultancy, hotel, insurance, architecture, interior design, pottery, recruitment, quarry, human resource, handyman, farmer, gynecology and obstetrics, and clergy.

Health Issues: Fatigue, sickness, contracting a chronic disease, mental confusion, too much coldness in the organs, weakness in body, cancer, oesophagus, intestines, digestive issues, no appetite, indigestion, dropping of stomach, constipation, toothache, skin disease, always feeling cold, spleen problems, typhoid, stomach infection and muscle pain.

3 Life-Gua

Gua Name: CHEN "The Arousing"
Element: WOOD
LIFE GROUP: East

Enterprising, Impatient, Self-Confident

Personality: Three Guas are extremely enterprising and have progressive ideas. They tend to be outspoken, direct, and organized. The 3 Gua's nature is one of nervousness punctuated by lots of energy and steam. Constantly crafting new inventions, new ventures or the latest thing, they love new beginnings and 'start ups'. When in a negative energy, the 3 Guas tend to self-punish, spread their energy too thin leading to collapse, and can be abrasive. However, they are full of surprises, 3 Guas have a sense of vitality and vigor that can overwhelm people.

The Best Occupations: Education, philosophy, social services, medicine, pharmaceuticals, print media, bookstores, gardening, farming, agriculture, textiles, fashion, telegraph operator, technician, musician, broadcast announcer, and transportation.

Health Issues: Liver disease, problems with the feet *(especially the left foot)*,vocal chords, gall bladder, nerve disease, too much heat/fire in stomach/body, very dry throat, teeth, ovary problems, nervous system issues lead to weight issues, face and head problems, always diseased and painful, head/hand injuries, obesity, headaches, and leg problems.

4 Life-Gua

Gua Name: XUN "The Gentle"
Element: WOOD
LIFE GROUP: East

Honest, Malleable, Progressive

Personality: Malleable, flexible, indecisive, the' 4 Gua's may 'blow with the wind' if not grounded, finding it hard to take a stand. In general, they usually are attractive people or may have movie-star qualities. The 4 Gua's are more prone to be sexually controlled by their partners than other Guas. They have progressive ideas and can become famous in writing or rich in the publishing business. The un-evolved 4's may self-destruct by refusing good advice. The 4 Gua's can somewhat remote and private, but they are also gentle people with an innocent purity.

The Best Occupations: Education, philosophy, social services, medicine, pharmaceuticals, print media, publishing, bookstores, gardening, farming, agriculture, textiles, fashion, telegraph operator, technician, musician, broadcast announcer, and transportation.

Health Issues: Liver issues, too much exercise causes problems, sickness, weak body, children undernourished, breathless, bald head, rheumatism, cold sickness, shivering, dizziness, coughing, and bitten by snake.

6 Life-Gua

Gua Name: CHIEN "The Creative"
Element: METAL
LIFE GROUP: West

Leaders, Solitary, Creative

Personality: The 6 Guas can easily step into positions of power and authority as they are natural leaders that seem to be blessed by the heavens. They make excellent lawyers, judges and CEO's as their energy commands respect. The 6 Gua's have a regal, royal air that is naturally unpretentious. Clear thinkers, lots of courage, possessing foresight, extremely creative, and they can hold their own in a debate. They need time alone as they often get caught up in over-thinking, which can lead to being sleep-deprived. Oozing with creativity, the 6 Guas are filled with ideas that involve large groups of people, a community or an organization.

The Best Occupations: Emperor, ruler, president, sovereign, dictator, leader, monarch, sage, founder of a religion, pope, church elder, prime minister, board chairman, military commander, director, governor, teacher, banker, statesman, CEO, chief, leader, head of government office, engineering, computers, gold, hardware, heavy machinery, lawyers, judges, sports equipment, clocks, and lecturers.

Health Issues: Bone fracture, stroke, insanity, neurosis, skin disease, baldness, head injury, Parkinson's disease, stroke, coughs, dry & sore throat, breathlessness, flu common, panting, arthritis, pain of bones, head & nose problems, and catches cold easily.

7 Life-Gua

Gua Name: DUI "The Joyful"
Element: METAL
LIFE GROUP: West

Charming, Excessive, Talkative

Personality: 7 Guas tend to be youthful in behavior or appearance. They are very attracted to metaphysical studies and arts; they can be talkative, lively, and nervous. The 7 female Guas are often blessed with very good looks, and sensuous beauty. Comfortable with a lot of 'stage', the 7 Gua's are good at acting, speaking, in front of the camera or on the radio. With a strong tendency to over indulge in the pleasures of life such as food, drink, money, and sex, they must keep a balanced life. They can be a fast-talker, smooth talker, or have a razor-sharp tongue. The 7 Guas are very social, charming, and charismatic; they create stimulating, informative conversation wherever they go.

The Best Occupations: Actors, celebrities, singers, Internet-related businesses, engineering, computers, gold, hardware, heavy machinery, lawyers, judges, sports equipment, clocks, artist, soldiers, and lecturers.

Health Issues: Catches colds easily, inflammation of the lungs, shortness of breath, hurt by knives, toothaches, mouth cancer, face and leg scars, cancer, miscarriage, difficulty giving birth, sex disease, and suicide by hanging.

8 Life-Gua

Trigram Name: GEN "Keeping Still"
Element: MOUNTAIN EARTH
LIFE GROUP: West

Successful, Hoarders, Dependable

Personality: The 8 Guas have a stubborn, dependable and steadfast nature. They tend to have a great deal of integrity and are vey attracted to all things spiritual. They can become spiritual seekers, and trek the mountains in search of 'answers' and to find themselves. Hardworking and loving things of the earth, the 8's are talented in construction, real estate, and landscaping. They also have a little of 'save the world' energy. While the 8 Guas tend to resist change, they can deftly handle trouble without falling apart. They are geared for success and often become very rich with worldly honors, recognition and status.

The Best Occupations: Property, real estate, construction, consultancy, hotel, landscape architect, insurance, architecture, interior design, pottery, quarry, human resources, farmer, gynecology and obstetrics, clergy, restaurateur, Taoist practitioner, and celebrity.

Health Issues: Backbone, stomach, haggard and tired, coccyx pain, bone fractures, gallstones, problems with the left leg, pain in the ribs, spinal and hip problems.

9 Life-Gua

Gua Name: LI "The Clinging"
Element: FIRE
LIFE GROUP: East

Adventurous, Rash, Brilliance

Personality: 9 Guas have a sharp, brilliant intellect; they can also be wise, loyal, and sentimental. Blessed with a fiery spirit and energy, these Guas have a decided adventurous streak. The female 9's are usually beautiful like a diva or goddess but can be argumentative, aggressive, and rash. With concentrated and focused effort, they can reach great height of achievements and standing in the world. The truly un-evolved 9 Guas will exhibit mental illness such as paranoia and psychotic, unstable behavior. When grounded and evolved, the 9's can light up a room with their radiant energy!

The Best Occupations: Acting, show business, public speaking, fuel, oil, chemicals, optical, cosmetics, advertising, television, restaurants, lighting, beauty, writers, war correspondence, soldiers, barbers, hairdressers, or welders.

Health Issues: Heart, eyes, eyesight, stroke, irritated mind, breast pain, high blood pressure, bleeding, electrical shock, gas poisoning, eye disease, heart failure, heart sickness, burning, and frequent illness.

The Four Categories of the Eight Life-Gua Personalities

To further explain the Eight Mansions Personality types, all eight can be placed into four (4) main categories; showing the energy *(fire, water etc)* and key words expressing driving energy:

The Intellectuals	The Modernists	The Rebels	The Dependables
1 and 9 Guas *Water and Fire energy*	**3 and 4 Guas** *Wood energy*	**6 and 7 Guas** *Metal energy*	**2 and 8 Guas** *Earth energy*
These Guas tend to have a highly developed and sharp intellect; they can be scholarly, full of creative ideas, may be bright visionaries, and are constantly developing the mind. Very attracted to communications. **Other Key Words:** *"I Feel"*	These Guas are modern and very progressive thinkers. These personalities tend to be highly organized, a bit outspoken and be full of surprises. They love to initiate start-up projects and thrive on growth or growing things. They are attracted to politics, acting and writing. **Other Key Words:** *"I Analyze"*	As natural leaders, these Guas tend to be rebels against authority. They have a talent for writing sharp papers or speaking out and can rally a group with their charm; they are often CEOs of firms. Attracted to metaphysics, corporate and military power. **Other Key Words**: *"I Desire"*	The earthy energy of these Guas marks them as steadfast, dependable, noble, and stubborn. They tend to gather wealth, are attracted to construction, healing arts and metaphysics. **Other Key Words:** *"I Know"*

Even though the Life-Gua gives great insights into our personalities (and the 4 categories), I noticed that not all Life Guas were created equal. While in general, for example, the 1 Life Guas are very intelligent, secretive, love freedom and are highly sensuous, they can be very different depending on the animal year in which they were born. For example a 1 Gua born in the *Year of the Snake* is very different than the 1 Gua born in the *Year of the Horse.* So, I decided to once again expand the Life Gua Personalities by matching them with the animal year of birth; this gave a more specific picture of the personality traits.

Chapter Eight
The 57 Life-Gua Zodiac Personalities

"An invisible thread connects those who are destined to meet."
~ Chinese Proverb

The Life-Guas matched up with the Animal Year of Birth gives specific details into a person's career choices, romance or martial partners, possible health issues and more. For example, a 1-Gua born in the *Year of the Pig* is quite different than a 1-Gua born in the *Year of the Horse*.

The 57 Life-Gua Zodiac Personalities
(The Life-Guas Combined with Animal Year of Birth)

In this chapter you will find all eight Life-Guas combined with the 12 Chinese Zodiac Animal signs. There are 96 possible combinations (8 Guas x 12 Animals). However some Life-Guas never match up with certain animal years; so there are actually only 57. For example, those born in either the Year of the Ox, Dragon, Goat or Dog will only be a 3, 6, or 9 Life-Gua. Other pairings will be exclusive to either men or women. This expanded version of the Life-Gua personalities, I've named The *Life-Gua Zodiac Personalities*. You will need your Life-Gua number and the animal year in which you were born to find your personality description; both may be found using the Eight Mansions chart on page 20.

Keep in mind the New Year according to the Chinese Solar calendar starts on February 4th in any given year about 99% of the time, on rare occasions it begins on February 3rd or 5th. If you were born on February 3rd, 4th or 5th refer to the chart in Appendix I on page 140 to see when the New Year actually began for your birth year. For everyone else just refer to your year of birth to locate your Life-Gua.

Also note that in the following descriptions, the 'elements' of the animals are not based on element of the year, for instance, *Year of the Water Snake*. For example, the Pig is water, the Dragon is earth, and the Monkey is metal energy and so forth using the Stems and Branch principles (aka Ganzhi System).

Year of the Rat

1 Gua as a Rat

Men Only!

Sensuous, High Strung, Survivors

Elements: Yang **Water** and Yang **Water**

Years occurring for Males: **1936, 1972, 2008, 2044**

No female 1 Guas are ever born in the Year of the Rat

Famous 1 Gua-Rat Men: Vidal Sassoon, Buddy Holly, Engelbert Humperdinck, Glen Campbell, Kris Kristofferson, Albert Finney, Wilt Chamberlain, Silvio Berlusconi, Robert Redford, Burt Reynolds, Bobby Darin, David Carradine, Jim Henson, John McCain, Bruce Dern, Yves Saint-Laurent, Louis Gossett Jr., Ben Affleck, Jude Law, Dwayne Johnson, Marlon Wayans, Eminem, Dwayne Johnson, Brad Paisley, Dane Cook, Josh Duhamel, Scott Peterson, Antonio Sabato Jr., Marlon Wayans, Notorious B.I.G, Billie Joe Armstrong, and Shaquille O'Neal

Personality and Romance: The 1 Gua men who are born in the *Year of the Rat* is a double water sign making them extremely emotional, sensuous, and high strung. These men are highly intelligent, imaginative, and very charming. The water-water combination also enhances their natural intuitive abilities in sizing people up; when provoked the 1 Gua-Rat can become very aggressive. With the appearance of being cool and dignified, deep down these men tend to be insecure and react very well to praise rather than being criticized.

The rat is one of the oldest survivors on the planet; their energy adapts, endures and overcomes almost any challenge presented. They love being free, mobile and the excitement of travel.

The 1 Gua-Rats tend to be very loyal in relationships and need a partner who can handle their deep sexuality, moodiness, high energy and intenseness. If they have love affairs, they are still loyal to their wives and family—these temptations are never *affairs of the heart*, just dalliances.

The best stuff: When the 1 Gua-Rats are fully exhibiting their best qualities, they are very intelligent, forthright, disciplined, systematic, meticulous, charismatic, charming, cool and dignified, hardworking, industrious, charming, eloquent, sociable and shrewd.

The worst stuff: When the 1 Gua-Rats move into the darker side of their nature, they can be manipulative, cruel, dictatorial, rigid, selfish, obstinate, critical, over-ambitious, ruthless, intolerant, scheming, and sturdy.

Career: Some of the best professions for the 1 Gua-Rats, where they may attain wealth, fame or fulfillment, are as/in writers, broadcasters, actors, advisors, lawyers, politicians, directors, administrators, entrepreneurs, musicians, stand-up comedians, researchers, historians, race car drivers, sales, spa, and enforcement.

2 Gua as a Rat

Women Only!

Calm, Intelligent, Intuitive

Elements: Yin **Earth** and Yang **Water**

Years occurring for Females:
1924, 1960, 1996, 2032
No Male 2 Guas are born in the Year of the Rat

Famous 2 Gua-Rat Women: Gloria Vanderbilt, Ruby Dee, Lauren Bacall, Eva Marie Saint, Kelly LeBrock, Kathy Griffin, Dorothy Stratten, Carol Alt, Emma Samms, Roma Downey, Meg Tilly, Robin Roberts, Jennifer Grey, Kristin Scott Thomas, Sarah Brightman, Daryl Hannah, Julianne Moore, Valerie Bertinelli, Carol Alt, Greta Scacchi, Amy Grant, Abigail Breslin, Sasha Pieterse, Kyla Ross and Zendaya.

Personality and Romance: The 2 Gua born in the *Year of the Rat* is a mix of earth and water energy bringing a bit more emotion to their normal, calm-nature. The 2 Gua-Rats are very intuitive, observing people with sharp accuracy. These women are attracted to the healing arts such as psychiatry in which they can use their energy and communicative skills. They make talented doctors with a compassionate, charming 'bedside' manner that is reassuring to those in their care.

The 2 Gua Rats are survivors, comfortable in dark spaces and have relaxed demeanors but can be rigid as well. Since their energy is very yin, if not kept in check, the 2 Gua Rats can suffer from depression. Focusing on their creative side and love of travel will keep their energy high and expressed in productive outlets.

The best stuff: When the 2 Gua-Rats are fully exhibiting their best qualities, they are forthright, disciplined, systematic, meticulous, charismatic, hardworking, industrious, charming, eloquent, sociable, and shrewd.

The worst stuff: When the 2 Gua-Rats move to the darker side of their nature, they can be manipulative, cruel, dictatorial, rigid, selfish, obstinate, critical, depressed, over-ambitious, ruthless, intolerant, scheming, and sturdy.

Career: Some of the best professions for the 2 Gua-Rats, where they may attain wealth, fame or fulfillment, are as/in writers, broadcasters, advisors, lawyers, politicians, designers, engineers, entrepreneurs, race car drivers, publishing, musician, real estate, construction, hotel, architecture, or OB-GYN.

4 Gua as a Rat

Men Only!

Gentle, Charming, Witty

Elements: Yin **Wood** and Yang **Water**

Years occurring for Males: **1924, 1960, 1996, 2032**

There are no 4 Gua females ever born in the Year of the Rat

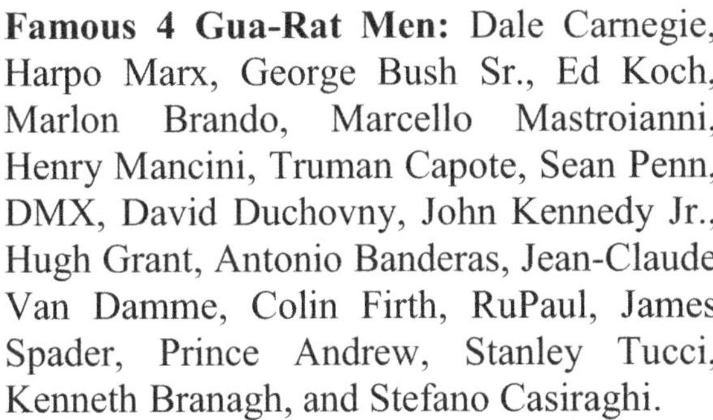

Famous 4 Gua-Rat Men: Dale Carnegie, Harpo Marx, George Bush Sr., Ed Koch, Marlon Brando, Marcello Mastroianni, Henry Mancini, Truman Capote, Sean Penn, DMX, David Duchovny, John Kennedy Jr., Hugh Grant, Antonio Banderas, Jean-Claude Van Damme, Colin Firth, RuPaul, James Spader, Prince Andrew, Stanley Tucci, Kenneth Branagh, and Stefano Casiraghi.

Personality and Romance: The 4 Gua men born in the *Year of the Rat* are a harmonious mix of wood and water energy; this creates sharp minded wit and irresistible charm! To the world, they have a cool and dignified persona, but deep down they are insecure. The 4 Gua-Rats thrive on praise, recognition and popularity. They resent being ordered around or made to feel small. If they are cornered or feel trapped, they can become aggressive, stay on their good side as their true nature is gentle. These men have very progressive energy and ideas; they often become famous in the writing, acting or as an entrepreneur. In dealing with these men, you must use diplomacy as they can be overly sensitive to any type of criticism. They are loyal in relationships finding it hard to break away and go forward. A good partner needs to be able to keep up with this high-energy personality. When the 4 Gua-Rats step into their negative side, they can be obstinate, ruthless, rigid and selfish. However, they are genuinely romantic and sentimental in relationships.

The best stuff: When the 4 Gua-Rats are fully exhibiting their best qualities, they are forthright, disciplined, systematic, meticulous, gentle, charismatic, hardworking, industrious, charming, eloquent, sociable and shrewd.

The worst stuff: When the 4 Gua-Rats move to the darker side of their nature, they can be indecisive, manipulative, cruel, dictatorial, critical, over-ambitious, wishy-washy, intolerant and scheming.

Career: Some of the best professions for the 4 Gua-Rats, where they may attain wealth, fame or fulfillment, are as/in writers, advisors, lawyers, politicians, designers, engineers, directors, entrepreneurs, researchers, historians, race car drivers, estate management, philosophy, chef, pharmaceuticals and publishing.

7 Gua as a Rat

Men Only!

Talkative, Sexual, Charming

Elements: Yin **Metal** and Yang **Water**

Years occurring for Males: **1948, 1984, 2020**

There are no 7 Gua females ever born in the Year of the Rat

Famous 7 Gua-Rat Men: Gene Kelly, Perry Como, Karl Malden, Art Linkletter, Steven Tyler, James Taylor, Ozzy Osbourne, Cat Stevens, Terry Bradshaw, Alice Cooper, Prince Charles, Ted Nugent, Mikhail Baryshnikov, Gérard Depardieu, Jeremy Irons, Al Gore, Andrew Lloyd Webber, Wolf Blitzer, Richard Simmons, Jean Reno, Trey Songz, Fernando Torres, Prince Harry Windsor, LeBron James, and Mark Zuckerberg.

Personality and Romance: The 7 Guas born in the *Year of the Rat* are a harmonious mix of metal and water energy; these men are charming, confident, witty, insecure, talkative, and have engaging personalities. They are usually very interesting men and make great partners and lovers. The 7 Gua Rats tend to be restless, impulsive and need a great deal of praise and flattery; be cognizant of not injuring their sensitive egos with direct or, even implied criticism. While these men are not great risk-takers, they make inventive entrepreneurs, good negotiators, and clever tacticians. The 7 Gua-Rats love the pleasures of life—good food, good sex, good conversation, and so forth. They can be fully charged at the beginning of a relationship, and romantic; they love to take care of their partners. These men take marriage very seriously and are faithful in romantic relationships. They can be charismatic, smooth-talking, or have a razor-sharp tongue—especially if backed into a corner where they may also become aggressive.

The best stuff: When the 7 Gua-Rats are fully exhibiting their best qualities, they are forthright, disciplined, systematic, meticulous, charismatic, hardworking, industrious, charming, eloquent, sociable and shrewd.

The worst stuff: When the 7 Gua-Rats move to the darker side of their nature, they can be manipulative, cruel, dictatorial, rigid, selfish, obstinate, critical, over-ambitious, ruthless, intolerant, scheming, and sturdy.

Career: Some of the best professions for the 7 Gua-Rats, where they may attain wealth, fame or fulfillment, are as/in writers, actors, advisors, politicians, engineers, directors, administrators, researchers, race car drivers, police office, metal mining, excavation, internet, lawyer, metal jewelry and lecturers.

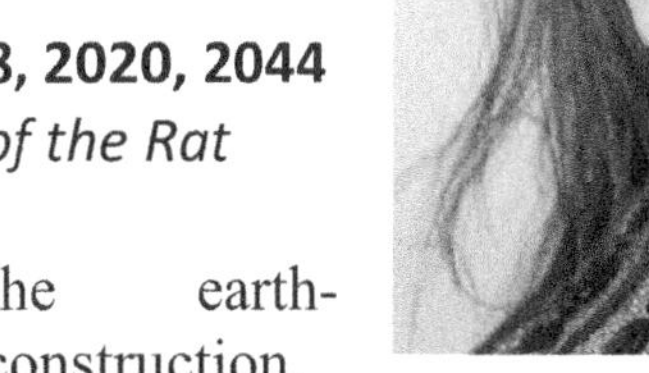

8 Gua as a Rat

Women Only!

Witty, Sexual, Magnetic

Elements: Yang **Earth** and Yang **Water**

Years occurring for Females: **1936, 1948, 1984, 2008, 2020, 2044**

There are no 8 Gua males ever born in the Year of the Rat

Famous 8 Gua-Rat Women: Eva Braun, Sonja Henie, Julia Child, Doris Duke, Ursula Andress, Mary Tyler Moore, Ruth Buzzi, Princess Elizabeth of Yugoslavia, Stevie Nicks, Grace Jones, Barbara Hershey, Margot Kidder, Kathy Bates, Barbara Mandrell, JoBeth Williams, Tina Sinatra, Scarlett Johansson, Katy Perry, Khloé Kardashian, Cheryl Burke, Ashlee Simpson, and Kelly Osbourne.

Personality and Romance: The 8 Gua women born in the *Year of the Rat* is a combination of earth and water energy; this will cause some emotional tension. These women are steadfast, witty, magnetic, hardworking, vivacious and dynamic. While the 8 Gua-Rats may resist change, they can deftly handle trouble without falling apart. They tend to be a bit old-fashioned in relationships wanting marriage and babies above a career.

They fear being alone and must always have a man in their life; even when life is bringing them success and independence, she will give it up to have a spouse and security. These women are full of energy, talkative, expressive, and charming; however they can become aggressive when provoked. They are talented with things of the earth-construction, real estate, and landscaping. They move a great deal—homes, jobs, and love to travel. They are loyal in relationships finding it hard to break away and go forward. A good partner needs to be able to keep up with this high-energy personality.

The best stuff: When the 8 Gua-Rats are fully exhibiting their best qualities, they are forthright, disciplined, systematic, meticulous, charismatic, hardworking, industrious, charming, eloquent, sociable, noble and shrewd.

The worst stuff: When the 8 Gua-Rats move to the darker side of their nature, they can be manipulative, cruel, dictatorial, rigid, selfish, obstinate, critical, stubborn, over-ambitious, ruthless, intolerant, scheming, and sturdy.

Career: Some of the best professions for the 8 Gua-Rats, where they may attain wealth, fame or fulfillment, are as writers, counselors, lawyers, politicians, designers, directors, entrepreneurs, stand-up comedians, historians, race car drivers, publishing, real estate, construction, architecture, HR, and OB-GYN.

Year of the Ox

The Year of the Ox only produces 3, 6, & 9 Life Guas

3 Gua as an Ox

Men and Women!

Enterprising, Steady, Outspoken

Elements: Yang **Wood** and Yin **Earth**

Years occurring for Males and Females:
1925, 1961, 1997, 2033

Famous 3 Gua-Oxen Men and Women: Prime Minister Margaret Thatcher, Rock Hudson, Tony Curtis, Angela Lansbury, Robert F. Kennedy, Princess Diana, George Clooney, Melissa Etheridge, Eddie Murphy, Enya, Nadia Comaneci, Mariel Hemingway, Laurence Fishburne, k.d. lang, Heather Locklear, Barack Obama, Dennis Rodman, Bonnie Hunt, Billy Ray Cyrus, and Jeremy Northam.

Personality and Romance: The 3 Guas born in the *Year of the Ox* are a mix of wood and earth energy causing a bit of inner turmoil; with the right outlet however, it is mitigated. With a dependable and steady nature, these men and women work hard with a methodical, focused determination. The 3 Gua-Oxens prefer to develop life-long relationships to casual ones. They will take their time finding the perfect partner in life as change is out of the comfort zone for them. These people are full of energy that is often punctuated with bursts of nervousness. Tending towards outspokenness, they often surprise or shock those around them. Because the 3 Gua-Oxens are prone to spreading their energy a little thin, committing to too much, they are often fall into overwhelm. When they move to the darker side of their nature, they can become demanding and rigid.

The best stuff: When the 3 Gua-Oxens are fully exhibiting their best qualities, they are dependable, calm, methodical, patient, organized, hardworking, ambitious, conventional, steady, modest, logical, resolute, and tenacious.

The worst stuff: When the 3 Gua-Oxens move to the darker side of their nature, they can be outspoken, stubborn, narrow-minded, brash, materialistic, nervous, rigid, demanding.

Career: Some of the best professions for the 3 Gua-Oxens, where they may attain wealth, fame or fulfillment, are in manufacturing, pharmacy, engineering, artistry, politics, philosophy, entertainers, chef, pharmaceuticals, publishing, fashion, technicians, musicians, broadcast announcers, and transportation.

6 Gua as an Ox

Men and Women!

Ambitious, Authoritative, Methodical

Elements: Yang **Metal** and Yin **Earth**

Years occurring for Males:
1913, 1949, 1985, 2009, 2021

Years occurring for Females:
1901, 1937, 1973, 2045

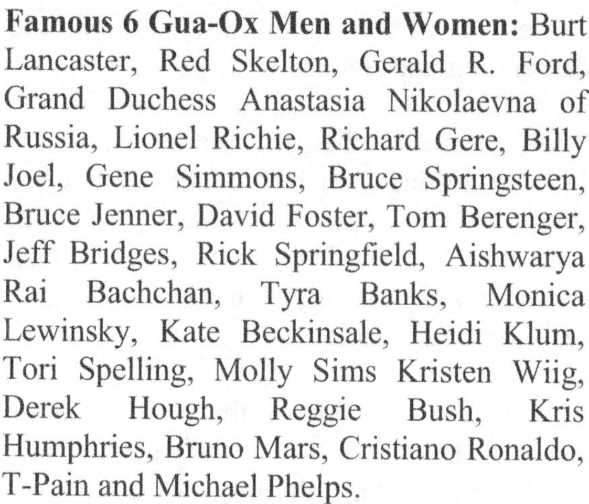

Famous 6 Gua-Ox Men and Women: Burt Lancaster, Red Skelton, Gerald R. Ford, Grand Duchess Anastasia Nikolaevna of Russia, Lionel Richie, Richard Gere, Billy Joel, Gene Simmons, Bruce Springsteen, Bruce Jenner, David Foster, Tom Berenger, Jeff Bridges, Rick Springfield, Aishwarya Rai Bachchan, Tyra Banks, Monica Lewinsky, Kate Beckinsale, Heidi Klum, Tori Spelling, Molly Sims Kristen Wiig, Derek Hough, Reggie Bush, Kris Humphries, Bruno Mars, Cristiano Ronaldo, T-Pain and Michael Phelps.

Personality and Romance: The 6 Guas born in the *Year of the Ox* are a harmonious mix of metal and earth energy; this makes these men and women steadfast, dependable and methodical. The 6 Gua-Oxens are not particularly romantic; however they can be very passionate and extraordinarily loyal to their partners. These men and women are highly principled and disciplined mixed with steely determination. Neither sex is showy; preferring to develop the intellect than to dress to 'strut you stuff' or as a seductress. The 6 Gua-Oxens do not like excess, frivolity and flaunting their wealth. The men can be ruthless, tough and the women judgmental as they cannot tolerate idle gossip or silly behavior; they are not naturally social preferring to stay at home. They feel comfortable with positions of power and authority, making righteous leaders.

The best stuff: When the 6 Gua-Oxens are fully exhibiting their best qualities, they are dependable, calm, methodical, patient, hardworking, ambitious, conventional, steady, modest, logical, resolute and tenacious.

The worst stuff: When the 6 Gua-Oxens move to the darker side of their nature, they can be stubborn, narrow-minded, judgmental, materialistic, rigid and demanding.

Career: Some of the best professions for the 6 Gua-Oxens, where they may attain wealth, fame or fulfillment, are in manufacturing, pharmacy, engineering, real estate, interior design, medicine, engineering, IT, goldsmith, metal mining, excavation, government service, sports equipment, and lecturers.

9 Gua as an Ox

Men and Women!

Confident, Brilliant, Loyal

Elements: Yin **Fire** and Yin **Earth**

Years occurring for Males: **1937, 1973, 2009, 2045**
Years occurring for Females: **1913, 1949, 1985, 2021**

Famous 9 Gua Oxen Men and Women: Walt Disney, Louis Armstrong, Rosa Parks, Vivien Leigh, Jack Nicholson, Warren Beatty, Morgan Freeman, Bill Cosby, Anthony Hopkins, Dustin Hoffman, George Carlin, Ridley Scott, Joyce DeWitt, Shelley Long, Whoopi Goldberg, Twiggy, Sigourney Weaver, Meryl Streep, Ivana Trump, Vera Wang, Leslie Van Houten, Yasmin Khan, Annie Leibovitz, Paul Walker, Akon, Adrien Brody, Nick Lachey, Peter Facinelli, Neil Patrick Harris, Peter Andre, Ashley Tisdale, Bar Refaeli, Ciara, Amanda Seyfried, Keira Knightley, and Carey Mulligan.

Personality and Romance: The 9 Gua men and women who were born in the *Year of the Ox* are an auspicious mix of fire and earth energy; this creates inner confidence and stability. These men and women are honest, patriotic, ambitious, family-oriented, free-spirited and highly intelligent. They are famously diligent, determined and hard-working. The 9 Gua-Oxens are not influenced by others and do things according to their own ideas and abilities; before taking action to do anything, they will have a specific plan and detailed steps, add to this their physical strength and these people will enjoy great success. The 9 Gua-Oxens have a sharp, brilliant intellect; they can also be wise, loyal, and sentimental. Blessed with a fiery spirit and energy, these people have a decided adventurous streak. They are not particularly romantic; rather will take a more practical approach to selecting a spouse. They prefer their own counsel over that of others, and would rather develop life-long relationships to casual ones. With concentrated and focused effort, they can reach great height of achievements and standing in the world.

The best stuff: When the 9 Gua-Oxens are fully exhibiting their best qualities, they are radiant, steadfast, loyal, social, methodical, patient, hardworking, ambitious, conventional, steady, modest, logical, resolute, and tenacious.

The worst stuff: When the 9 Gua-Oxens move to the darker side of their nature, they can be paranoid, unforgiving, ruthless, domineering, psychotic, unstable, stubborn, narrow-minded, materialistic, rigid, demanding.

Career: Some of the best professions for the 9 Gua-Oxens, where they may attain wealth, fame or fulfillment, are in medicine, religion, manufacturing, pharmacy, engineering, politics, real estate, interior design, public speaking, chemicals, optical, cosmetics, television, beauty, war correspondence and soldiers.

Year of the Tiger

1 Gua as a Tiger

Women Only!

Leaders, Risk-Takers, Raw Energy

Elements: Yang **Water** and Yang **Wood**

Years occurring for Females: **1950, 1986, 2022**

No 1 Guas males are ever born in the Year of the Tiger

Famous 1 Gua-Tiger Women: Dorothy Lamou, Karen Carpenter, Cybill Shepherd, Natalie Cole, Joan Lunden, Susan Anton, Arianna Huffington, Princess Anne, Deniece Williams, Cristina Ferrare, Patti Austin, Christina Onassis, Dianna Agron, Leighton Meester, Camilla Belle, Amber Heard, Lea Michele, Ellie Goulding, Megan Fox, Amanda Bynes, Lindsay Lohan, Lady Gaga, and Mary-Kate and Ashley Olsen.

Personality and Romance: The 1 Gua born in the *Year of the Tiger* is a mix of water and wood elements, making their energy progressive, powerful, commanding and usually the 'smartest person in the room'. These women are gutsy and are natural leaders due to their highly developed intelligence. They exhibit and have a natural, primal and raw energy that is almost palatable. The 1 Gua-Tigers are huge risk-takers, spontaneous using their charm and independent nature to influence people in any setting to always come out on top.

Despite their powerful energy, they can be very vulnerable, and often become victims of their own outrageous, unchecked passions. They can get bored with their partners quite easily and may move from lover to lover, all in the pursuit of finding true love. In general, they are very talented at making money; they also may squander it. In relationships, the 1 Gua-Tiger women never bore their partners; they are intensely passionate and are protective of their mates, employees, children and anyone under their care.

The best stuff: When the 1 Gua-Tigers are fully exhibiting their best qualities, they are powerful, passionate, daring, stimulating, sincere, affectionate, humanitarian and generous.

The worst stuff: When the 1 Gua-Tigers move to the darker side of their nature, they can be restless, reckless, impatient, secretive, quick-tempered, moody, obstinate, and selfish.

Career: Some of the best professions for the 1 Gua-Tigers, where they may attain wealth, fame or fulfillment, are as/ in advertising, artist, airline pilot, travel, design, politics, travel writer, explorer, advertising, business executive, sales, freight, shipping, fishing or firefighting.

2 Gua as a Tiger

Men Only!

Primal Energy, Protective, Passionate

Elements: Yin **Earth** and Yang **Wood**

Years occurring for Males:

1926, 1950, 1962, 1986, 1998, 2022, 2034

No female 2 Guas are ever born in the Year of the Tiger

Famous 2 Gua-Tiger Men: Joe DiMaggio, Jack LaLanne, Andy Griffith, Chuck Berry, Hugh Hefner, Fidel Castro, Tony Bennett, Jerry Lewis, David Cassidy, Stevie Wonder, Huey Lewis, Bruce Boxleitner, Gabriel Byrne, Peter Frampton, William Hurt, Jay Leno, Ed Harris, Teddy Pendergrass, Bill Murray, Sir Richard Branson, Dr. Phil McGraw, Axl Rose, William H. Macy, Jon Bon Jovi, Tom Cruise, Tommy Lee, Ralph Fiennes, Garth Brooks, M.C. Hammer, Clint Black, Usain Bolt, Shia LaBeouf and Robert Pattinson.

Personality and Romance: The 2 Gua-Tiger is a mix of earth and wood energy making them intense, but with a calm, self-assured and primal energy. Like the powerful cat always aware of his natural environment, they are deeply sensitive and intuitive. They have a great deal of influence in any setting—personal or business—and they are natural, instinctive leaders. The 2 Gua-Tigers are men that are huge risk-takers, spontaneous, independent and they thrive by being on top! As they tend to be very passionate in relationships, they never bore their partners. Their natural, nurturing energy makes them very protective of what 'belongs' to them.

The best stuff: When the 2 Gua-Tigers are fully exhibiting their best qualities, they are nurturing, unpredictable, colorful, powerful, passionate, daring, vigorous, stimulating, sincere, affectionate, humanitarian, and generous.

The worst stuff: When the 2 Gua-Tigers move to the darker side of their nature, they can be rebellious, impulsive, restless, reckless, impatient, quick-tempered, obstinate, and selfish.

Career: Some of the best professions for the 2 Gua-Tigers, where they may attain wealth, fame or fulfillment, as/are in advertising agent, actor, airline pilot, comedian, design, politics, military, explorer, advertising, business executive, property, real estate, consultancy, architecture, human resources, and OB-GYN.

4 Gua as a Tiger

Women Only!

Intense, Protective, Sex-Appeal

Elements: Yin **Wood** and Yang **Wood**

Years occurring for Females: **1962, 1998, 2034**

There are no 4 Guas males born in Tiger years

Famous 4 Gua-Tiger Women: Marilyn Monroe, Queen Elizabeth II, Demi Moore, Jodie Foster, Sheryl Crow, Paula Abdul, Kelly Preston, Felicity Huffman, Taylor Dayne, Dina Lohan, Star Jones, Genie Francis, Kristy McNichol, Gina Gershon, and Laura San Giacomo.

Personality and Romance: The 4 Guas born in the *Year of the Tiger* is pure wood energy making these women extremely progressive and exciting with lots of potent sex-appeal! Old-fashioned Chinese parents do not like their sons marrying Tiger women believing it ill-fated as these ladies have such intense, indecisive and flamboyant energy. While it is true that the 4 Gua Tigers are all about passion and excitement, they are very protective of those who are lucky enough to win their heart. So fiercely passionate, these ladies tend to be their own worst enemy with their do or die approach to life and relationships. While they are easily influenced, often blowing with the wind, the 4 Gua-Tiger women can still make very devoted, protective and responsible mothers and wives. These ladies are huge risk-takers, spontaneous, direct, honest, and independent—they love being on top.

The best stuff: When the 4 Gua-Tigers are fully exhibiting their best qualities, they are unpredictable, rebellious, colorful, powerful, passionate, daring, impulsive, vigorous, stimulating, sincere, affectionate, humanitarian and generous.

The worst stuff: When the 4 Gua-Tigers move to the darker side of their nature, they can be restless, reckless, impatient, quick-tempered, indecisive, obstinate, and selfish.

Career: Some of the best professions for the 4 Gua-Tigers, where they may attain wealth, fame or fulfillment, as/are in advertising agent, office manager, actor, writer, artist, airline pilot, musician, politics, explorer, advertising, executives, entrepreneurs, philosophy, entertainers, chef, pharmaceuticals and print media.

7 Gua as a Tiger

Women Only!

Impulsive, Sexy, Passionate

Elements: Yin **Metal** and Yang **Wood**

Years occurring for Females: **1974, 2010, 2046**

There are no 7 Gua males born in Tiger years

Famous 7 Gua-Tiger Women: Natalie Wood, Claudia Cardinale, Diana Rigg, Connie Stevens, Eva Mendes, Victoria Beckham, Penélope Cruz, Kate Moss, Jenna Jameson, Jillian Michaels, Hilary Swank, Kimberly 'Lil' Kim' Jones, Amy Fisher, Alanis Morissette, Elizabeth Banks, and Victoria Silvstedt.

Personality and Romance: The 7 Gua women born in the *Year of the Tiger* is an inauspicious mix of metal and wood energy; causing inner turbulence and unrest. These women are passionate, impulsive, protective, enthusiastic, and excessive with exciting, powerful sexual allure! The 7 Gua-Tigers tackle things with enthusiasm, optimism and determination that ensure their success in work or projects.

They make talented and efficient leaders and are the most loyal and generous of friends. They are huge risk-takers, spontaneous, independent and they like to be on top! In the areas of love and romance, these women often get carried away with their passions, making them victims of love gone bad; at times they can fall into the charms of manipulative and immoral men.

The 7 Gua-Tigers may tend towards the 'excessive' and extremes—too much sex, too much food, too many radical ideas or opinions and so forth. They may have many lovers as they get bored very easily especially if the heartthrob of the moment turns out to be predictable. In the end, they long for a mate that is constant, steady and allows the natural instincts of a tigress to blossom—protective mothers and loyal, passionate wives.

The best stuff: When the 7 Gua-Tigers are fully exhibiting their best qualities, they are unpredictable, rebellious, colorful, powerful, passionate, daring, impulsive, vigorous, stimulating, sincere, affectionate, humanitarian and generous.

The worst stuff: When the 7 Gua-Tigers move to the darker side of their nature, they can be restless, reckless, impatient, quick-tempered, obstinate and selfish.

Career: Some of the best professions for the 7 Gua-Tigers, where they may attain wealth, fame or fulfillment, are in advertising, travel agent, artist, comedian, chauffeur, medicine, chef, engineering, IT, goldsmith, excavation, internet, judging, metal jewelry and sports equipment.

8 Gua as a Tiger
Men Only!
Risk-takers, Dazzling, Independent
Elements: Yang **Earth** and Yang **Wood**

Years occurring for Males: **1938, 1974, 2010, 2046**
No 8 Gua females ever born in the Year of the Tiger

Famous 8 Gua Tiger Men: John Steinbeck, Bobby Jones, Oliver Reed, Ted Turner, Karl Lagerfeld, Bill Withers, Peter Jennings, Elliott Gould, Leonardo DiCaprio, Joaquin Phoenix, Ryan Seacrest, Ryan Phillippe, Jimmy Fallon, and CeeLo Green.

Personality and Romance: The 8 Gua men born in the *Year of the Tiger* are an inauspicious mix of earth and wood energy; this creates inner turmoil and restlessness. These men are action-oriented, big risk-takers, tempestuous, independent and unpredictable. The 8 Gua-Tigers can be quite irresistible; you'll always feel an air of excitement around them and may get carried away by their confidence and ambitions. They are adventurous, highly social, and they have unforgettable charm!

These men have energy so intense and primal, that it can overpower people. However, they are deeply sensitive and protective—never boring; but be prepared if you fall in love with these enigmatic men. They are high-maintenance and will require lots of energy and attention.

The 8 Gua-Tigers crave excitement, love the outdoors, nature, and building things where their dynamic energy can find an outlet.

The best stuff: When the 8 Gua-Tigers are fully exhibiting their best qualities, they are unpredictable, rebellious, colorful, powerful, passionate, daring, impulsive, vigorous, stimulating, sincere, affectionate, humanitarian and generous.

The worst stuff: When the 8 Gua-Tigers move to the darker side of their nature, they can be restless, reckless, impatient, quick-tempered, obstinate, stubborn and selfish.

Career: Some of the best professions for the 8 Gua-Tigers, where they may attain wealth, fame or fulfillment, are/as in design, politics, police officer, travel writer, explorer, business executive, acting, property, real estate, construction, consultancy, hotel, architecture, pottery, quarry, and OB-GYN.

Year of the Rabbit

1 Gua as a Rabbit

Men Only!

Highly Sexual, Refined, Very Clever

Elements: Yang **Water** and Yin **Wood**

Years occurring for Males: **1927, 1963, 1999, 2035**

No female 1 Guas are ever born in the Year of the Rabbit

Famous 1 Gua-Rabbit Men: Clint Walker, Harry Belafonte, Tom Bosley, Bob Fosse, Jerry Stiller, Doc Severinsen, Robert Shaw, Neil Simon, Pope Benedict XVI, Peter Falk, Roger Moore, Sidney Poitier, George C. Scott, Brad Pitt, Michael Jordan, Bret Michaels, John Stamos, Seal, George Michael, Dermot Mulroney, Kevin Sorbo, Marc Jacobs, Conan O'Brien, David Thewlis, Mike Myers, Charles Barkley, James Hetfield, George Michael, Donnie Yen, Johnny Depp, Jet Li, Quentin Tarantino and Benjamin Bratt.

Personality and Romance: The 1 Gua men who are born in the *Year of the Rabbit* is a mix of water and wood elements, giving them lightening quick intelligence, accentuated by acute cleverness. Highly social, they are classy and refined men that are well-mannered with high style. The 1 Gua-Rabbits are low-profile, extremely tactful, accommodating and always correct and well-groomed. They are known for their good judgment and tend to be very shrewd about people and their character.

These men are very concerned with how they are perceived and must have the right address, the right woman, the right kind of car; image is very important. They tend to be insecure by nature and are not risk-takers at all--prone to being on the cautious side of investments, relationships and feelings. The 1 Gua-Rabbits are naturally sensuous and highly sexual. These men are proficient at holding on to their money, ideas, and concepts; they are also skillful at hiding secrets.

The best stuff: When the 1 Gua-Rabbits are fully exhibiting their best qualities, they are gracious, kind, sensitive, soft-spoken, amiable, elegant, reserved, cautious, artistic, thorough, tender, self-assured, astute, compassionate, and flexible.

The worst stuff: When the 1 Gua-Rabbits move to the darker side of their nature, they can be moody, detached, superficial, self-indulgent, opportunistic, and lazy.

Career: Some of the best professions for the 1 Gua-Rabbits, where they may attain wealth, fame or fulfillment, are in design, cultivation, education, medicine, culture, judiciary, public relations, judge, life coach, adviser, shipping, communications, entertainment, sex industry, or a diplomat.

2 Gua as a Rabbit

Women Only!

Quick, Sexual, Intuitive

Elements: Yin **Earth** and Yin **Wood**

Years occurring for Females: **1951, 1987, 2023**

No 2 Guas males are ever born in the Year of the Rabbit

Famous 2 Gua-Rabbit Women: Ingrid Bergman, Billie Holiday, Beverly D'Angelo, Lynda Carter, Jane Seymour, Anjelica Huston, Olivia Hussey, Crystal Gayle, Jean Smart, Jo Jo Starbuck, Melissa Manchester, Suze Orman, Kathryn Bigelow, Queen Noor, Morgan Brittany, Cheryl Ladd, Blake Lively, Ashley Greene, Hilary Duff, Rosie Huntington-Whiteley, Ellen Page, Joss Stone and Maria Sharapova.

Personality and Romance: The 2 Gua-Rabbits are always on the alert and are very sensitive, soft and vulnerable. They tend to be honest, calm-natured, dependable, highly intelligent, clever, and their minds move lightening quick. The 2 Gua-Rabbits are generally insecure, and are not risk-takers at all. However, they are highly social, refined and classy women with superior manners and high style.

The 2 Gua-Rabbits are ladies that are naturally sensuous and highly sexual. They may have unrealistic expectations such as a "Cinderella complex", and need a partner that will not take advantage of them as the disappointment could lead to depression. Since their energy is really yin, at times they may be moody and detached.

The best stuff: When the 2 Gua-Rabbits are fully exhibiting their best qualities, they are gracious, kind, sensitive, soft-spoken, amiable, elegant, nurturing, reserved, cautious, artistic, thorough, tender, self-assured, astute, compassionate, and flexible.

The worst stuff: When the 2 Gua-Rabbits move to the darker side of their nature, they can be moody, detached, superficial, depressed, self-indulgent, opportunistic, and lazy.

Career: Some of the best professions for the 2 Gua-Rabbits, where they may attain wealth, fame or fulfillment, are in cultivation, medicine, judiciary, politics, public relations, literature, lawyers, advisors, property, real estate, construction, consultancy, architecture, interior design, recruitment, or an OB-GYN.

4 Gua as a Rabbit

Men Only!

Sexual, Self-Assured, Progressive

Elements: Yin **Wood** and Yin **Wood**

Years occurring for Females: **1951, 1987, 2023**

No 4 Guas females ever born in the Year of the Rabbit

Famous 4 Gua-Rabbit Men: Frank Sinatra, Orson Welles, Anthony Quinn, Luther Vandross, Mark Harmon, Phil Collins, Sting, John Mellencamp, Michael Keaton, Kurt Russell, Peabo Bryson, Stedman Graham, Robin Williams, Lou Ferrigno, Dan Fogelberg, Tony Danza, Stellan Skarsgård, Rob Halford, and Treat Williams.

Personality and Romance: The 4 Guas born in the *Year of the Rabbit* is pure wood energy making these men progressive, self-assured and easy-going. The 4 Gua Rabbits are clever, highly intelligent and their minds can move quickly as lightening. These men are classy, refined, and stylish with wonderful manners. Always aware of how they are perceived, the 4 Gua Rabbits pay a great deal attention to being polished and image is very important. They can even be snobs about the status of others and their standing in the world.

These men are naturally sensuous and highly sexual; they are not risk takers in love or any other area of their life. Since they may have unrealistic expectations and may be easily influenced by lovers, they need a partner that will not take advantage of them. However, free-loving women need not apply, these men will only attached themselves to women they consider having the right caliber and status; sexy sirens will not win a husband here.

The best stuff: When the 4 Gua-Rabbits are fully exhibiting their best qualities, they are gracious, kind, sensitive, soft-spoken, amiable, elegant, reserved, cautious, artistic, thorough, tender, self-assured, astute, gentle, compassionate and flexible.

The worst stuff: When the 4 Gua-Rabbits move to the darker side of their nature, they can be moody, detached, superficial, self-indulgent, indecisive, opportunistic, and lazy.

Career: Some of the best professions for the 4 Gua-Rabbits, where they may attain wealth, fame or fulfillment, are in health care, travel, public relations, judge, lawyers, diplomats, design, explorer, estate management, farming, entertainers, publishing, fashion, technicians, and broadcast announcers.

7 Gua as a Rabbit

Men Only!

Refined, Charming, Nervous

Elements: Yin **Metal** and Yin **Wood**

Years occurring for Females:
1939, 1975, 2011, 2047
No 7 Gua females are born in Rabbit years

Famous 7-Gua Rabbit Men: Bob Hope, Bing Crosby, Marvin Gaye, Neil Sedaka, George Hamilton, Francis Ford Coppola, Enrique Iglesias, David Beckham, Tiger Woods, Tobey Maguire, 50 Cent, Ray Lewis, Russell Brand, Michael Buble, and Johnny Galecki.

Personality and Romance: The 7 Gua men born in the *Year of the Rabbit* is an inauspicious mix of metal and wood energy; causing some internal chaos and instability. These men are diplomatic, well-mannered, shrewd, sensuous, and stylish. They are always conscious of their image, making sure that they come off impeccable. The 7-Gua Rabbit males tend to be very materialistic and could even be described as a genuine snob; having the right address, right clothes, the best associates and so forth are essential.

Not known for being spontaneous, these men are careful planners in almost all areas of their life. This would include romantic relationships as well. He will only choose a spouse that in his estimation is worthy and suitable, meeting all the criteria to secure the right image. The 7 Gua-Rabbits must be alert not to overindulge in the pleasures of life such as food, drink, money, and sex; they must keep a balanced lifestyle. While extremely charming, they can be a fast-talker, smooth talking, or have a razor-sharp tongue. These men are also naturally sensuous and highly sexual. However they will powerfully commit to the right partner.

The best stuff: When the 7 Gua-Rabbits are fully exhibiting their best qualities, they are gracious, kind, sensitive, soft-spoken, amiable, elegant, reserved, cautious, artistic, thorough, tender, self-assured, astute, compassionate and flexible.

The worst stuff: When the 7 Gua-Rabbits move to the darker side of their nature, they can be moody, detached, superficial, self-indulgent, opportunistic and lazy.

Career: Some of the best professions for the 7 Gua-Rabbits, where they may attain wealth, fame or fulfillment, are in cultivation, health care, judiciary, politics, estate management, engineering, IT, goldsmith, machinery, metal, mining, hi-tech goods, lawyer, and metal jewelry.

8 Gua as a Rabbit

Women Only!

Virtuous, Materialistic, Social

Elements: Yang **Earth** and Yin **Wood**

Years occurring for Females: **1963, 1975, 1999, 2011**

There are no 8 Gua males are born in Rabbit years

Famous 8 Gua Rabbit Women: Claudette Colbert, Tina Turner, Ali MacGraw, Dusty Springfield, Dixie Carter, Elizabeth Ashley, Whitney Houston, Elle Macpherson, Brigitte Nielsen, Vanessa Williams, Nicollette Sheridan, Lisa Kudrow, Keely Shaye Smith, Tatum O'Neal, Jeanne Tripplehorn, Natasha Richardson, Angelina Jolie, Charlize Theron, Eva Longoria, Drew Barrymore, and Kate Winslet.

Personality and Romance: The 8 Gua women born in the *Year of the Rabbit* are an inauspicious mix of earth and wood energy; this will trigger inner conflict and insecurities. These women are virtuous, diplomatic, modest, tactful, soft-spoken and elegant. Social acceptance is very important to them and they desire material things in the world—grand home, good marriage, successful husband who brings status, good career—the objective is to look picture perfect. Later in life, they may even become hoarders.

However, the 8 Gua-Rabbits are down to earth, enjoying a life of order and peace. Their energy is quick as lightening, however they make excellent listeners and you may feel calmed in their presence.

These women may have unrealistic expectations and need a partner that will not take advantage of them. They are attracted and talented with things of the earth—real estate (especially raw land and mountainous regions), construction, landscaping and planting. These ladies will need time alone to recharge their energy; otherwise they may tend towards depression.

The best stuff: When the 8 Gua-Rabbits are fully exhibiting their best qualities, they are diplomatic, intuitive, social, refined, classy, soft-spoken, elegant, reserved, well-mannered, stylish, clever and naturally sensuous.

The worst stuff: When the 8 Gua-Rabbits move to the darker side of their nature, they can be stubborn, moody, detached, superficial, self-indulgent, opportunistic, and lazy.

Career: Some of the best professions for the 8 Gua-Rabbits, where they may attain wealth, fame or fulfillment as or are in literature, public relations, judge, lawyer, cultivation, education, culture, politics, real estate, construction, consultancy, hotel, architecture, HR, farmers and OB-GYN.

Year of the Dragon

The Year of the Dragon only produces 3, 6 & 9 Guas

3 Gua as a Dragon

Men and Women!

Powerful, Steady, Outspoken

Elements: Yang **Wood** and Yang **Earth**

Years occurring for Males/Females: **1952, 1988, 2024**

Famous 3 Gua-Dragon Men and Women: Betty Grable, Kirk Douglas, George Strait, Grace Jones, Liam Neeson, Patrick Swayze, Isabella Rossellini, Steven Seagal, Christopher Reeve, Beverly Johnson, Dan Aykroyd, Susan Dey, Mr. T, Sharon Osbourne, Mickey Rourke, Marilu Henner, Jeff Goldblum, Beverly Johnson, Roseanne, David Hasselhoff, John Goodman, Bob Costas, John Tesh, Emma Stone, Julianne Hough, Rihanna, Rupert Grint, Vanessa Hudgens, Candice Swanepoel, Nikki Reed, Haley Joel Osment, Michael Cera, Adele, Sergio Aguero, and Petra Ecclestone Stunt.

Personality and Romance: The 3 Guas born in the *Year of the Dragon* have a mix of wood and earth giving them power and confidence, yet they are grounded as well. In the Chinese culture the mythical dragon is the most potent and revered creature, therefore it is considered one of the most auspicious signs to be born under. The 3 Guas can exude power, progressive and enterprising energy; the mix is indeed intense. These people have lots of vigor, fiery passion, decisive and zealous ambition. The 3 Gua-Dragons feel most alive when they are inventing new things, starting new businesses, or off on a new adventure as their energy is very progressive and modern, no matter their age. When they have their creative juices flowing they exhibit their best qualities of being loyal, dignified and generous. In relationships they are charming and draw in their chosen partner/s with their charisma. They easily find lovers, but it's harder for them to settle down as they like a challenge even in love. When and if they marry, they will need lots of space.

The best stuff: When the 3 Gua-Dragons are fully exhibiting their best qualities, they are magnanimous, vigorous, strong, self-assured, proud, noble, direct, dignified, zealous, fiery, passionate, decisive, pioneering, ambitious, generous and loyal.

The worst stuff: When the 3 Gua-Dragons move to the darker side of their nature, they can be arrogant, imperious, tyrannical, demanding, eccentric, grandiloquent and extremely bombastic, prejudiced, dogmatic, over-bearing, brash, outspoken, violent, impetuous, and brash.

Career: Some of the best professions for the 3 Gua-Dragons, where they may attain wealth, fame or fulfillment, are as a journalist, inventor, lawyer, engineer, architect, law, religion, the arts, entrepreneurs, actors, estate management, entertainers and pharmaceuticals.

6 Gua as a Dragon
Men and Women!
Confident, Powerful, Loyal

Elements: Yang **Metal** and Yang **Earth**

Years occurring for Males:
1940, 1976, 2012, 2044
Years occurring for Females:
1928, 1964, 2000

Famous 6 Gua-Dragon Men and Women: Dr. Suess, Robert Oppenheimer, Shirley Temple, Maya Angelou, Rosemary Clooney, Al Pacino, Chuck Norris, Smokey Robinson, Bruce Lee, Frank Zappa, Ringo Starr, John Gotti, Richard Pryor, Martin Sheen, Sandra Bullock, Sarah Palin, Courteney Cox, Elle Macpherson, Melissa Gilbert, Tracy Chapman, Wynonna Judd, Juliette Binoche, Trisha Yearwood, Ville Valo, Ryan Reynolds, Colin Farrell, Alexander Skarsgård, Ronaldo, Benedict Cumberbatch and Blake Shelton.

Personality and Romance: The 6 Guas born in the *Year of the Dragon* are a harmonious mix of metal and earth energy; this makes these men and women very confident and powerful. They are vibrant and captivating—you will notice these people whenever they enter a room! The 6 Gua-Dragons shine in positions of leadership and authority such as senators, governors, entrepreneurs, CEO's, or Supreme Court judges. These men and women play by their own rules; they also like to 'play big', no acting small or shy in the world for these lucky people.

In romantic relationships, the women are very desirable, stunningly sexy with brilliant intelligence—she will have many suitors and admirers.

In order to win her heart, she will have to be properly courted and dazzled before she selects her mate for life. The 6 Gua-Dragon men have huge egos, are usually highly successful and will want a partner worth winning—a real trophy before he gives up his notoriously unfaithful ways. Both sexes need their independence to some degree; dragons can have hot tempers, they need a tough-skinned mate, but they themselves make loyal life partners.

The best stuff: When the 6 Gua-Dragons are fully exhibiting their best qualities, they are magnanimous, stately, vigorous, strong, self-assured, proud, noble, direct, dignified, zealous, fiery, passionate, decisive, pioneering, ambitious, generous and loyal.

The worst stuff: When the 6 Gua-Dragons move to the darker side of their nature, they can be arrogant, imperious, tyrannical, demanding, eccentric, grandiloquent and extremely bombastic, prejudiced, dogmatic, over-bearing, violent, over-thinkers, impetuous, and brash.

Career: Some of the best professions for the 6 Gua-Dragons, where they may attain wealth, fame or fulfillment, are as an inventor, lawyer, engineer, architect, broker, medicine, philosopher, goldsmith, metal mining, excavation, and hi-tech goods.

9 Gua as a Dragon
Men and Women!
Powerful, Brilliant, Loyal

Elements: Yin **Fire** and Yang **Earth**

Years occurring for Males: **1928, 1964, 2000, 2036**
Years occurring for Females: **1940, 1976, 2012, 2048**

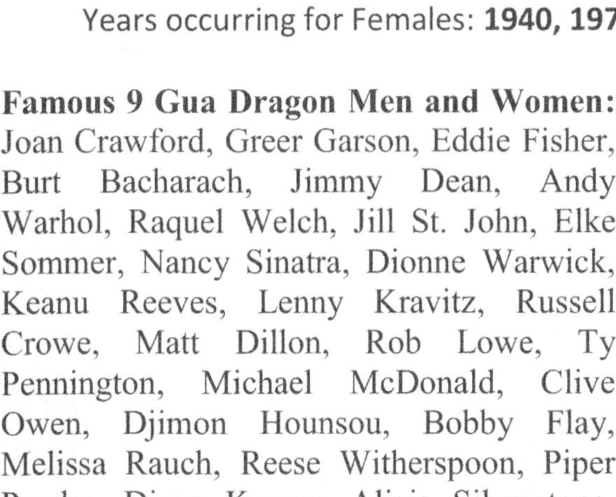

Famous 9 Gua Dragon Men and Women: Joan Crawford, Greer Garson, Eddie Fisher, Burt Bacharach, Jimmy Dean, Andy Warhol, Raquel Welch, Jill St. John, Elke Sommer, Nancy Sinatra, Dionne Warwick, Keanu Reeves, Lenny Kravitz, Russell Crowe, Matt Dillon, Rob Lowe, Ty Pennington, Michael McDonald, Clive Owen, Djimon Hounsou, Bobby Flay, Melissa Rauch, Reese Witherspoon, Piper Perabo, Diane Kruger, Alicia Silverstone, Rashida Jones, Kelly Clarkson, Keri Russell, Isla Fisher and Naomie Harris.

Personality and Romance: The 9 Gua men and women born in the *Year of the Dragon* are an auspicious mix of fire and earth energy; this brings great personal power. The Chinese culture revere the mythical dragon is the mightiest and most revered creatures. These men and women enjoy things on a grand scale, and play by their own rules. They are vibrant, courageous, tenacious, intelligent, enthusiastic, confident, impetuous and charismatic. 9 Guas have a sharp, brilliant intellect; they can also be wise, loyal, and sentimental. The 9 Gua-Dragon women are captivating and are not modest or unassuming—you *will* notice her as she enters a room. The male 9 Gua-Dragons have supreme egos; they are dashing, hugely ambitious, and born winners. Blessed with a fiery spirit and energy, these Guas have a permanent adventurous streak. The female 9's are usually beautiful like a diva or goddess. The 9 Gua-Dragons may have their head in the clouds at times, they are nevertheless very grounded. In the search for the ideal partner, they might find themselves often hesitating to move forward in a relationship and/or unwilling to make a permanent commitment. When they do, however, it is their intention that it be lasting. The 9 Gua-Dragons are likely to have a warm, giving personality. They can be very generous to their loved ones. Because dragons can have hot tempers, they need a tough-skinned spouse, but make loyal life partners.

The best stuff: When the 9 Gua-Dragons are fully exhibiting their best qualities, they are intellectual, magnanimous, stately, vigorous, strong, self-assured, brilliant, proud, noble, direct, dignified, zealous, fiery, passionate, decisive, pioneering, ambitious, generous and loyal.

The worst stuff: When the 9 Gua-Dragons move to the darker side of their nature, they can be paranoid, unstable, rash, psychotic, arrogant, imperious, tyrannical, demanding, eccentric, grandiloquent, extremely bombastic, prejudiced, dogmatic, over-bearing, violent, impetuous and brash.

Career: Some of the best professions for the 9 Gua-Dragons, where they may attain wealth, fame or fulfillment, are in law, the arts, entrepreneur, doctors, inventor, lawyer, engineer, architect, broker, television, restaurants, beauty and war correspondence.

Year of the Snake

1 Gua as a Snake

Women Only!

Seductive, High-Strung, Intelligent

Elements: Yang **Water** and Yin **Fire**

Years occurring for Females: **1941, 1977, 2013, 2049**

No 1 Guas males are ever born in the Year of the Snake

Famous 1 Gua-Snake Women: Joan Crawford, Greta Garbo, Julie Christie, Linda McCartney, Helen Reddy, Martha Stewart, Sally Kirkland, Juliet Mills, Vikki Carr, Ann Margret, Faye Dunaway, Nora Ephron, Sophia Rossi, Sarah Michelle Gellar, Maggie Gyllenhaal, Gaby Espino, Jaime Pressly, Katheryn Winnick, Irina Voronina, Melanie Jayne Lynskey, Brittany Murphy, and Liv Tyler.

Personality and Romance: The 1 Gua women who were born in the *Year of the Snake* is a mix of water and fire elements, both are volatile types of energy that makes this personality almost impossible to pin down. Usually blessed with beauty, allure, dignity and charm, they have lovely manners and are rarely short of admirers. These women are masters at the waiting game, and they will take their time finding the right job, the right house and the right spouse.

The 1 Gua-Snakes are extremely intelligent, high-strung, and know how to get what they want from people using their incredible seductive skills. It's wise not to make an enemy of this personality, they will get their revenge. They tend to be highly sexual, sensuous and emotional in nature. They are adept in using their internal energy for powerful results in all areas of their life.

The best stuff: When the 1 Gua-Snakes are fully exhibiting their best qualities, they are deep thinkers, wise, mystical, graceful, soft-spoken, sensual, creative, secretive, prudent, shrewd, ambitious, elegant, cautious, responsible, calm, strong, constant, and purposeful.

The worst stuff: When the 1 Gua-Snakes move to the darker side of their nature, they can be a loner, bad communicator, possessive, moody, emotional, hedonistic, self-doubting, distrustful, and mendacious.

Career: Some of the best professions for the 1 Gua-Snakes, where they may attain wealth, fame or fulfillment, are as a scientist, analyst, astrologer, politics, law, archaeologist, entrepreneur, philosopher, banking, freight, entertainment, firefighting, diplomat, or in the publishing industry.

2 Gua as a Snake

Men Only!

Seductive, Possessive, Intuitive

Elements: Yin **Earth** and Yin **Fire**

Years occurring for Males: **1953, 1977, 1989, 2013**

No female 2 Guas are born in Snake years

Famous 2 Gua-Snake Men: President John F. Kennedy, Dean Martin, Dezi Arnaz, Franco Nero, Ryan O'Neal, Michael Bolton, Bob Dylan, Paul Simon, Nick Nolte, Jesse Jackson, Pierce Brosnan, John Malkovich, Hulk Hogan, Alex Van Halen, Keith Hernandez, Bill Pullman, Tim Allen, John Mayer, Kanye West, Jonathan Rhys Meyers, Travis Alexander, Tom Hardy, John Cena, Ludacris, Joe Jonas, Daniel Radcliffe, Chris Brown, David Henrie and Prince George Alexander Louis.

Personality and Romance: The 2 Guas born in the *Year of the Snake* have an interesting combination of very earthy energy mixed with fire! Men born under these signs are grounded, sensitive, and intelligent and are masters at the waiting game. They also know how to get what they want from people, making them consummate seducers. The 2 Gua-Snake men are often soft-spoken (or use seductive speech), shrewd, cautious, calm-natured, and responsible. They can be possessive in relationships and of their possessions. Generally distrusting of everyone, they use their intuitive abilities to weed out the bad characters. One of their best qualities is how they reserve and use their internal energy for powerful results.

The best stuff: When the 2 Gua-Snakes are fully exhibiting their best qualities, they are deep thinkers, wise, mystic, graceful, soft-spoken, sensual, creative, prudent, shrewd, ambitious, elegant, cautious, responsible, calm, strong, constant, nurturing and purposeful.

The worst stuff: When the 2 Gua-Snakes move to the darker side of their nature, they can be a loner, bad communicator, possessive, depressed, hedonistic, self-doubting, distrustful, and mendacious.

Career: Some of the best professions for the 2 Gua-Snakes, where they may attain wealth, fame or fulfillment, are as a scientist, investigator, jeweler, magician, politics, law, astrologer, archaeologist, entrepreneur, spelunker, psychologist, philosopher, architecture, interior design or human resources.

4 Gua as a Snake

Women Only!

Seductive, Mystical, Intelligent

Elements: Yin **Wood** and Yin **Fire**

Years occurring for Females: **1953, 1989, 2025**

No 4 Guas males ever born in the Year of the Snake

Famous 4 Gua-Snake Women: Phyllis Diller, Zsa Zsa Gabor, Lena Horne, Kim Basinger, Bebe Buell, Kathie Lee Gifford, Benazir Bhutto, Cyndi Lauper, Chaka Khan, Kate Capshaw, Mary Steenburgen, Patti Scialfa, Marcia Clark, Oprah Winfrey, Bess Armstrong, Joanna Kerns, Tracy Scoggins, Amy Irving, Kathleen Sullivan, Meredith Vieira, Jordin Sparks, Hayden Panettiere, Chelsie Hightower and Taylor Swift. *Note: Oprah was born January 1954; the Chinese New Year does not start until February 4th, 1954 which places her in the Year of the Snake (1953).*

Personality and Romance: Those 4 Guas born in the *Year of the Snake* are a powerful mix of wood and fire energy; this makes these ladies consummate seducers, even if it's innocently. These women are highly intelligent, deep thinkers, alluring, and very dignified. Often unaware of their potent attraction, they move through life casting a spell with their charm and feminine sexuality everywhere they go. If they pursue an academic or scholastic profession, they will achieve great success and fame.

The 4 Gua-Snake women love exquisite things—homes, jewelry, clothes, jets—all the trappings of a life saturated in luxury and beauty. They are masters of the waiting game, and it often pays off with a brilliant marriage that brings them wealth and status. While they are flexible in ideas, they often struggle with making decisions. These women can have movie-star looks and may be obsessed with their appearance. Progressive, but not naturally independent, most will seek a partner in life that can bring them stability and status.

The best stuff: When the 4 Gua-Snakes are fully exhibiting their best qualities, they are deep thinkers, wise, mystical, graceful, soft-spoken, sensual, creative, prudent, shrewd, ambitious, elegant, cautious, responsible, calm, strong, constant and purposeful.

The worst stuff: When the 4 Gua-Snakes move to the darker side of their nature, they can be a loner, bad communicator, wishy-washy, possessive, hedonistic, indecisive, self-doubting, distrustful and mendacious.

Career: Some of the best professions for the 4 Gua-Snakes, where they may attain wealth, fame or fulfillment, are as a scientist, analyst, investigator, astrologer, public relations, archaeologist, psychologist, the arts, entrepreneurs, medicine, publishing, real estate management, and transportation.

7 Gua as a Snake

Women Only!

Seductive, Talkative, Regal

Elements: Yin **Metal** and Yin **Fire**

Years occurring for Females: **1929, 1965, 2001, 2037**

No 7 Gua males ever born in the Year of the Snake

Famous 7 Gua-Snake Women: Audrey Hepburn, Grace Kelly, Jacqueline Kennedy, Barbara Walters, Shania Twain, Katarina Witt, Brooke Shields, Elizabeth Hurley, Sarah Jessica Parker, Linda Evangelista, Paulina Porizkova, Princess Stéphanie of Monaco, Connie Nielsen, Kyra Sedgwick, Heidi Fleiss, Constance Marie and J.K. Rowling.

Personality and Romance: The 7 Gua women born in the *Year of the Snake* is an inauspicious mix of metal and fire energy; causing some emotional, inner turmoil. These women are highly intelligent, deep thinkers, alluring, and very dignified. Often unaware of their potent attraction, they move through life innocently casting a spell with their charm and feminine sexuality. If they pursue an academic or scholastic profession, they will achieve great success and fame. The 7 Gua-Snake women love exquisite things—homes, jewelry, clothes, jets—all the trappings of a life filled with luxury and beauty.

They are masters of the waiting game, and it often pays off with a brilliant marriage that brings them wealth and status. These women are often irresistible and men can fall passionately in love with them; they tend to be youthful in behavior or appearance. They are comfortable with a lot of 'stage' and are good at acting, speaking, in front of the camera or on the radio. In romantic relationships, the 7 Gua-Snakes enjoy being wooed and lavished with attention. In marriage they make good partners with no particular need for deep independence, rather security is what they crave.

The best stuff: When the 7 Gua-Snakes are fully exhibiting their best qualities, they are deep thinkers, wise, mystic, graceful, soft-spoken, sensual, creative, prudent, shrewd, ambitious, elegant, cautious, responsible, calm, strong, constant and purposeful.

The worst stuff: When the 7 Gua-Snakes move to the darker side of their nature, they can be a loner, bad communicator, possessive, hedonistic, self-doubting, distrustful and mendacious.

Career: Some of the best professions for the 7 Gua-Snakes, where they may attain wealth, fame or fulfillment, are in scientist, investigator, astrologer, magician, sociologist, farming, medicine, engineering, computers, excavation, hi-tech goods, lawyer, metal jewelry, government service, sports equipment and lecturers.

8 Gua as a Snake

Men Only!

Seducers, Intelligent, Sensitive

Elements: Yang **Earth** and Yin **Fire**

Years occurring for Males: **1929, 1965, 2001, 2037**

No 8 Gua males ever born in the Year of the Snake

Famous 8 Gua Snake Men: Ike Jones, Christopher Plummer, Bob Newhart, Max von Sydow, André Previn, Salman Khan, Charlie Sheen, Slash, Robert Downey Jr., Ben Stiller, Sean Patrick Flanery, Chris Rock, Martin Lawrence, Dougray Scott, Scottie Peppin, Kevin James and Shahrukh Khan.

Personality and Romance: The 8 Gua men born in the *Year of the Snake* are a mix of earth and fire energy; this auspicious mix brings lots of personal power. These men are sensitive, stubborn, intelligent, and they're masters at the waiting game. They can become spiritual seekers, and trek the mountains in search of 'answers' or to find themselves. They are consummate seducers, and in relationships with lovers and partners tend to be possessive and jealous.

One of their best qualities is how they reserve and use their internal energy for powerful results. The 8 Gua-Snakes tend to resist change; they can deftly handle trouble without falling apart. These men work very hard; however, they have a tendency to get bored with routine and will regularly job hop. They are great thinkers and solving complex problems is stimulating to them; they do well under pressure and deadlines. They are geared for success and often become very rich with worldly honors, recognition and status.

The best stuff: When the 8 Gua-Snakes are fully exhibiting their best qualities, they are deep thinkers, wise, mystic, sensual, creative, shrewd, ambitious, elegant, cautious, responsible, calm, strong, dependable and purposeful.

The worst stuff: When the 8 Gua-Snakes move to the darker side of their nature, they can be hoarders, stubborn, self-righteous, short-tempered, a bad communicator, possessive, hedonistic, self-doubting, distrustful, and mendacious.

Career: Some of the best professions for the 8 Gua-Snakes, where they may attain wealth, fame or fulfillment, are in or as a scientist, analyst, astrologer, dietician, politics, law, entrepreneur, real estate, construction, consultancy, hotel, architecture, recruitment, quarry, farmers, and OB-GYN.

Year of the Horse

1 Gua as a Horse

Men Only!

Confident, Proud, Intelligent

Elements: Yang **Water** and Yang **Fire**

Years occurring for Males: **1954, 1990, 2026**

There are no female 1 Guas born in Horse years

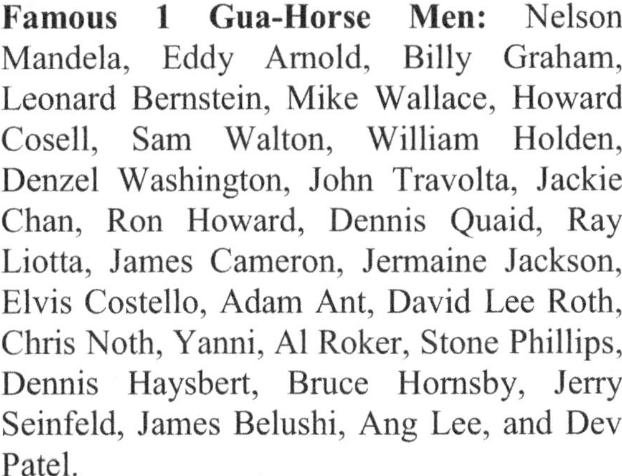

Famous 1 Gua-Horse Men: Nelson Mandela, Eddy Arnold, Billy Graham, Leonard Bernstein, Mike Wallace, Howard Cosell, Sam Walton, William Holden, Denzel Washington, John Travolta, Jackie Chan, Ron Howard, Dennis Quaid, Ray Liotta, James Cameron, Jermaine Jackson, Elvis Costello, Adam Ant, David Lee Roth, Chris Noth, Yanni, Al Roker, Stone Phillips, Dennis Haysbert, Bruce Hornsby, Jerry Seinfeld, James Belushi, Ang Lee, and Dev Patel.

Personality and Romance: The 1 Gua born in the *Year of the Horse* is a mix of water and fire elements, both unpredictable energies that can be powerful and yet unstable. The 1 Gua-Horse personalities are that of strength and persistence. They are highly intelligent, high-speed and analytical thinkers, but deep inside they have a rich emotional and varied landscape. These men have tremendous inner confidence, love to be the center of attention and are stimulated by the next challenge.

The 1 Gua Horses are proud and independent but still long for a life partner who can match their deeply sensuous nature. They prefer to live in harmony with a good mate that can bring stability and where they can exhibit their full power and spirit. The 1 Gua-Horse men tend to fall hard and fast in relationships but get a great deal mellower late in life.

The best stuff: When the 1 Gua-Horses are fully exhibiting their best qualities, they are cheerful, popular, quick-witted, changeable, earthy, perceptive, talkative, agile both mentally and physically, magnetic, intelligent, astute, flexible, open-minded and intelligent.

The worst stuff: When the 1 Gua-Horses move to the darker side of their nature, they can be moody, fickle, anxious, rude, gullible, stubborn, lack perseverance and emotionally unstable.

Career: Some of the best professions for the 1 Gua-Horses, where they may attain wealth, fame or fulfillment, are in journalist, language instructor, performer, pilot, librarian, politics, sports, construction, geographer, executive, finance, banking, communications, entertainment, or a diplomat.

2 Gua as a Horse

Women Only!

Persistent, Confident, Magnetic

Elements: Yin **Earth** and Yang **Fire**

Years occurring for Females: **1942, 1978, 2014**

No male 2 Guas are ever born in Horse years

Famous 2 Gua-Horse Women: Mary Astor, Josephine Baker, Jean Shrimpton, Carole King, Sandra Dee, Penny Marshall, Annette Funicello, Linda Evans, Barbara Streisand, Aretha Franklin, Carole King, Geneviève Bujold, Rachael McAdams, Katie Holmes, Katherine Heigl, Maria Menounos, Ginnifer Goodwin, Nicole Scherzinger, Stana Katic, Zoe Saldana and Karina Smirnoff.

Personality and Romance: The 2 Gua women born in the *Year of the Horse* bring a powerful combination of earth and fire energy making them both grounded and exciting to be around! They thrive on being the center of attention, have incredible inner confidence, and are always looking to be stimulated by the next big thing or challenge.

The 2 Gua-Horses are very proud, calm, dependable and supportive of all in their inner circle. However, they need their independence even when they choose a life partner. They prefer to live in harmony with a good mate where they can feel safe to give free rein to their full potential. While they may fall hard and fast in relationships, they do mellow out as they age. If they are not fully able to influence their life and living environment, they tend towards depression and melancholy episodes

The best stuff: When the 2 Gua-Horses are fully exhibiting their best qualities, they are nurturing, cheerful, popular, quick-witted, changeable, earthy, perceptive, talkative, agile both mentally and physically, magnetic, intelligent, astute, flexible, and open-minded.

The worst stuff: When the 2 Gua-Horses move to the darker side of their nature, they can be stubborn, fickle, anxious, rude, depressed, gullible, lack stability and perseverance.

Career: Some of the best professions for the 2 Gua-Horses, where they may attain wealth, fame or fulfillment, are as a publicist, journalist, translator, performer, librarian, politics, sports, archaeologist, entrepreneur, psychologist, real estate, construction, architecture, interior design, human resources or OB-GYN.

4 Gua as a Horse

Men Only!

Strength, Proud, Earthy Sensuality

Elements: Yin **Wood** and Yang **Fire**

Years occurring for males: **1942, 1978, 2014, 2050**

No 4 Guas females ever born in the Year of the Horse

Famous 4 Gua-Horse Men: Bugsy Siegel, Billy Wilder, Jimi Hendrix, Paul McCartney, Harrison Ford, Brian Jones, Isaac Hayes, Brian Wilson, Wayne Newton, Billy Connolly, Jerry Garcia, Larry Flynt, Roger Ebert, Martin Scorsese, Calvin Klein, Ian McShane, Enrique Iglesias, Lou Reed, Ian Somerhalder, Josh Hartnett, Usher Raymond, Ashton Kutcher, James Franco, and Kobe Bryant.

Personality and Romance: The 4 Gua men born in the *Year of the Horse* are a powerful mix of wood and fire; this energy gives them a remarkable drive in life. They also have strength, persistence, inner confidence and a very proud air. The 4-Gua Horses can be very restless, always needing something to do or a project to start. Deeply honest, he may be a man of few words who values people being direct and forthcoming. These men have immense energy, but they are not aggressive, though they do come across as being strong and macho. They are attracted to sophisticated women who are a bit glamorous. When they fall in love, it is hard and fast-and forever. The 4 Gua Horse men can carry a torch for years for the same woman and they enjoy being the leader in a relationship. They have a wonderful, earthy sensuality and tend to be very faithful in a romantic relationship; seldom if ever, do they stray from their chosen mate.

The best stuff: When the 4 Gua-Horses are fully exhibiting their best qualities, they are cheerful, popular, quick-witted, changeable, earthy, perceptive, talkative, agile both mentally and physically, magnetic, intelligent, astute, flexible and open-minded.

The worst stuff: When the 4 Gua-Horses move to the darker side of their nature, they can be fickle, anxious, rude, gullible, stubborn, indecisive, lack stability and perseverance.

Career: Some of the best professions for the 4 Gua-Horses, where they may attain wealth, fame or fulfillment, are as a publicist, journalist, librarian, pilot, politics, sports, construction, geographer, entrepreneurs, philosophy, chef, education, pharmaceuticals, publishing and fashion.

7 Gua as a Horse

Men Only!

Independent, Magnetic, Talkative

Elements: Yin **Metal** and Yang **Fire**

Years occurring for Females: **1930, 1966, 2002, 2038**

No 7 Gua females born in the Year of the Horse

Famous 7 Gua-Horse Men: Jack Benny, Clint Eastwood, Ray Charles, Sean Connery, Shel Silverstein, Richard Harris, Warren Buffett, John Cusack, Adam Sandler, Mike Tyson, Luke Perry, Troy Aikman, Kiefer Sutherland, David Schwimmer, Billy Zane, Jon Favreau , Michael Imperioli, Billy Burke, Donal Logue, Jeffery Dean Morgan and Matthew Fox.

Personality and Romance: The 7 Gua men born in the *Year of the Horse* is an inauspicious mix of metal and fire energy; causing some internal chaos and instability. These men are fiercely independent, proud, outspoken and may have a firey or touchy temperament. They tend to be restless and need an outlet for their incredible energy and spirit. The 7 Gua-Horse men tend to act on inspired ideas without hesitation, often getting carried away by the excitement of something new.

Due to the fact that these men are often brimming with ideas, energy and time may get scattered. In romantic relationships, they love the thrill and exhilaration of romance; they may set aside their normal responsible and hard-working self to pursue the whirlwind of new emotions. However, when they settled down, they make excellent husbands and great providers.

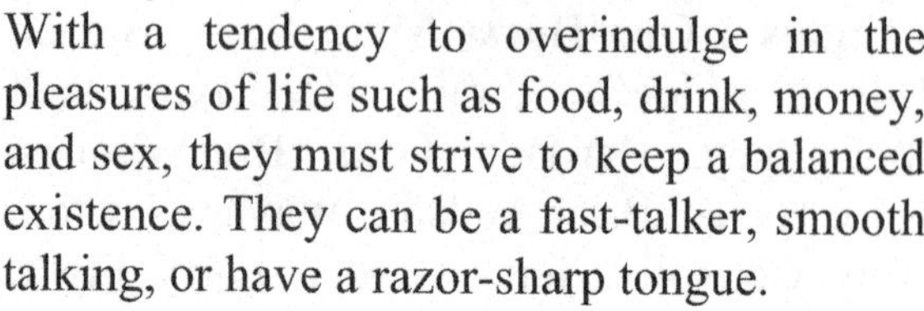

With a tendency to overindulge in the pleasures of life such as food, drink, money, and sex, they must strive to keep a balanced existence. They can be a fast-talker, smooth talking, or have a razor-sharp tongue.

The best stuff: When the 7 Gua-Horses are fully exhibiting their best qualities, they are cheerful, popular, quick-witted, changeable, earthy, perceptive, talkative, agile both mentally and physically, magnetic, intelligent, astute, flexible and open-minded.

The worst stuff: When the 7 Gua-Horses move to the darker side of their nature, they can be fickle, anxious, rude, gullible, stubborn, cutting speech, lack stability and perseverance.

Career: Some of the best professions for the 7 Gua-Horses, where they may attain wealth, fame or fulfillment, are as a publicist, sales representative, journalist, translator, performer, librarian, philosopher, teacher, chef, police office engineering, goldsmith, judging, metal jewelry, government service, sports equipment and lecturers.

8 Gua as a Horse

Women Only!

Confident, Proud, Stubborn

Elements: Yang **Earth** and Yang **Fire**

Years occurring for Females: **1954, 1966, 1990, 2002**
There are no 8 Gua males born in Horse years

Famous 8 Gua Horse Women: Rita Hayworth, Pearl Bailey, Ingmar Bergman, Betty Ford, Tippi Hedren, Joanne Woodward, Princess Margaret, Lesley-Anne Down, Ellen Barkin, Kathleen Turner, Chris Evert, Annie Lennox, Condoleezza Rice, Margaux Hemingway, Halle Berry, Samantha Fox, Salma Hayek, Janet Jackson, Sophie Marceau, Cindy Crawford, Sinéad O'Connor, Robin Wright, Cynthia Nixon, Kristen Stewart, Emma Watson and Jennifer Lawrence.

Personality and Romance: The 8 Gua women born in the *Year of the Horse* are an auspicious mix of earth and fire energy; this gives them a great deal of self-assurance and self-worth. These ladies are warm-hearted and generous but they are fiercely independent; trying to control or break her spirit will not end well. The 8 Gua-Horses are champions of causes, require lots of activity, and have a desire for adventure. They have a mind of their own and are usually highly principled and moral—lying and being dishonest is not part of her character.

These women are rather bossy and earthy; usually very successful, they have no need to parade around their material wealth. They tend to be hyper sensitive, complex, stubborn and dependable—making good wives and spouses only when they respect their strong, patient mate. These principled females have a little of 'save the world' energy as well. They tend to fall hard and fast in relationships, but get a great deal mellower later in life.

The best stuff: When the 8 Gua-Horses are fully exhibiting their best qualities, they are cheerful, popular, quick-witted, changeable, earthy, stubborn, perceptive, talkative, agile both mentally and physically, magnetic, intelligent, astute, flexible, open-minded.

The worst stuff: When the 8 Gua-Horses move to the darker side of their nature, they can be fickle, anxious, rude, gullible, stubborn, overly sensitive, lack stability, intolerant, bossy, and perseverance.

Career: Some of the best professions for the 8 Gua-Horses, where they may attain wealth, fame or fulfillment, are in or as a sales representative, journalist, language instructor, librarian, pilot, real estate, construction, consultancy, hotel, insurance, architecture, pottery, recruitment, quarry, farmers and OB-GYN.

Year of the Goat

The Year of the Goat only produces 3, 6 & 9 Guas

3 Gua as a Goat

Men and Women!

Generous, Steady, Outspoken

Elements: Yang **Wood** and Yin **Earth**

Years occurring for Males and Females:
1943, 1979, 2015, 2051

Famous 3 Gua-Dragon Men and Women: John Wayne, Katherine Hepburn, Jim Morrison, Janis Joplin, Mick Jagger, Robert De Niro, Julio Iglesias, George Benson, Chevy Chase, Penny Marshall, Malcolm McDowell, John Kerry, Geraldo Rivera, Lynn Redgrave, Jim Croce, Joe Namath, Jennifer Love-Hewitt, Kourtney Kardashian, Kate Hudson, Heath Ledger, Norah Jones, Rose Byrne, Adam Levine, Coco Austin, Jason Momoa and Pink.

Personality and Romance: The 3 Guas born in the *Year of the Goat* is a mix of wood and earth energy causing some internal unrest; with a purposeful and focused life however, it is eased. The 3 Gua-Goats are extremely reliable and steadfast; even under undo pressure they remain calm. They have nurturing personalities, are generous, and sensitive to the world around them. Intensely private people, it takes some time and effort to know them. Having projects and creating new ventures is most rewarding to them.

The 3-Gua Goats have lots of nervous energy and need an outlet, but they often have 'too many irons in the fire'. This can leave them feeling overwhelmed, exhausted and unfulfilled. Regarding romantic love, they can be insecure or shy. They do not like to be overpowered in relationships and too many 'rules' will make them feel repressed. While the 3 Gua-Goats are at times brash and outspoken, they have kind and gentle hearts.

The best stuff: When the 3 Gua-Goats are fully exhibiting their best qualities, they righteous, sincere, sympathetic, mild-mannered, shy, artistic, organized, creative, gentle, compassionate, understanding, mothering, determined, peaceful, generous and seeks security.

The worst stuff: When the 3 Gua-Goats move to the darker side of their nature, they can be outspoken, brash, moody, indecisive, worrier, over-sensitive, and a complainer.

Career: Some of the best professions for the 3 Gua-Goats, where they may attain wealth, fame or fulfillment, are as a pediatrician, actor, interior designer, florist, musician, entrepreneurs, actors, estate management, philosophy, entertainers, chef, medicine, print media, agriculture, textiles, and transportation.

6 Gua as a Goat
Men and Women!
Cunning, Patient, Creative
Elements: Yang **Metal** and Yang **Earth**

Years occurring for Males:
1931, 1967, 2003, 2039

Years occurring for Females:
1919, 1955, 1991, 2027

Famous 6 Gua-Goat Men and Women: Eva Gabor, Eva Perón, James Dean, Ike Turner, Larry Hagman, William Shatner, Kris Kardashian-Jenner, Reba McEntire, Isabelle Adjani, Whoopi Goldberg, Tanya Roberts, Connie Sellecca, Iman, Debra Winger, Maria Shriver, Vin Diesel, Jason Statham, Tim McGraw, Jamie Foxx, Kurt Cobain, Criss Angel, Anderson Cooper, Keith Urban, Rufus Sewell, Matt LeBlanc, Vanilla Ice, Liev Schreiber, Jimmy Kimmel, Rhys Ifans, Emma Roberts and Jamie Lynn Spears.

Personality and Romance: The 6 Guas born in the *Year of the Goat* are a harmonious mix of metal and earth energy; these men and women are cunning, long-suffering, outwardly innocent, self-disciplined and dignified. The 6 Gua-Goats are immensely creative in manipulating things, circumstances and people for advantageous outcomes. They are cunning and crafty but will give the aura of innocence or detachment; do not make an enemy of these people as they will patiently and seemingly blameless, *annihilate* you.

You will not see this coming as they are famous for avoiding confrontations and

arguments; even if they are in positions of authority where their will may be imposed. The 6 Gua Goat women are supremely feminine and deceptively compliant—however she is not a push-over or empty-headed. These women are powerful, ethereally beautiful and serene. The 6 Gua Goat men desire power and are ambitious, unpredictable, adventurous and at times, ruthless. In romantic relationships, these men and women, are patient and may involve schemes and dreams to find the right life partner. Intensely private people, it takes some time and effort to know them.

The best stuff: When the 6 Gua-Goats are fully exhibiting their best qualities, they are righteous, sincere, sympathetic, mild-mannered, shy, creative, gentle, compassionate, peaceful, generous, and they seek security.

The worst stuff: When the 6 Gua-Goats move to the darker side of their nature, they can be indecisive, worrier, pessimistic, over-sensitive and a complainer.

Career: Some of the best professions for the 6 Gua-Goats, where they may attain wealth, fame or fulfillment, are as a pediatrician, interior designer, estate management, chef, engineering, computers, excavation, hi-tech goods, internet, lawyer, and metal jewelry.

9 Life Gua as a Goat

Men and Women!

Gentle, Cunning, Classy

Elements: Yin **Fire** and Yin **Earth**

Years occurring for Males: **1955, 1991, 2027**
Years occurring for Females: **1931, 1967, 2003, 2039**

Famous 9 Gua Goat Men and Women: Nat 'King' Cole, Liberace, Jack Palance, Anita Ekberg, Angie Dickinson, Mitzi Gaynor, Leslie Caron, Rita Moreno, Della Reese, Steve Jobs, Bill Gates, Billy Idol, Bruce Willis, David Lee Roth, Billy Bob Thornton, Dodi Fayed, Tom Bergeron, Gary Sinise, Kelsey Grammer, Yun-Fat Chow, Willem Dafoe, Jeff Daniels, Dana Carvey, Pamela Anderson, Nicole Kidman, Courtney Thorne-Smith, Faith Hill, Anna Nicole Smith, Toni Braxton, Julia Roberts, Carrie-Anne Moss, Mira Sorvino, Laura Dern, Kristen Johnston, Joely Fisher, Rebecca Ramos, Mitchel Musso, Jason Dolley and Hunter Hayes.

Personality and Romance: The 9 Gua men and women born in the *Year of the Goat* are a mix of fire and earth energy; this gives them inner confidence and stability. They are shy, gentle, calm, intelligent, cunning, charming, crafty, sympathetic, and tend to be dreamers. While they love being social, they do not crave attention as they prefer to be observant and autonomous. The 9 Gua-Goats like to be fashionable and will spend money on presenting a first-class appearance; however they are not snobbish about material wealth.

9 Guas have a sharp, brilliant intellect; they can also be wise, loyal, and sentimental. The 9 Gua-Goat women are usually very beautiful like a diva or goddess and may even have an ethereal air about her. These men and women are extremely reliable and steadfast; even under undo pressure they remain calm. They have nurturing personalities and are very giving people; intensely private, it takes some time and effort to know them. They have a small inner circle, but will work hard for friends and loved ones.

The best stuff: When the 9 Gua-Goats are fully exhibiting their best qualities, they are righteous, sincere, sympathetic, mild-mannered, shy, artistic, creative, gentle, compassionate, understanding, mothering, determined, peaceful, and generous.

The worst stuff: When the 9 Gua-Goats move to the darker side of their nature, they can be crafty, cunning, moody, indecisive, over-passive, worrier, pessimistic, over-sensitive, and a complainer.

Career: Some of the best professions for the 9 Gua-Goats, where they may attain wealth, fame or fulfillment, are in law, religion, entrepreneur, doctors, journalist, inventor, computer analyst, lawyer, engineer, architect, chemicals, optical, and cosmetics.

Year of the Monkey

1 Gua as a Monkey

Women Only!

Quick, Highly Intelligent, Sexual

Element: Yang **Water** and Yang **Metal**

Years occurring for Females: **1932, 1968, 2004, 2040**
No 1 Guas males are born in Monkey years

Famous 1 Gua-Monkey Women: Wallis Simpson *(Duchess of Windsor)*, Elizabeth Taylor, Debbie Reynolds, Loretta Lynn, Patsy Cline, Ellen Burstyn, Catherine Bell, Vanessa Marcil, Stephanie Seymour, Yasmine Bleeth, Helena Christensen, Lucy Lawless, Gillian Anderson, Patricia Arquette, Ricki Lake, Naomi Watts, Lucy Lui, Ashley Judd, Rachel Ray, Celine Dion, Lisa Marie Presley, Debra Messing, and Traci Lords.

Personality and Romance: The 1 Gua born in the *Year of the Monkey* is water and metal energy, making it mercurial in nature. These women's personalities can be moody, quick, highly intelligent and at certain times of their life, promiscuous, as they can get easily bored with their lovers.

The 1 Gua-Monkeys are always hatching new ideas, concepts or inventing new systems. They are playful and may be hard to pin down in relationships and won't settle down quickly. However, with an excellent partner, they will commit to that person in every way. The 1 Gua-Monkey ladies can be secretive, could have arcane aspects to their lives or may live a whole other life.

The best stuff: When the 1 Gua-Monkeys are fully exhibiting their best qualities, they are inventive, motivators, improviser, quick-witted, inquisitive, flexible, innovative, problem solver, self-assured, sociable, polite, dignified, competitive, objective, factual and intellectual.

The worst stuff: When the 1 Gua-Monkeys move to the darker side of their nature, they can be egotistical, vain, selfish, cunning, jealous, and suspicious.

Career: Some of the best professions for the 1 Gua-Monkeys, where they may attain wealth, fame or fulfillment, are in the media, banking, science, engineering, stock market, film directing, jewelry, public relations, surveyor, sports, construction, geographer, communications, entertainment, sex industry or in the publishing industry.

2 Gua as a Monkey

Men Only!

Sexual, Lightening Quick, Intuitive

Elements: Yin **Earth** and Yang **Metal**

Years occurring for Males:
1944, 1968, 1980, 2016, 2040, 2052
No female 2 Guas are born in Monkey years

Famous 2 Gua-Monkey Men: Nelson Rockefeller, Louis L'Amour, James Stewart, Ian Fleming, Alistair Cooke, Joe Cocker, Sam Elliott, Robert Kardashian, Michael Douglas, George Lucas, Barry White, Sir Richard Branson, Kenny Chesney,' Hugh Jackman, Will Smith, Daniel Craig, Marc Anthony, Edward Burns, Eric Bana, Ryan Gosling and Channing Tatum.

Personality and Romance: The 2 Guas born in the *Year of the Monkey* are a mix of earth and metal and they are quick as lightening! Inside, however they are calm, steady, dependable and altogether persistent. They are fond of creating concepts that give a new spin on old ideas/paradigms. The 2 Gua-Monkeys make caring and talented health professionals as their nurturing nature coupled with their natural intuition are a winning combination.

These men feel comfortable in dark spaces such as caves or may have a 'man-cave' in their home in which to retreat. In relationships, they will not settle on a partner quickly and may give the appearance of being playful, promiscuous or cavalier. When they do find an excellent mate for life, they will commit 100% and be very devoted.

The best stuff: When the 2 Gua-Monkeys are fully exhibiting their best qualities, they are quick-witted, inventive, motivators, improviser, inquisitive, nurturing, flexible, innovative, problem solver, self-assured, sociable, polite, dignified, competitive, objective, factual, and intellectual.

The worst stuff: When the 2 Gua-Monkeys move to the darker side of their nature, they can be moody, egotistical, vain, selfish, cunning, depressed, jealous, and suspicious.

Career: Some of the best professions for the 2 Gua-Monkeys, where they may attain wealth, fame or fulfillment, are in accounting and banking, science, engineering, stock market trading, film directing, jewelry, media, public relations, designer, real estate, construction, consultancy, architecture, interior design, or an OB-GYN.

4 Gua as a Monkey

Women Only!

Highly Sexual, Quick-Witted, Modern

Elements: Yin **Wood** and Yang **Metal**

Years occurring for females:
1944, 1980, 2016, 2052

No 4 Guas males born in Monkey years

Famous 4 Gua-Monkey Women: Bette Davis, Carole Lombard, Joey Heatherton, Jacqueline Bisset, Diana Ross, Patti LaBelle, Pattie Boyd, Sondra Locke, Gladys Knight, Stockard Channing, Michelle Phillips, Teri Garr, Kim Kardashian, Jessica Simpson, Christina Aguilera, Olivia Munn, Gisele Bündchen, Kristen Bell, Christina Ricci, and Venus Williams.

Personality and Romance: The 4 Gua women born in the *Year of the Monkey* are a mix of metal and wood energy; this may cause some internal conflict, usually in the form of self-doubt. These women are of high intelligence and have lightening quick minds. Their energy is very progressive, full of ideas, concepts or inventing new things. The 4-Gua Monkey women love their freedom and may be hard to pin down in relationships; she is playful, slippery and very quick-witted. These women are generous to a fault, are interested in everyone's business, and definitely have an opinion about everything and everybody.

At certain times in their life, they may be promiscuous as they can get easily bored with their lovers. However, with an excellent partner, they will commit to that person in every way. Their chosen mate must always be aware that if they feel confined or 'jailed' in the relationship, they will exit in a flash!

The best stuff: When the 4 Gua-Monkeys are fully exhibiting their best qualities, they are inventive, motivating, improviser, quick-witted, inquisitive, flexible, innovative, problem solver, self-assured, sociable, polite, dignified, competitive, objective, factual and intellectual.

The worst stuff: When the 4 Gua-Monkeys move to the darker side of their nature, they can be egotistical, vain, selfish, indecisive, cunning, jealous and suspicious.

Career: Some of the best professions for the 4 Gua-Monkeys, where they may attain wealth, fame or fulfillment, are in banking, science, engineering, stock market trading, film directing, jewelry, media, entrepreneurs, philosophy, farming, entertainers, medicine, publishing, technicians and musicians.

7 Gua as a Monkey

Women Only!

Lightening Quick, Unconventional, Playful

Elements: Yin **Metal** and Yang **Metal**

Years occurring for Females: **1920, 1956, 2010, 2028**

No 7 Gua males are born in the Year of the Monkey

Famous 7 Gua-Monkey Women: Maureen O'Hara, Shelley Winters, Bo Derek, Dana Delany, Kim Cattrall, Patti Hansen, Carrie Fisher, Geena Davis, Sela Ward, Lisa Hartman, Linda Hamilton, Jerry Hall, Paula Zahn, LaToya Jackson, Dorothy Hamill, Lisa Niemi Swayze, Koo Stark and Rita Wilson.

Personality and Romance: The 7 Gua women born in the *Year of the Monkey* is an auspicious mix of yin and yang metal; this brings a radiant inner confidence! These ladies are gracious, generous, unconventional and make a loyal and entertaining friend. They also can be talkative, lively, and nervous. The 7 Gua-Monkey's are often blessed with very good looks, and sensuous beauty. Comfortable with a lot of 'stage', the 7 Gua's are good at acting, speaking, in front of the camera or on the radio. These women also love their freedom and may be hard to pin down; they're quick witted and will slip through your fingers at any attempt of constraint.

The 7 Gua-Monkeys also have a strong tendency to overindulge in the pleasures of life such as food, drink, money, and sex; they must strive to keep balanced. If you bore these charming ladies, they may move onto a new lover; however, with an excellent partner, they will commit to that person in every way.

The best stuff: When the 7 Gua-Monkeys are fully exhibiting their best qualities, they are inventive, motivating, improviser, quick-witted, inquisitive, flexible, innovative, problem solver, self-assured, sociable, polite, dignified, competitive, objective, factual and intellectual.

The worst stuff: When the 7 Gua-Monkeys move to the darker side of their nature, they can be egotistical, vain, selfish, cunning, jealous, excessive and suspicious.

Career: Some of the best professions for the 7 Gua-Monkeys, where they may attain wealth, fame or fulfillment, are in banking, science, engineering, stock market trading, film directing, medicine, engineering, IT, goldsmith, hardware, lawyer, judging, metal jewelry, sports equipment and lecturers.

8 Gua as a Monkey

Men Only!

Lightening Quick, Playful, Generous

Elements: Yang **Earth** and Yang **Metal**

Years occurring for males: **1920, 1956, 1992, 2028**

There are no 8 Gua males born in the Year of the Monkey

Famous 8 Gua Monkey Men: Yul Brynner, Montgomery Clift, Mickey Rooney, Walter Matthau, Tony Randall, Dwight Yoakam, Chris Isaak, Tom Hanks, Andy Garcia, Kenny G, David Copperfield, Eric Roberts, Björn Borg, David E. Kelley, Randy Jackson, Joe Montana, Bryan Cranston, Sugar Ray Leonard, Taylor Lautner, Josh Hutcherson and Nick Jonas.

Personality and Romance: The 8 Gua men who are born in the *Year of the Monkey* are an auspicious mix of earth and metal energy; they have a great deal of inner power and confidence. These men are witty, intelligent and have a magnetic personality. Although they can be playful, mischievous and love a practical joke, they are also stubborn and competitive. While these men can often be extravagant suitors—champagne, diamonds and furs--they love their freedom and will not settle down in marriage easily. The 8 Gua-Monkeys are hardworking, great risk-takers and are survivors of difficult situations usually due to their charm and enormous social skills.

They have integrity and may become spiritual seekers, and trek the mountains in search of 'answers' or to find themselves. These men are fast learners and crafty opportunists; they have many interests and need partners who are capable of stimulating them. Later in life they may become eccentric or hoarders. While the 8 Gua-Monkeys tend to resist change, they can deftly handle trouble without falling apart. They are geared for success and often become very rich with worldly honors, recognition and status.

The best stuff: When the 8 Gua-Monkeys are fully exhibiting their best qualities, they are inventors, motivators, improvisers, quick-witted, inquisitive, flexible, innovative, problem solver, self-assured, sociable, polite, dignified, competitive, successful, earthy, objective, factual, and intellectual.

The worst stuff: When the 8 Gua-Monkeys move to the darker side of their nature, they can be hoarders, self-righteous, stubborn, short-tempered, egotistical, vain, selfish, cunning, jealous, impudent, impulsive, and suspicious.

Career: Some of the best professions for the 8 Gua-Monkeys, where they may attain wealth, fame or fulfillment, are in accounting science, engineering, stock market trading, film directing, jewelry, sales representative, real estate, construction, earthenware, consultancy, hotel, insurance, architecture, quarry, human resources, and OB-GYN.

Year of the Rooster

1 Gua as a Rooster

Men Only!

Creative, Trustworthy, Very Social

Element: Yang **Water** and Yin **Metal**

Years occurring for Males: **1945, 1981, 2017, 2053**
No female 1 Guas are born in Rooster years

Famous 1 Gua-Rooster Men: James Mason, Burl Ives, Benny Goodman, Steve Martin, Bob Seger, Bob Marley, Henry Winkler, Eric Clapton, Bubba Smith, Neil Young, John Lithgow, John Fogerty, Barry Bostwick, Van Morrison, Pete Townshend, Michael Nouri, Richard Thomas, José Feliciano, Phil Jackson, John Heard, Davy Jones, Joseph Gordon-Levitt, Josh Groban, Ben Barnes, and Jay Sean.

Personality and Romance: The 1 Gua born in the *Year of the Rooster* is also a mix of metal and water energy; however this mix is grounded. The 1 Gua-Roosters have the strength of persistence and formidable personal power. They tend to be very social, and are loyal and trustworthy with family, friends and business associates. Since these men tend to *tell it like it is*, the best life partners for the 1 Gua Roosters is one that understands that under their 'crowing' and gruffness lies a heart of gold.

These personalities are more transparent and less secretive than most 1 Guas. The 1 Gua-Roosters are excellent is ferreting people out, and have very sharp opinions. Filled with a sensuous nature, sex and loyalty are paramount to these sensitive, social creatures.

The best stuff: When the 1 Gua-Roosters are fully exhibiting their best qualities, they are neat, meticulous, organized, self-assured, decisive, conservative, perfectionist, alert, zealous, practical, scientific and responsible.

The worst stuff: When the 1 Gua-Roosters move to the darker side of their nature, they can be secretive, moody, overzealous and critical, puritanical, egotistical, abrasive, and opinionated.

Career: Some of the best professions for the 1 Gua-Roosters, where they may attain wealth, fame or fulfillment, are as an author, restaurateur, athlete, journalist, dentist, surgeon, soldier, fireman, entertainer, news anchor, military, politics, banking, communications, or a diplomat.

2 Gua as a Rooster

Women Only!

Honest, Opinionated, Nurturing

Elements: Yin **Earth** and Yin **Metal**

Years occurring for Females: **1933, 1969, 2005, 2041**
No male 2 Guas are born in the Year of the Rooster

Famous 2 Gua-Rooster Women: Amelia Earhart, Grand Duchess Tatiana Nikolaevna of Russia, Jayne Mansfield, Yoko Ono, Joan Collins, Carol Burnett, Joan Rivers, Jennifer Lopez, Catherine Zeta-Jones, Gwen Stefani, Pauley Perrette, Jennifer Aniston, Lara Spencer, Rachel Hunter, Renée Zellweger, Rachel Hunter, Cate Blanchett, Anne Heche and Honey Boo Boo.

Personality and Romance: The 2 Guas who were born in the *Year of the Rooster* are earth and metal energy. They have a strong independent, calm and confident nature. One minute they enjoy being the center of attention, the next they want to retreat as they can be intensely private. They are naturally intuitive, loyal, trustworthy and social. Since they tend to be painfully honest with strong, often abrasive opinions, their partners and friends cannot be overly sensitive. However, under their gruffness and sharp opinions beats a heart of gold. These women can be very clear thinkers with logical, grounded and earthy energy. Their character is nurturing and if those choose, makes them talented healers or physician. When exhibiting the dark side of their nature, they tend towards moodiness or depression—even this may be overcome with a purposeful life.

The best stuff: When the 2 Gua-Roosters are fully exhibiting their best qualities, they are neat, meticulous, organized, self-assured, decisive, conservative, nurturing, critical, perfectionist, alert, zealous, practical, scientific and responsible.

The worst stuff: When the 2 Gua-Roosters move to the darker side of their nature, they can be overzealous and critical, puritanical, depressed, egotistical, reclusive, abrasive, and opinionated.

Career: Some of the best professions for the 2 Gua-Roosters, where they may attain wealth, fame or fulfillment, are in sales, restaurateur, public relations officer, athlete, journalist, travel writer, dentist, surgeon, public relations, politics, writer, entertainer, real estate, construction, architecture, or in interior design.

4 Gua as a Rooster

Men Only!

Personal Power, Organized, Blunt

Elements: Yin **Wood** and Yin **Metal**

Years occurring for males:
1933, 1969, 2005, 2041
No 4 Guas females are born in Rooster years

Famous 4 Gua-Rooster Men: Willie Nelson, James Brown, Michael Caine, Quincy Jones, Larry King, Gene Wilder, Conway Twitty, Lou Rawls, Jay Z, Ice Cube, Triple H, Gerad Butler, Matthew McConaughey, Tyler Perry, Jack Black, and Zach Galifianakis.

Personality and Romance: The 4 Gua men born in the *Year of the Rooster* are a mix of wood and metal energy; this makes him emotionally complex. These men are very much the 'rooster', showing off their beautiful masculinity every chance they get. Highly social and deep thinkers, the 4 Gua-Roosters make excellent leaders, CEO's, or anywhere they may use their potent energy being very comfortable with power. In his love-life, he can be a skillful and passionate lover which is chiefly for physical pleasure, not necessarily romantic. It is not natural for a 4-Gua Rooster man to limit himself to a single partner. Expect that he may have many sexual partners without guilt; if he does settled down, he will make an excellent provider. After marriage, while they may be lovers, they rarely desert their partners or family. Under their gruffness lies a heart of gold.

The best stuff: When the 4 Gua-Roosters are fully exhibiting their best qualities, they are neat, meticulous, organized, self-assured, decisive, conservative, critical, perfectionist, alert, zealous, practical, scientific and responsible.

The worst stuff: When the 4 Gua-Roosters move to the darker side of their nature, they can be overzealous and critical, puritanical, indecisive, egotistical, abrasive and opinionated.

Career: Some of the best professions for the 4 Gua-Roosters, where they may attain wealth, fame or fulfillment, are in sales, restaurateur, athlete, journalist, travel writer, dentist, surgeon, fireman, military, chef, education, pharmaceuticals, publishing, musicians, and transportation.

7 Gua as a Rooster
Men Only!
Lightening Quick, Sexual, Charming
Elements: Yin **Metal** and Yin **Metal**

Years occurring for Males: **1921, 1956, 1993, 2029**
There are no 7 Gua females born in Rooster years

Famous 7 Gua-Rooster Men: Charles Bronson, Louis Jourdan, Mario Lanza, Prince Philip, Peter Ustinov, Sugar Ray Robinson, Vince Gill, Dolph Lundgren, Daniel Day-Lewis, Donny Osmond, Christopher Lambert, Matt Lauer, Falco, Ray Romano, and Spike Lee.

Personality and Romance: The 7 Gua men born in the *Year of the Rooster* are an auspicious mix of yin and yang metal energy; this brings a steely confidence! These men are resilient, clever, and very macho; they enjoy strutting around and crowing, but under their gruffness beat a heart of gold. However, they are no 'dandy', they have substance and depth. The 7 Gua-Roosters can be amazingly creative, rebellious, productive, and use speech to their advantage; they can be a fast-talker, smooth talker, or have a razor-sharp tongue. They may be talented in imitating voices as well. These men are very comfortable with power making great leaders and CEOs,--anywhere their considerable management and organizational skills may be exploited.

In romantic relationships, they tend towards infidelity; they are quite guilt-free and comfortable courting several women at a time—a real heart-breaker! However, if they do marry, they seldom desert their families and make great providers. With a strong tendency to overindulge in the pleasures of life such as food, drink, money, and sex, they must make an effort to keep a balanced. The 7 Gua-Roosters are very social, charming, and charismatic; they create stimulating, informative conversation wherever they go.

The best stuff: When the 7 Gua-Roosters are fully exhibiting their best qualities, they are neat, meticulous, organized, self-assured, decisive, conservative, critical, perfectionist, alert, zealous, practical, scientific and responsible.

The worst stuff: When the 7 Gua-Roosters move to the darker side of their nature, they can be overzealous and critical, puritanical, excessive, egotistical, abrasive, and opinionated.

Career: Some of the best professions for the 7 Gua-Roosters, where they may attain wealth, fame or fulfillment, are in/as a restaurateur, public relations officer, athlete, journalist, travel writer, fireman, medicine, philosopher, computers, metal mining, lawyer, metal jewelry, government service, sports equipment, and lecturers.

8 Gua as a Rooster

Women Only!

Confident, Purposeful, Social

Elements: Yang **Earth** and Yin **Metal**

Years occurring for Females: **1957, 1981, 1993, 2017**

There are no 8 Gua females born in Rooster years

Famous 8 Gua Rooster Women: Queen Juliana, Jessica Tandy, Jane Russell, Lana Turner, Priscilla Presley, Jaclyn Smith, Carly Simon, Goldie Hawn, Bette Midler, Diane Sawyer, Rita Coolidge, Linda Hunt, Vanna White, Faye Resnick, Rachel Ward, Melanie Griffith, Denise Austin, Caroline Kennedy, Gloria Estefan, Jessica Alba, Beyoncé Knowles, Britney Spears, Duchess Kate Middleton, Paris Hilton, Serena Williams, Natalie Portman, Anna Kournikova, Jennifer Hudson, Ivanka Trump and Victoria Justice.

Personality and Romance: The 8 Gua women born in the *Year of the Rooster* are an auspicious mix of earth and metal energy; this brings purpose and great inner confidence. These ladies are hardworking, talented, charming, resourceful, loyal, honest and open; they're very comfortable with power and prestige. The 8 Gua-Roosters love deeply, when she is wounded or disappointed, will create a wall of protection against the offenders. However, she does not wear her heart on her sleeve; you'll not see a drama queen display of emotions. They generally take life seriously; and are filled with laser-sharp purpose and efficiency. These women distain snobby, superior-acting people and they are equally unimpressed with blatant social climbers.

The 8 Gua-Roosters love a challenge and will tackle it with vigor, intimidation if necessary, and with her considerable power. While they are famously stubborn, they are not vindictive, nor do they hold grudges. So talented are these ladies, there is almost no profession that they can't excel in or master; and she will manage it with efficiently and resolute independence. They are geared for success and often become very rich with worldly honors, recognition and status. Prone to 'tell it like it is', they will need a partner who is not overly sensitive.

The best stuff: When the 8 Gua-Roosters are fully exhibiting their best qualities, they are purposeful, neat, meticulous, organized, self-assured, decisive, conservative, perfectionist, observant, zealous, practical, scientific, talented, social, honest, loyal, responsible and have hearts of gold.

The worst stuff: When the 8 Gua-Roosters move to the darker side of their nature, they can be stubborn, overzealous, critical, puritanical, intimidating, egotistical, abrasive, and opinionated.

Career: Some of the best professions for the 8 Gua-Roosters, where they may attain wealth, fame or fulfillment, are in or as a restaurateur, hairdresser, public relations officer, athlete, journalist, dentist, surgeon, soldier, fireman, real estate, construction, consultancy, hotel, architecture, quarry and OB-GYN.

Year of the Dog

The Year of the Dog only produces 3, 6 & 9 Guas

3 Gua as a Dog

Men and Women!

Enterprising, Loyal, Restless

Elements: Yang **Wood** and Yang **Earth**

Years occurring for Males and Females:
1934, 1970, 2006, 2042

Famous 3 Gua-Dragon Men and Women: George Gershwin, Golda Meir, Louis Armstrong, Enzo Ferrari, Irene Dunne, Elvis Presley, Sophia Loren, Bridgett Bardot, Maggie Smith, Pat Boone, Giorgio Armani, Carl Sagan, Gloria Steinem, Mariah Carey, Matt Damon, Leah Remini, Naomi Campbell, Heather Graham, Queen Latifah, Uma Thurman, Vince Vaughn, Rachel Weisz, Claudia Schiffer, River Phoenix, Giada De Laurentiis, Shemar Moore, and DMX

.

Personality and Romance: The 3 Guas born in the *Year of the Dog* have a mix of wood and earth energy; this may cause some inner tension or feeling restless. They are loyal and ready to fight for the 'underdog' or to leap into action when needed. The 3 Gua-Dogs are very enterprising and resourceful, wherever they turn their attention, it is sure to thrive.

Blessed with lots of vigor, energy and vitality they are in their element with inventions, new ventures or being involved in the 'latest' thing.

In relationships they have trouble trusting others, and are often frightened off by the dog's insecure, worrisome and anxious nature. The 3 Gua-Dogs tend to be faithful and loyal; they do not enjoy the excitement of the chase nor do they take pleasure in jealous scenes.

The best stuff: When the 3 Gua-Dogs are fully exhibiting their best qualities, they are honest, intelligent, straightforward, loyal, sense of justice and fair play, attractive, organized, surprising, amiable, unpretentious, sociable, open-minded, idealistic, moralistic, practical, and affectionate.

The worst stuff: When the 3 Gua-Dogs move to the darker side of their nature, they can be dogged, cynical, lazy, cold, brash, judgmental, pessimistic, outspoken, worrier, stubborn, and quarrelsome.

Career: Some of the best professions for the 3 Gua-Dogs, where they may attain wealth, fame or fulfillment, are as a scientist, professor, politician, nurse, judge, law, entrepreneurs, philosophy, chef, medicine, publishing, bookstores, fashion, technicians, musicians and transportation.

6 Gua as a Dog

Men and Women!

Loners, Loyal, Anxious

Elements: Yang **Metal** and Yang **Earth**

Years occurring for *Males*: **1922, 1958, 1994, 2030**

Famous 6 Gua-Dog Men and Women: Mother Teresa, Redd Foxx, Sid Ceaser, Jack Klugman, Carl Reiner, Dolly Parton, Cher, Linda Ronstadt, Suzanne Somers, Susan Sarandon, Sally Field, Diane Keaton, Liza Minnelli, Patti Smith, Susan Lucci, Naomi Judd, Connie Chung, Gilda Radner, Diane von Fürstenberg, Michael Jackson, Prince, Viggo Mortensen, Marg Helgenberger, Dr. Drew Pinsky, Andie MacDowell, Alec Baldwin, Gary Oldman, Andrea Bocelli, Ice-T, Tim Robbins, Prince Albert of Monaco, Tim Burton, Kevin Bacon, Kevin Sorbo, Nicki Minaj, Jessica Biel, Anne Hathaway, Kirsten Dunst, Kelly Clarkson, LeAnn Rimes.

Personality and Romance: The 6 Guas born in the *Year of the Dog* are a harmonious mix of metal and earth energy; these men and women are affectionate, loyal, attractive, anti-social/loners and have a keen sense of justice. They are by and large, cynical of the world. However, they shine when they engage in noble, charitable works or 'feel good' causes. While the 6 Gua-Dogs are not overly ambitious or materialistic they are diligent and dedicated workers, often rising to great heights due to this. The 6 Gua-Dogs can be blissfully naïve and innocent which can make them vulnerable or even fragile in romantic relationships. Although these men and women make the most loyal and best of friends, they tend to be self-righteous; taking a great deal of pride being honest, faithful, correct and proper- that it often comes across as 'holier than thou'. While the 6 Gua-Dogs are warm and personable, they generally have a very pessimistic view of life and are always expecting the worst to happen. They make devoted and loving partners; however they do require lots of reassurance and attention in the relationship.

The best stuff: When the 6 Gua-Dogs are fully exhibiting their best qualities, they are honest, intelligent, straightforward, loyal, sense of justice and fair play, attractive, amiable, unpretentious, sociable, open-minded, idealistic, moralistic, practical, affectionate and *dogged* (determined).

The worst stuff: When the 6 Gua-Dogs move to the darker side of their nature, they can be cynical, lazy, cold, judgmental, over-thinkers, loners, pessimistic, worrier, stubborn, and quarrelsome.

Career: Some of the best professions for the 6 Gua-Dogs, where they may attain wealth, fame or fulfillment, are as a scientist, interior designer, professor, politician, nurse, judge, medicine, teacher, IT, goldsmith, excavation, hi-tech goods, lawyer, judging, government service and lecturers.

9 Gua as a Dog

Men and Women!

Social, Loyal, Passionate

Elements: Yin **Fire** and Yang **Earth**

Years occurring for *Males*: **1946, 1982, 2018, 2054**
Years occurring for *Females*: **1922, 1958, 1994, 2030**

Famous 9 Gua Dog Men and Women: Jacques Cousteau, David Niven, Artie Shaw, Ava Gardner, Doris Day, Judy Garland, Betty White, Cyd Charisse, Sylvester Stallone, David Gilmour, Bill Clinton, Al Green, Tim Curry, Alan Rickman, Timothy Dalton, Jimmy Buffett, Donald Trump, Daryl Hall, Tommy Lee Jones, Steven Spielberg, George W. Bush, Danny Glover, Ben Vereen, Madonna, Sharon Stone, Jamie Lee Curtis, Michelle Pfeiffer, Ellen DeGeneres, Marg Helgenberger, Andie MacDowell, Annette Bening, Angela Bassett, Nancy Grace, Ne-Yo, Prince William Windsor, and Justin Bieber.

Personality and Romance: The 9 Gua men and women born in the *Year of the Dog* are a mix of earth and fire energy; this creates an inner, firey passion and stability. They are generous, faithful, loyal, pessimistic, introspective, sincere, amiable, loving, kind and devoted. Due to bearing a strong sense of loyalty and sincerity, they will do everything for the person who they think is most important. The 9 Gua-Dogs are born with a good nature; they are not inclined towards criminal behavior or to seeking gain through dishonest means.

They simply require a quite life and a good family to help them forget the ugliness and evil in the world. They are always ready to help others, even to the determent of their own interest, and when they find themselves betrayed by cunning people, they will feel shocked and hurt.

The 9 Gua-Dogs are consummate worriers and are generally pessimistic about the world around them; always fully expecting something bad is around the corner. However, they have a sharp, brilliant intellect; they can also be wise, loyal, and sentimental. Whatever they focus and turn their attention to, they will develop competence; they'll always find a way to complete an assignment. In romantic relationships, the 9 Gua-Dogs require lots of emotional support and attention as they find it difficult to trust others and are often scared off by the dog's insecure, worrisome and anxious nature.

The best stuff: When the 9 Gua-Dogs are fully exhibiting their best qualities, they are intelligent, loyal, have a strong sense of justice, unpretentious, and sociable.

The worst stuff: When the 9 Gua-Dogs move to the darker side of their nature, they can be cynical, lazy, cold, paranoid, judgmental, *dogging*, pessimistic, worrier, and stubborn.

Career: Some of the best professions for the 9 Gua-Dogs, where they may attain wealth, fame or fulfillment, are in research, interior designer, professor, nurse, and beauty.

Year of the Pig

1 Gua as a Pig
Women Only!
Generous, Sexual, Intelligent
Elements: Yang **Water** and Yin **Water**

Years occurring for Females: **1923, 1959, 1995, 2031**
No male 1 Guas are ever born in the Year of the Pig

Famous 1 Gua-Pig Women: Rhonda Fleming, Maria Callas, Lorrie Morgan, Marie Osmond, Rebecca De Mornay, Rosanna Arquette, Sheena Easton, Sean Young, Emma Thompson, Patricia Clarkson, Kelly Emberg, Nancy Grace, Irene Cara, Mackenzie Phillips, Marcia Gay Harden, Sarah Ferguson *(Duchess of York),* Aphrodite Jones, Jordyn Wieber, Kendall Jenner, Gabrielle Douglas, and Missy Franklin.

Personality and Romance: The 1 Guas born in the *Year of the Pig* is double water making them very emotionally, sensuous, and intelligent. These women are very generous and are keenly perceptive. The 1 Gua-Pigs are affectionate, highly sexual and make great partners. They possess an inner power that makes them reliable and wise in times of a great crisis. Those born under these energies are great accumulators of wealth, energy or wisdom (the pot belly of the pig). They are studious, diligent, and compassionate. The double water of the 1 Gua-Pig females will make them very anxious, nervous and a bit high strung. These ladies love their freedom, and even in a solid marriage will need lots of space; keeping tight reins will lead to rebellion, remoteness or an exit.

The best stuff: When the 1 Gua-Pigs are fully exhibiting their best qualities, they are honest, sturdy, sociable, peace-loving, patient, loyal, hard-working, trusting, sincere, calm, understanding, thoughtful, scrupulous, passionate and intelligent.

The worst stuff: When the 1 Gua-Pigs move to the darker side of their nature, they can be naive, secretive, over-reliant, self-indulgent, gullible, moody, fatalistic, too emotional and materialistic.

Career: Some of the best professions for the 1 Gua-Pigs, where they may attain wealth, fame or fulfillment, are in medicine, entertainer, caterer, doctor, veterinarian, interior decorator, banking, scientist, horticulturist, fishing, firefighting, sex industry, or in the publishing industry.

2 Gua as a Pig

Men Only!

Inner Power, Affectionate, Intuitive

Elements: Yin **Earth** and Yin **Water**

Years occurring for Males:
1935, 1959, 1971, 1995, 2007, 2031, 2043
No female 2 Guas are ever born in the *Year of the Pig*

Famous 2 Gua-Pig Men: Hank Williams, Henry Kissinger, Woody Allen, Sony Bono, Luciano Pavarotti, Bryan Adams, Val Kilmer, Simon Cowell, Kenneth 'Babyface' Edmonds, John McEnroe, Kyle MacLachlan, Magic Johnson, Tupac Shakur, Mark Wahlberg, Josh Lucas, Ricky Martin, Chris Tucker, and Paul Bettany.

Personality and Romance: The 2 Guas born in the *Year of the Pig* are a mix of water and earth that can create an inner tension. These men are honest and affectionate with a tolerant and peaceful side to their nature. The 2 Gua-Pigs are naturally grounded, confident and dependable with a calm demeanor making them everyone's friend. However, only those in the intimate inner circle will hear their true thoughts and feelings. They are highly intelligent and perceptive who are also in possession of a great inner power; this makes them invaluable in a time of crisis. They enjoy nurturing and can make excellent doctors or practitioners of alternate healing arts such as chiropractry, massage therapy, and acupuncture.

In relationships they are loving and affectionate, yet allowing a great deal of freedom, which they too must have in order not to feel trapped. However, a little time spent in introspection will set things back in balance; some 'cave' time is important for these men.

The best stuff: When the 2 Gua-Pigs are fully exhibiting their best qualities, they are honest, gallant, sturdy, sociable, peace-loving, patient, loyal, hard-working, nurturing, natural healers, trusting, sincere, calm, understanding, thoughtful, scrupulous, passionate and intelligent.

The worst stuff: When the 2 Gua-Pigs move to the darker side of their nature, they can be reclusive, depressed, naive, over-reliant, self-indulgent, gullible, fatalistic, and materialistic.

Career: Some of the best professions for the 2 Gua-Pigs, where they may attain wealth, fame or fulfillment, are in as an entertainer, doctor, veterinarian, interior decorator, transportation, entertainment, retail, medicine, scientist, horticulturist, artist, real estate, construction, consultancy, architecture, or an OB-GYN.

4 Gua as a Pig

Women Only!

Generous, Accumulators, Highly Sexual

Elements: Yin **Wood** and Yin **Water**

Years occurring for males: **1935, 1971, 2007, 2043**

No 4 Guas males ever born in the Year of the Pig

Famous 4 Gua-Pig Women: Julie Andrews, Loretta Lynn, Diahann, Carroll, Jada Pinkett Smith, Christina Applegate, Wionna Ryder, Thalía, Denise Richards, Dido, Jenna Elfman, Sandra Oh, Carla Gugino, Amy Poehler, Sanaa Lathan, Shannen Doherty, and Selena.

Personality and Romance: The 4 Guas born in the *Year of the Pig* are a harmonious mix of wood and water; this makes these ladies highly intelligent and very perceptive people. The 4-Gua Pigs make very good friends as they are compassionate, supportive and devoted. These women are great accumulators—the pot belly of the pig—of wealth, energy or wisdom. Whatever work they engage in, they are diligent and generous. In the matters of love, they dream of a *knight in shining amour* to sweep them off their feet. When they let go of this fantasy, which may hurt them at times, they make wonderfully affectionate and highly sexual partners to the men who deserve them. The 4-Gua Pigs are extremely reliable and wise in times of a crisis; they are always ready to support and serve their friends.

The best stuff: When the 4 Gua-Pigs are fully exhibiting their best qualities, they are honest, gentle, gallant, sturdy, sociable, peace-loving, patient, loyal, hard-working, trusting, sincere, calm, understanding, thoughtful, scrupulous, passionate and intelligent.

The worst stuff: When the 4 Gua-Pigs move to the darker side of their nature, they can be indecisive, naive, over-reliant, self-indulgent, wishy-washy, gullible, fatalistic, and materialistic.

Career: Some of the best professions for the 4 Gua-Pigs, where they may attain wealth, fame or fulfillment, are as an entertainer, veterinarian, interior decorator, retail or hospitality, researcher, scientist, philosophy, entertainers, pharmaceuticals, print media, agriculture, fashion, technicians and musicians.

7 Gua as a Pig

Women Only!

Accumulators, Intelligent, Affectionate

Elements: Yin **Metal** and Yin **Water**

Years occurring for Males: **1947, 1983, 2019, 2055**

No 7 Gua males are ever born in the Year of the Pig

Famous 7 Gua-Pig Women: Lucille Ball, Ginger Rogers, Jaclyn Smith, Cheryl Tiegs, Teri Garr, Barbara Bach, Hillary Rodham Clinton, Sally Struthers, Glenn Close, Camilla Parker-Bowles, Marisa Berenson, Danielle Steel, Elisabeth Broderick, Deidre Hall, Emmylou Harris, Mila Kunis, Emily Blunt, and Amy Winehouse.

Personality and Romance: The 7 Gua women born in the *Year of the Pig* are a very auspicious mix of metal and water energy; this brings unexpected blessings and unique gifts and talents. These women are affectionate, peace-loving, hardworking, intelligent and passionate. The 7 Gua-Pigs are often blessed with very good looks, and sensuous beauty; however they tend to be naïve and can be used by unscrupulous, immoral men. These women are very social, charming, and charismatic; they create stimulating, informative conversation wherever they go. They can be a fast-talker, smooth talker, or have a razor-sharp tongue; they may also use their voice as a way to fame.

The 7 Gua-Pigs can be vulnerable in the mouth, throat or lungs and must be careful not to smoke or engage in drug use. With a strong tendency to overindulge in the pleasures of life such as food, drink, money, and sex, they must strive to keep things and their bodies balanced.

The best stuff: When the 7 Gua-Pigs are fully exhibiting their best qualities, they are honest, simple, gallant, sturdy, sociable, peace-loving, patient, loyal, hard-working, trusting, sincere, calm, understanding, thoughtful, scrupulous, passionate and intelligent.

The worst stuff: When the 7 Gua-Pigs move to the darker side of their nature, they can be naive, over-reliant, self-indulgent, gullible, fatalistic, excessive and materialistic.

Career: Some of the best professions for the 7 Gua-Pigs, where they may attain wealth, fame or fulfillment, are in medicine, philosopher, teacher, chef, police office engineering, computers, goldsmith, hi-tech goods, internet, lawyer, judging, metal jewelry, government service, sports equipment and lecturers.

8 Gua as a Pig

MEN ONLY!

Accumulators, Intelligent, Affectionate

Elements: Yang **Earth** and Yin **Water**

Years occurring for Males:
1911, 1947, 1983, 2019, 2055
No 8 Gua females ever born in the Year of the Pig

Famous 8 Gua Pig Men: Ronald Regan, L. Ron Hubbard, Jack Ruby, Arnold Schwarzenegger, Carlos Santana, Don Henley, Elton John, Meat Loaf, O.J. Simpson, David Letterman, Kevin Kline, Larry David, Salman Rushdie, Stephen King, Sam Neill, **Henry Cavill,** Andrew Garfield, Aaron Rodgers, Chris Hemsworth and Jesse Eisenberg.

Personality and Romance: The 8 Gua men who are born in the *Year of the Pig* are an inauspicious mix of earth and water energy; this cause inner turmoil and insecurity. These men are intelligent, perceptive, affectionate, highly sexual and make great partners. The pot belly of the pig makes them great accumulators—wealth, energy, or wisdom. Although these men can be stubborn, they have a dependable steadfast nature. They tend to have a great deal of integrity and are vey attracted to all things spiritual. They can become spiritual seekers, and trek the mountains in search of 'answers' or to find themselves. Professionally, these men are industrious, and productive; with a great sense of responsibility, creativity and rich imagination, they're not afraid to try to do what interest them. They are geared for success and often become very rich with worldly honors, recognition and status.

The best stuff: When the 8 Gua-Pigs are fully exhibiting their best qualities, they are honest, gallant, sturdy, noble, sociable, peace-loving, patient, loyal, hard-working, trusting, sincere, calm, understanding, thoughtful, scrupulous, passionate, and intelligent.

The worst stuff: When the 8 Gua-Pigs move to the darker side of their nature, they can be naive, over-reliant, materialistic, procrastinator, gullible, passive, lazy, overly meek/apologetic, fatalistic, depressed and self-indulgent.

Career: Some of the best professions for the 8 Gua-Pigs, where they may attain wealth, fame or fulfillment, are in or as an entertainer, caterer, doctor, veterinarian, transportation, entertainment, retail, hospitality, real estate, construction, consultancy, architecture, pottery, human resources, farmers and OB-GYN.

Summary

The Life-Gua Zodiac Personalities is a unique way in which to peer into our energy and that which attracts and repels us. The information is useful, not only in romantic relationships, but with family members, co-workers, children, bosses, business partners and previous spouses or lovers. Having insights into our proclivities is sometimes disconcerting; no one wants to admit that at times our behavior can veer towards the negative. Remember, the Life-Gua Zodiac Personalities aspect of Eight Mansions is not about using your good and bad directions, rather is all about the relationship with ourselves and others in our sphere.

Chapter Nine
The 64 Life-Gua Compatibilities

"A bit of fragrance clings to the hand that gives flowers".
~ Chinese Proverb

The following information is a unique way to compare the energy of each of the 8 Guas with each other. I like to call these relationships, **Life-Gua Compatibility**. It is a mostly romantic perspective. Each of the 64 comparisons includes general and sexual compatibility.

There are said to be four (4) perfect matches for couples in the Eight Mansions system; 1 &4; 2 & 8; 3 & 9; and 6 & 7. I've put a little heart to indicate these matches and they are always in the same Life Group.

Please bear in mind that while some of the comments may be perceived as negative aspects of the personality, these refer to those who are not very evolved. We all have moments when we are not exhibiting the most developed part of our consciousness. Meanwhile, enjoy the romantic compatibility or lack thereof for yourself, family members and friends' significant other. It is also valuable to examine the compatibility of past relationships. It may give you some clues and insights as to their successful and failing aspects. The term 'Peach Blossom' has a sexual connotation.

"Secretive, Emotional and Scholarly"
The 1 Gua in Romantic Relationships or Marriages with other Guas:

1 Gua with a 1 Gua
Elemental relationship: WATER-WATER

The 1 Gua with another 1 indicates "friends and lovers." This is a compatible mix but things can get a bit emotional at times since the 1's tend to be moody, hard to pin down and secretive. While the 1's can be good communicators, in romantic relationships they often have difficulty expressing themselves clearly and need time alone to process their feelings. However, this couple will hit it off having *like minds* and an

affinity toward the intellect, developing the mind, scholarly pursuits, and hatching brilliant ideas. Sexual union will be emotional and sensuous. *This couple both belong to the East Life Group.*

1 Gua with a 2 Gua
Elemental relationship: WATER-EARTH

In general, the 1 Gua with a 2 Gua can indicate strife and conflict. Even if the couple has a long-term marriage it can be riffed with arguments and disagreements with the 2 trying to control/influence the 1 Gua. Often these relationships end in divorce, and a bitter one at that. Even in the bedroom, there could be conflict with *"who's on top"*. On bad days—the 1 Gua can go into moodiness and the 2 will slip into reclusiveness. For more evolved individuals, the 2 would only offer his/her advice or opinions when the 1 ask for it. The 2 Gua would then respect the need of their partner to process emotions at their own pace and not offer their keen, intuitive insights until approached. This would allow the 1 Gua to *flow* towards the grounded earthiness of the 2. Sexual union can be rather lusty which could keep the couple connected. *This couple belongs to opposite groups.*

1 Gua with a 3 Gua
Elemental relationship: WATER-WOOD

The 1 Gua with a 3 Gua is a very harmonious relationship. The 1 Gua will indeed be a supportive life partner to the progressive thinking of the 3 Gua. These two people will be very much into organizing ideas, and can be very creative together. If both step into the negative aspects of their personalities, the 3 Gua's progressive ways and raw ambition may clash with the 1 Gua's intellectual and strong intuitive abilities. Sexual union can be very compatible as well as creatively diverse. *This couple both belong to the East Life Group.*

♥ 1 Gua with a 4 Gua
Elemental relationship: WATER-WOOD
Sexy, 'Peach Blossom' Energy

The 1 Gua with a 4 Gua is said to be a "perfect match". The 1 Gua will be totally supportive and feed energy to the 4. Under this type of attention, the 4 Gua will blossom and grow. This can be a highly sexual and romantic union, with both partners feeling the harmonic energy. These couples often enjoy tantric sexual practices. If the couple is not evolved, both can be tempted by affairs outside the partnership. This union has a very sexy, 'peach blossom' energy, each partner needs to stay on their toes to present their best sides. Stepping into a negative energy could have the 1 Gua going into emotional, irrational behavior to sexually control the 4 Gua. Evolved couples will enjoy a wonderful, loving connection that grows more deeply over time that may put them into 'their own world'—so focused they are on each other. *This couple both belong to the East Life Group.*

1 Gua with a 6 Gua
Elemental relationship: WATER- METAL
Sexy, 'Peach Blossom' Energy

The 1 Gua with a 6 Gua can indicate a "heavenly combination". Normally, the 1 Gua will make the 6 Gua feel drained. And when the couple is not grounded, this can *rust out* or *corrode* a perfectly good relationship. The 6 Guas are natural leaders, but often need time to "marinate" in their feelings. The 1 Gua also can be moody and introspective; wanting some time alone as well. As both partners tend to be in their head, they will need to take time to hear each other and connect in the heart. However, if the couple is evolved, the combination is good with the 6 Gua helping their partner *give birth* to creative ideas and projects. Sexual union can be compatible, and sensuous. *This couple belongs to opposite groups.*

1 Gua with a 7 Gua
Elemental relationship: WATER- METAL
Sexy, 'Peach Blossom' Energy

The 1 Gua with a 7 Gua will indicate a great deal of sex and romance with *peachy, sexy* energy. In this relationship, the 7 Gua's natural joyfulness could turn sour as the 1 Gua's energy can be somewhat emotionally demanding. If the couple is grounded and evolved, the physical part of the relationship can be quite wonderful. Both Gua's tend to be highly sexual, but the match indicates that taking time to find a great spouse can result in being very focused and committed to the other. If not, both could be prone to affairs of the heart, unrequited love, extra martial affairs and intimate encounters. *This couple belongs to opposite groups.*

1 Gua with an 8 Gua
Elemental relationship: WATER-EARTH

The 1 Gua with an 8 Gua indicates conflict, fighting and general competitiveness. The fixed stubbornness of the 8 can try to control the 1. The 1 Gua will feel "out of control" when confronted with stubborn earthiness of the 8 Gua. Sexual union can also have frustrations and conflict, but still may be very sensuous. When both souls are evolved and grounded, the 8 Gua will allow his/her emotional, life partner to process without interference. The 1 Gua can then *flow* towards their "rock of Gibraltar" that is constant and noble for support, love and acceptance. *This couple belongs to opposite groups.*

1 Gua with a 9 Gua
Elemental relationship: WATER-FIRE

The 1 Gua with a 9 Gua is oddly enough very compatible, often creating "steamy" love affairs and hot romance. However, the 1 Gua can completely put out the *fiery* nature of the 9 Gua if they are not in succinct with the energy of their partners or not grounded. If the souls are spiritually evolved, the high emotions/intellect of the 1 Gua will be well-received by the brilliant, fiery goddess energy of the 9's. Sexual union can be highly charged, sensuous and create a lot of *heat* that would be apparent even to casual onlookers. *This couple both belong to the East Life Group.*

"Persistent, Reclusive, and Dependable"
The 2 Gua in Romantic Relationships or Marriages with other Guas:

2 Gua with a 1 Gua
Elemental relationship: EARTH -WATER

The 2 Gua with a 1 Gua indicates strife and conflict. Even if the couple has a long-term marriage it can be riddle with arguments and disagreements with the 2 trying to control the 1. Often these relationships end in divorce, and a bitter one at that. For highly evolved individuals, the 2 would only offer his/her advice/opinion when the 1 ask for it. The 2 Gua would then respect the need of his/her partner to process emotions at their own speed and not offer their keen, intuitive insights until approached. This would allow the 1 Gua to *flow* towards the earthiness of the 2. *This couple belongs to opposite groups.*

2 Gua with a 2 Gua
Elemental relationship: EARTH-EARTH

The 2 Gua with another 2 indicates "friends and lovers". With the intuitive energy of the 2 Guas, they will be in tune with each other's needs and feelings. The energy is earthy, and they will enjoy hiking, gardening, earthy or outdoor sex, constructing things together, and have an interest in healing arts and medicine.

2 Gua with a 3 Gua
Elemental relationship: EARTH-WOOD

The 2 Gua with a 3 Gua can indicate lots of fighting and conflict with the energy of the 3 trying to control the 2. If the couple is grounded, these relationships can be quite good with the progressive energy of the 3 Gua giving direction to the feeling and intuitive 2. Otherwise, there can be constant conflict, like two bulls fighting. Sexual union can be intense, even if is not frequent. *This couple belongs to opposite groups.*

2 Gua with a 4 Gua
Elemental relationship: EARTH-WOOD

The 2 Gua with a 4 Gua can be a difficult match. The 4 Gua will try to control the 2, often manipulating them using sex. These relationships can be tumultuous, and if the 2 cannot come to terms, divorce and break-ups are common. If they are grounded and evolved, the 4 Gua can bring a feeling of safety to the relationship and the sexual union can be quite intense. *This couple belongs to opposite groups.*

2 Gua with a 6 Gua
Elemental relationship: EARTH -METAL

The 2 Gua with a 6 Gua can be wonderfully compatible. The 2 Gua and the 6 represent pure yin and pure yang energy, and this makes this couple very well-matched. The 6 is the real leader here with the 2 as the follower, however the 2 Gua is a complete supporter of their mate. The energy of the 2 will assist the 6 to be all they can be! Sexual union can be both heavenly and earthy all at once! *This couple both belong to the West Life Group.*

2 Gua with a 7 Gua
Elemental relationship: EARTH-METAL

The 2 Gua with a 7 Gua will indicate a very good match. The quieter, more serious nature of the 2 Gua is a good match for the more vibrant, talkative and fun nature of the 7 Gua. The 7 Gua brings beauty to the relationship, while the 2 Gua gives his/her calmness to balance things out. Sex is earthy, and highly sensuous. *This couple both belong to the West Life Group.*

♥2 Gua with an 8 Gua
Elemental relationship: EARTH-EARTH

The 2 Gua with an 8 Gua indicate are the "perfect match" for each other. These Guas are both earthy, with the calmness of the 2 and the noble/stubbornness of the 8. Both Guas have an intense interest in the spiritual/metaphysics and will have this as an aspect of the relationship. Sex can be earthy, playful and spiritual. *This couple both belong to the West Life Group.*

2 Gua with a 9 Gua
Elemental relationship: EARTH-FIRE

The 2 Gua with a 9 Gua is a good match. The 2 Gua is really supported and fired up by the 9's energy. The 9 will enjoy the naturally calm nature of the 2 which perfectly complements the wild, fiery nature of the 9. These energies balance and feed each other beautifully. Sexual union can be hot, unconventional and exciting. *This couple belongs to opposite groups.*

"Enterprising, Impatient and Self-Confident"
The 3 Gua in Romantic Relationships or Marriages with other Guas:

3 Gua with a 1 Gua
Elemental relationship: WOOD-WATER

The 3 Gua with a 1 Gua is a very harmonious relationship. The 1 Gua will indeed be a supportive life partner to the progressive thinking 3 Gua. These two people will be very much into organizing ideas, and can be very creative together. Sexual union can be very compatible as well as creatively diverse. *This couple both belong to the East Life Group.*

3 Gua with a 2 Gua
Elemental relationship: WOOD-EARTH

The 2 Gua with a 3 Gua can indicate lots of fighting and conflict with the energy of the 3 trying to control the 2. If the couple is grounded, these relationships can be quite good with the progressive energy of the 3 Gua giving direction to the feeling and intuitive 2. Otherwise, there can be constant conflict, like two bulls fighting. Sexual union can be intense, even if is not frequent. *This couple belongs to opposite groups.*

3 Gua with a 3 Gua
Elemental relationship: WOOD-WOOD

The 3 Gua with a 3 Gua can indicate 'friends and lovers'. There could be difficulty with both having the tendency to be outspoken and overly direct. However, if both are grounded this couple could enjoy open communication with each other making them closer. This couple will delight in creating many ventures together which could enhance their natural vitality and high energy. Sexual union will be compatible, invigorating and can have many delightful surprises. *This couple both belong to the East Life Group*

3 Gua with a 4 Gua
Elemental relationship: WOOD-WOOD

The 3 Gua with a 4 Gua can be a can be a very good match. The progressive thinking with their multitude of ideas will perfectly suit the flexible energy of the 4's. Since the 4, at times, can be manipulated by their partners, the 3 Gua would need to use caution not to overwhelm his/her mate with too much aggressive energy. All in all, it is a highly compatible match and sexual union can be inventive and sensuous. *This couple both belong to the East Life Group*

3 Gua with a 6 Gua
Elemental relationship: WOOD-METAL

The relationship of the 3 Gua with a 6 Gua can be confrontational and difficult. The 6 Gua, if un-evolved, will cut down their partners especially concerning their ideas and point of views. The natural leadership/bossiness of the 6 can bring out nervousness and impatience of the 3 Gua. However, if these souls are developed and have worked on themselves, it can work out extremely well. The 6 Gua has a real opportunity here to help "carve out" the progressive thinking 3's ideas and help him/her put them into action. Sexual union can be deeply satisfying and creative. *This couple belongs to opposite groups.*

3 Gua with a 7 Gua
Elemental relationship: WOOD-METAL

The 3 Gua with a 7 Gua can indicate strife and discord. The 7 Gua, who is usually joyous, can get his/her "digs" into their partner especially using critical words and speech. The 3 Gua would feel *cut down* and could then step into their outspoken nature and fighting would get progressively worse. If both Guas have awareness, the relationship can be tantalizing in spite of their differences. With the natural vitality of the 3 and the sensuous nature/beauty of the 7, sexual union can be wonderful and full of surprises. *This couple belongs to opposite groups.*

3 Gua with an 8 Gua
Elemental relationship: WOOD-EARTH

The 3 Gua with an 8 Gua indicate a natural *tug of war* with the 3 Gua trying to wrestle control over the 8. The stubborn nature of the 8 Gua would frustrate the 3's effort to be the controlling partner in the relationship. However, if both people are evolved souls the relationship can be deeply satisfying. The 3 Gua's deep-rooted, steady nature would mix well with the noble energy of the 8. Both tend to be organized and progressive thinkers, and *constructing* things together is the surest way of remaining close as a couple. Sexual union can be very intense, earthy and creative. *This couple belongs to opposite groups, one is East Life and the other is West Life.*

♥3 Gua with a 9 Gua
Elemental relationship: WOOD-FIRE

The 3 Gua with a 9 Gua are considered one of the "perfect matches". The high-energy 3 Gua is a true supporter of the 9's fiery nature. The super intellect of the 9 and the progressive thinking 3's can be unstoppable. They are perfectly suited to capture whatever they are focused on as a couple and often this is fame for them both. If they are un-evolved, they can create a raging fire together and burn anyone in their path! Sexual union will be hot and intense. *This couple both belong to the East Life Group.*

"Honest, Malleable, and Progressive"
The 4 Gua in Romantic Relationship or Marriages with other Guas:

♥ 4 Gua with a 1 Gua
Elemental Relationship: WOOD-WATER
Sexy, 'Peach Blossom' Energy

The 1 Gua with a 4 Gua is said to be the "perfect match". The 1 Gua will be totally supportive and feed energy to the 4. Under this type of attention, the 4 Gua will blossom and grow. This can be a highly sexual and romantic union, with both partners feeling the harmonic energy. These couples often enjoy tantric sexual practices. *This couple both belong to the East Life Group.*

4 Gua with a 2 Gua
Elemental relationship: WOOD-EARTH

The 2 Gua with a 4 Gua can be a difficult match. The 4 Gua will try to control the 2, often manipulating them using sex. These relationships can be tumultuous, and if the 2 cannot come to terms, divorce and break-ups are common. If they are grounded and evolved, the 4 Gua can bring a feeling of safety to the relationship and the sexual union can be quite intense. *This couple belongs to opposite groups.*

4 Gua with a 3 Gua
Elemental relationship: WOOD-WOOD

The 4 Gua with a 3 Gua is a good match of energy. The 3 Gua is a natural leader, while the 4 Gua is flexible, a good consort or follower. The energy can yield collaboration in progressive ideas, expansion, and beginning new things. This can be a very harmoniousness union filled with growth and vitality. Romance can blossom throughout the marriage if they take care to honor each other's unique qualities. Sexual union can be satisfying and creative. *This couple both belong to the East Life Group.*

4 Gua with a 4 Gua
Elemental relationship: WOOD-WOOD

The 4 Gua with another 4 Gua will indicate 'friends and lovers'. These highly romantic, and often scholarly people, can have a joyful union of souls. Like the 3 Guas, the 4's can also be very progressive thinkers. Even in late life, these Gua tend to be display youthful vigor and ideas. They keep in touch with the times, and are often highly physical and sexual. Needless to say that sexual union can be intense, often, and at times playful. If the couple is not evolved or deeply connected and committed to each other, there could be affairs, divorce or love triangles. *This couple both belong to the East Life Group.*

4 Gua with a 6 Gua
Elemental relationship: WOOD-METAL

The 4 Gua with a 6 Gua could be a changeling relationship. The 6 Guas often are authoritative and have powerful energy, and this can overwhelm the malleable 4. If the couple is not evolved, the 6 energy can *cut* down the natural romantic and creative ideas of the 4. And sexually, it could be masochistic or may involve roles of domination. However, with more spiritual awareness, the insightful guidance of the 6 can help mold the 4 who often tend to 'blow with the wind' with lots of indecision. The 6 and the 4 both indicate a level of fame if desired. Couples with awareness can thrive in this union, if not; the couple could end in a bitter divorce. Sexual union can be highly intense. *This couple belongs to opposite groups.*

4 Gua with a 7 Gua
Elemental relationship: WOOD-METAL

The 4 with a 7 Gua can be very much like the 4 and 6 Gua, it will have difficult aspects. The 4 Gua may find themselves at the bitter end of the sharp, critical tongue of the 7. The union can be rewarding if the couple are sufficiently evolved however. Then, the 7 Gua can 'carve out' the best of the 4 Gua. Creative ideas will flourish between them. Both Guas have a lot of sexual energy and a youthful take on life. The relationship can be highly rewarding when there is commitment and respect. If not, both have a tendency to stray out of boredom or not being sufficiently supported by their partner. Sexual union can be joyful, fun and rewarding. *This couple belongs to opposite groups.*

4 Gua with an 8 Gua
Elemental relationship: WOOD-EARTH

The 4 Gua with an 8 Gua indicate a natural *tug of war* with the 4 Gua trying to wrestle control over the 8. The stubborn nature of the 8 would frustrate the 4's effort to be the controlling partner in the relationship. However, if both people are evolved souls, the relationship can be deeply satisfying. The 4 Gua's malleable nature would mix well with the noble energy of the 8. The romantic nature of the 4 can win over, rather than control, the stable energy of the 8 Gua. Sexual union can be very intense, earthy and romantic. *This couple belongs to opposite groups.*

4 Gua with a 9 Gua
Elemental relationship: WOOD-FIRE

The 4 Gua with a 9 Gua is a highly compatible match. The 4 Gua provides loyal support to the 9, making them the 'giver' in the relationship. The fiery intellect of the 9 Gua is an excellent match for the romantic and often scholarly 4. On the negative side, with the indecisive 4 and the rashness of the 9, sparks can fly. These two Guas are indicative of fame, and there could be some unhealthy competitiveness if the couple is not connected. The best way for a long marriage is the meeting of minds and hearts through clear communication. Sexual union can be intense and hot! *This couple both belong to the East Life Group.*

"Leaders, Solitary and Creative"
The 6 Gua in Romantic Relationships or Marriages with other Guas:

6 Gua with a 1 Gua
Elemental Relationship: METAL-WATER
Sexy, 'Peach Blossom' Energy

The 1 Gua with a 6 Gua can indicate a "heavenly combination". Normally, the 1 Gua will make the 6 Gua feel drained. And when the couple is not grounded, this can *rust out* or *corrode* a perfectly good relationship. The 6 Guas are natural leaders, but often need time to "marinate" in their feelings. The 1 Gua can also be moody and want some time alone. However, if the couple is evolved, the combination is good with the 6 Gua helping their partner *give birth* to creative ideas and projects. Sexual union can be emotional, compatible, and creative. *This couple belongs to opposite groups, one is East Life and the other is West Life.*

6 Gua with a 2 Gua
Elemental relationship: WOOD-EARTH

The 2 Gua with a 6 Gua can be wonderfully compatible. The 2 Gua and the 6 represent pure yin and pure yang energy, and this makes this couple very well-matched. The 6 is the real leader here with the 2 as the follower, however the 2 Gua is a complete supporter of their mates. The energy of the 2 will assist the 6 to be all they can be! Sexual union can be both heavenly and earthy all at once! *This couple both belong to the West Life Group.*

6 Gua with a 3 Gua
Elemental relationship: METAL-WOOD

The relationship of the 3 Gua with a 6 Gua can be difficult and riddled with conflict. The 6 Gua, if un-evolved, will cut down their partners especially concerning their ideas and point of views. The natural leadership/bossiness of the 6 can bring out nervousness and impatience of the 3 Gua. However, if these souls are developed and have worked on themselves, it can be rewarding. The 6 Gua has a real opportunity here to help "carve out" the progressive thinking 3's ideas and help him/her put them into action. Sexual union can be deeply satisfying and creative. *This couple belongs to opposite groups.*

6 Gua with a 4 Gua
Elemental relationship: METAL-WOOD

The 6 Gua with a 4 Gua could be a changeling relationship. The 6 Guas often are authoritative and have powerful energy, and this can overwhelm the malleable 4. If the couple is not evolved, the 6 energy can *cut* down the natural romantic and creative ideas of the 4. And sexually, it could be masochistic or may involve roles of domination. However, with more spiritual awareness, the insightful guidance of the 6 can help mold the 4 who often tend to 'blow with the wind' with lots of indecision. The 6 and the 4 both indicate a level of fame if desired. Couples with awareness can thrive in this union, if not; the couple could end in a bitter divorce. Sexual union can be highly intense. *This couple belongs to opposite groups.*

6 Gua with a 6 Gua
Elemental relationship: METAL-METAL

The 6 Gua with another 6 Gua can be considered a desirable match. However, it is not without its difficult aspects. Both parties have powerful, authoritative energy and when they butt heads, it will be about belief systems, ideas and the perspectives each holds. Both tend to over-think things and both have the energy to lead people. Sexual union could be blissful, imaginative and may involve fun, role-playing. *This couple both belong to the West Life Group.*

♥6 Gua with a 7 Gua
Elemental relationship: METAL-METAL

The 6 Gua with a 7 Gua is considered one of the "perfect matches" but can be clashing at the same time. In very traditional Feng Shui terms, it means the older man with the younger woman. The natural playfulness of the 7 may get on the nerves of the more serious, self-absorbed and over-thinking 6 Gua. As the charismatic 7 is prone to indulge in excess, the 6 Gua could be tempted to boss or correct their mate. If the couple were evolved however, the match can be very rewarding. They could create successful businesses that may involve products of sensuality, jewelry, travel, or metaphysics. Sexual union could be very expressive, non-traditional, and involve playful 'dirty talk'. *This couple both belong to the West Life Group.*

6 Gua with a 8 Gua
Elemental relationship: METAL-EARTH

The 6 Gua matched with an 8 Gua is considered very compatible energy. The steady and noble energy of the 8 is a good compliment to the authoritative energy of the 6. This is heaven and earth energy, however at times the 6 Gua can slightly deplete the 8 who would be the supporter in the relationship. On a more negative note, un-evolved 8's can be hoarders, and the 6 can be self-absorbed—this would cause a great deal of conflict. If the souls were very developed and clear, the match can have heavenly aspects with both people leaning to all things spiritual. Sexual union can be deep, earthy and extremely connected. *This couple both belong to the West Life Group.*

6 Gua with a 9 Gua
Elemental relationship: METAL-FIRE

In general, the match of a 6 Gua with a 9 Gua is not a compatible and could be difficult. Nevertheless, they will be attracted by their shared high intellect and thinking power. The 9's can totally 'melt' down the energy of the 6. Naturally this will cause a conflict with the 6 whose nature is to rule and exert power. Sparks could fly, sharp words and hot debates over ideas could happen on a regular basis. However, if both people are advanced in consciousness, the union can be quite titillating and exciting with a spectacular exchange of ideas—a true power couple. Sexual union can be just as exciting with each submitting to their passionate natures. *This couple belongs to opposite groups.*

"Charming, Excessive, and Talkative"
The 7 Gua in Romantic Relationships or Marriages with other Guas:

7 Gua with a 1 Gua
Elemental Relationship: METAL-WATER
Sexy, 'Peach Blossom' Energy

The 1 Gua with a 7 Gua will indicate a great deal of sex and romance with *peachy* energy, sweet and juicy. In this relationship, the 7 Gua's natural joyfulness could turn sour as the 1 Gua's energy can be somewhat demanding. If the couple is grounded, the physical part of the relationship can be quite wonderful. If not, both could be prone to affairs of the heart and even step out of the marriage for what their hearts long for. *This couple belongs to opposite groups.*

7 Gua with a 2 Gua
Elemental relationship: METAL-EARTH

The 2 Gua with a 7 Gua will indicate a very good match. The quieter, more serious nature of the 2 Gua is a good match for the more vibrant, talkative and fun nature of the 7 Gua. The 7 Gua brings beauty to the relationship, while the 2 Gua gives his/her calmness to balance things out. Sex is earthy, and highly sensuous. *This couple both belong to the West Life Group.*

7 Gua with a 3 Gua
Elemental relationship: METAL-WOOD

The 3 Gua with a 7 Gua can indicate strife and discord. The 7 Gua, who is usually joyous, can get his/her "digs" into their partner especially using critical words and speech. The 3 Gua would feel *cut down* and could then step into their outspoken nature and fighting would get progressively worse. If both Guas have awareness and are evolved, the relationship can be tantalizing in spite of their differences. With the natural vitality of the 3 and the sensuous nature/beauty of the 7, sexual union can be wonderful and full of surprises. *This couple belongs to opposite groups.*

7 Gua with a 4 Gua
Elemental relationship: METAL-WOOD

The 4 with a 7 Gua can be very much like the 4 and 6 Gua, it will have difficult aspects. The 4 Gua may find themselves at the bitter end of the sharp, critical tongue of the 7. The union can be rewarding if the couple are sufficiently evolved however. Then, the 7 Gua can 'carve out' the best of the 4 Gua. Creative ideas will flourish between them. Both Guas have a lot of sexual energy and a youthful take on life. The relationship can be highly rewarding when there is commitment and respect. If not, both have a tendency to stray out of boredom or not being sufficiently supported by their partner. Sexual union can be joyful, fun and rewarding. *This couple belongs to opposite groups.*

♥7 Gua with a 6 Gua
Elemental relationship: METAL-METAL

The 6 Gua with a 7 Gua is considered both compatible and clashing at the same time; it is one of the 'perfect matches". In very traditional terms, it means the younger woman with an older man. The natural playfulness of the 7 may get on the nerves of the more serious, self-absorbed and over-thinking 6 Gua. As the charismatic 7 is prone to indulge in excess, the 6 Gua could be tempted to boss or correct their mate, if this is the man in the relationship, it is doubly so. If the couple were evolved, the match can be very rewarding. They could create successful businesses that may involve products of sensuality, jewelry, travel, or metaphysics. Sexual union could be very expressive, non-traditional, and involve 'dirty talk'. *This couple both belong to the West Life Group.*

7 Gua with a 7 Gua
Elemental relationship: METAL-METAL

This is considered a highly compatible match of 'lovers and friends'. If the couple is not evolved, there could be too much indulgence in the pleasures of life, and the couple could exhaust and loose themselves in pursuing them. With no counterbalance or grounding energy, there could be over-spending, flirtations, and too many parties. However, if the couple is highly developed they could both be attracted to spiritual and metaphysical interests. They could be speakers and champions of human concerns, planetary issues, and political rightness. Sexual union can be playful and highly sensuous with possible interests in the tantric practices. *This couple both belong to the West Life Group.*

7 Gua with a 8 Gua
Elemental relationship: METAL-EARTH

The 7 Gua with an 8 Gua is excellent and considered very well-matched. The earthiness of the 8 grounds the nervous energy of the 7. The 7 brings the beauty and liveliness to the relationship, as the 8's can be more serious and stubborn. However, the 8 is considered the 'giver' in the relationship as the 7 does slightly deplete their energy. If the 8 is not developed they will lean towards greed, and the 7 will go to excesses and affairs. Sexual union can be highly sensuous, earthy and deeply gratifying for both parties. *This couple both belong to the West Life Group.*

7 Gua with a 9 Gua
Elemental relationship: METAL-FIRE

In general, the 7 Gua matched up with a 9 Gua is considered extremely negative and ill-suited. The 9 may try to control their partner with their passionate opinions and ideas, and the 7 will rebel using their sharp tongues. If not sufficiently evolved, conflict could be a daily event. However, if they are advanced in consciousness, the relationship can be exciting on several levels—the intellect, sexual, and spiritual. Both the 9 and the 7 bring passion, sensuousness, and brilliance. These Guas can be a powerful couple when the energy is directed to the greater good. Sexual union can be intense, beautiful and deeply sensual. *This couple belongs to opposite groups.*

"Successful, Hoarders, and Dependable"
The 8 Gua in Romantic Relationships or Marriages with other Guas:

8 Gua with a 1 Gua
Elemental relationship: METAL-WATER

The 8 Gua with a 1 Gua indicates conflict, fighting and general competitiveness. The fixed stubbornness of the 8 can try to control the 1. The 1 Gua will feel "out of control" when confronted with mountain earthiness of the 8. Sexual union can also have frustrations and conflict, but still can be very sensuous. When both are evolved souls and are grounded, the 8 will allow his/her emotional life partner to process without interference. The 1 Gua can then *flow* towards their "rock of Gibraltar" that is constant and noble. *This couple belongs to opposite groups.*

♥8 Gua with a 2 Gua
Elemental relationship: EARTH-EARTH

The 8 Gua with an 2 Gua indicate are the "perfect match" for each other. These Guas are both earthy, with the calmness of the 2 and the noble/stubbornness of the 8. Both Guas have an intense interest in the spiritual/metaphysics and will have this as an aspect of the relationship. Sex can be earthy, playful and spiritual. *This couple both belong to the West Life Group.*

8 Gua with a 3 Gua
Elemental relationship: EARTH-WOOD

The 8 Gua with an 3 Gua indicate a natural tug a war with the 3 Gua trying to wrestle control over the 8. The stubborn nature of the 8 would frustrate the 3's effort to be the controlling partner in the relationship. However, if both people are evolved souls the relationship can be deeply satisfying. The 3 Gua's deep-rooted, steady nature would mix well with the noble energy of the 8. Both tend to be organized and progressive thinkers, and *constructing* things together is the surest way of remaining close as a couple. Sexual union can be very intense, earthy and creative. *This couple belongs to opposite groups.*

8 Gua with a 4 Gua
Elemental relationship: EARTH-WOOD

The 8 Gua with an 4 Gua indicate a natural tug a war with the 4 Gua trying to wrestle control over the 8. The stubborn nature of the 8 would frustrate the 4's effort to be the controlling partner in the relationship. However, if both people are evolved souls, the rélationship can be deeply satisfying. The 4 Gua's malleable nature would mix well with the noble energy of the 8. The romantic nature of the 4 can win over, rather than control, the stable energy of the 8 Gua. Sexual union can be very intense, earthy and romantic. *This couple belongs to opposite groups.*

8 Gua with a 6 Gua
Elemental relationship: EARTH-METAL

The 8 Gua matched with an 6 Gua is considered very compatible energy. The steady and noble energy of the 8 is a good compliment to the authoritative energy of the 6. This is heaven and earth energy, however at times the 6 Gua can slightly deplete the 8 who would be the supporter in the relationship. On a more negative note, un-evolved 8's can be hoarders, and the 6 can be self-absorbed—this would cause a great deal of conflict. If the souls were very developed and clear, the match can have heavenly aspects with both people leaning to things spiritual. Sexual union can be deep, earthy and extremely connected. *This couple both belong to the West Life Group.*

8 Gua with a 7 Gua
Elemental relationship: EARTH-METAL

The 8 Gua with an 7 Gua is excellent and considered very well-matched. The earthiness of the 8 grounds the nervous energy of the 7. The 7 brings the beauty and liveliness to the relationship, as the 8's can be more serious and stubborn. However, the 8 is considered the 'giver' in the relationship as the 7 does slightly deplete their energy. If the 8 is not developed they will lean towards greed, and the 7 will go to excesses and affairs. Sexual union can be highly sensuous, earthy and deeply gratifying for both parties. *This couple both belong to the West Life Group.*

8 Gua with an 8 Gua
Elemental relationship: EARTH-EARTH

The 8 Gua with another 8 Gua indicates 'friends and lovers.' The noble and steadfast nature of the 8's can bring harmony and stability if the couple is developed. If not, head butting over how things should be done will occur with a digging in the heels and being implacable. Greed, hoarding and being remote will leave each other feeling deprived in the relationship. If the couple is higher in consciousness, each will bring out the nobleness, generosity and spirituality that is possible for these Guas. Sexual union can be very intense and earthy. *This couple both belong to the West Life Group.*

8 Gua with a 9 Gua
Elemental relationship: EARTH-FIRE

The 8 Gua with an 9 Gua is considered very well-matched with lots of potential. The 9 would be the 'giver' in the relationship supporting his/her spouse extremely well. They will fire up, fuel and support their mates with all that they have to offer—ideas, money and love. The 8 Gua will bring their stable, earth energy to the fiery, rasher nature of the 9. When these Guas are not very evolved the stubbornness of the 8 can totally irritate the 9's sharp intellect and superior attitude. Sexual union can be very intense, and these people can be very loyal and passionate lovers. *This couple belongs to opposite groups.*

"Adventurous, Rash, and Brilliance"
The 9 Gua in Romantic Relationships or Marriages with other Guas:

9 Gua with a 1 Gua
Elemental relationship: FIRE & WATER

The 1 Gua with a 9 Gua is oddly enough very compatible, often creating "steamy" love affairs and hot romance. However, the 1 Gua can completely put out the *fiery* nature of the 9 Gua if they are not in succinct or not grounded. If the souls are spiritually evolved, the high emotions/intellect of the 1 Gua will be well-received by the brilliant, fiery passionate energy of the 9's. Sexual union can be highly charged, sensuous and create a lot of *heat* that would be apparent even to casual onlookers. *This couple both belong to the East Life Group.*

9 Gua with a 2 Gua
Elemental relationship: FIRE & EARTH

The 2 Gua with a 9 Gua is a good match. The 2 Gua is really supported and fired up by the 9's energy. The 9 will enjoy the naturally calm nature of the 2 which perfectly complements the wild, fiery nature of the 9. These energies balance and feed each other beautifully. Sexual union can be hot, unconventional and exciting. *This couple belongs to opposite groups.*

♥ 9 Gua with a 3 Gua
Elemental relationship: FIRE & WOOD

The 3 Gua with a 9 Gua are considered a "perfect match". The high-energy 3 Gua is a true supporter of the 9's fiery nature. The super intellect of the 9 and the progressive thinking 3's can be unstoppable. They are perfectly suited to capture whatever they are focused on as a couple—often this is fame for them both. If they are un-evolved, they can create a raging fire together and burn anyone in their path! Sexual union will be hot and intense. *This couple both belong to the East Life Group.*

9 Gua with a 4 Gua
Elemental relationship: FIRE & WOOD

The 4 Gua with a 9 Gua is a highly compatible match. The 4 Gua provides loyal support to the 9, making them the 'giver' in the relationship. The fiery intellect of the 9 Gua is an excellent match for the romantic and often scholarly 4. On the negative side, with the indecisive 4 and the rashness of the 9, sparks can fly. These two Guas are indicative of fame, and there could be some unhealthy competitiveness if the couple is not connected. The best way for a long marriage is the meeting of minds and hearts through clear communication. Sexual union can be intense and hot! *This couple both belong to the East Life Group.*

9 Gua with a 6 Gua
Elemental relationship: FIRE-METAL

In general, the match of a 6 Gua with a 9 Gua is not a compatible and could be difficult. Nevertheless, they will be attracted by their shared high intellect and thinking power. The 9's can totally 'melt' down the energy of the 6; naturally this will cause a conflict with the 6 whose nature is to rule and exert power. Sparks could fly, sharp words and hot debates over ideas could happen on a regular basis. However, if both people are advanced in consciousness, the union can be quite titillating and exciting with a spectacular exchange of ideas—a true power couple. Sexual union can be just as exciting with each succumbing to their passionate natures. *This couple belongs to opposite groups.*

9 Gua with a 7 Gua
Elemental relationship: FIRE-METAL

In general, the 7 Gua matched up with a 9 Gua is considered extremely negative and ill-suited. The 9 may try to control their partner with their passionate opinions and ideas, and the 7 will rebel using their sharp tongues. If not sufficiently evolved, conflict could be a daily event. However, if they are advanced in consciousness, the relationship can be exciting on several levels—the intellect, sexual, and spiritual. Both the 9 and the 7 bring passion, beauty, sensuousness, and brilliance. These Guas can be a powerful couple when the significant energy is directed to the greater good. Sexual union can be intense, beautiful and deeply sensual. *This couple belongs to opposite groups.*

9 Gua with an 8 Gua
Elemental relationship: FIRE-EARTH

The 9 Gua with an 8 Gua is considered very well-matched with lots of potential. The 9 would be the 'giver' in the relationship supporting his/her spouse extremely well. They will fire up, fuel and support their mates with all that they have to offer—ideas, money and love. The 8 Gua will bring their stable, earth energy to the fiery, rasher nature of the 9. When these Guas are not very evolved the stubbornness of the 8 can totally irritate the 9's sharp intellect and superior attitude. Sexual union can be very intense, and these people can be very loyal and passionate lovers. *This couple belongs to opposite groups.*

9 Gua with a 9 Gua
Elemental relationship: FIRE-FIRE

The match of the 9 Guas can be a something to behold, and generally it is considered to be a good match. The energy of this couple has the potential to be great—each bringing out the best in each other—or disaster. The 9's who are not developed can exhibit paranoia, rashness and very aggressive behavior. These people can start revolutions and stir up trouble. When they are advanced in consciousness however, they can have a powerful influence on people with their noble and wise ideas and deliver them with passion. Sexual union can be *fiery* in capital letters! *This couple both belong to the East Life Group.*

Appendix I

Check the Year of Birth for those Born on Feb 3rd, 4th, or 5th

Life Gua Determination if you were born on Feb 3, 4 or 5th

Using dates/times based on universal time—the time at the Greenwich Meridian to avoid the confusion that can be caused by different time zones and the international date line

Animal	Year	Feb	Time The Year Began	Animal	Year	Feb	Time The Year Began	Animal	Year	Feb	Time The Year Began
Rooster	**1933**	4	2:10 pm	Dragon	**1964**	5	3:05 am	Pig	**1995**	4	3:14 pm
Dog	**1934**	4	8:04 pm	Snake	**1965**	4	8:46 am	Rat	**1996**	4	9:08 pm
Pig	**1935**	5	1:49 am	Horse	**1966**	4	2:38 pm	Ox	**1997**	4	3:04 am
Rat	**1936**	5	7:30 am	Goat	**1967**	4	8:31 pm	Tiger	**1998**	4	8:53 am
Ox	**1937**	4	1:26 pm	Monkey	**1968**	5	2:08 am	Rabbit	**1999**	4	2:42 pm
Tiger	**1938**	4	7:15 pm	Rooster	**1969**	4	7:59 am	Dragon	**2000**	4	8:32 pm
Rabbit	**1939**	5	1:11 am	Dog	**1970**	4	1:46 pm	Snake	**2001**	4	2:20 am
Dragon	**1940**	5	7:08 am	Pig	**1971**	4	7:26 pm	Horse	**2002**	4	8:08 am
Snake	**1941**	4	12:50 pm	Rat	**1972**	5	1:20 am	Goat	**2003**	4	1:57 pm
Horse	**1942**	4	6:49 pm	Ox	**1973**	4	7:04 am	Monkey	**2004**	4	7:46 pm
Goat	**1943**	5	12:41 am	Tiger	**1974**	4	1:00 pm	Rooster	**2005**	4	1:34 am
Monkey	**1944**	5	6:23 am	Rabbit	**1975**	4	6:59 pm	Dog	**2006**	4	7:25 am
Rooster	**1945**	4	12:20 pm	Dragon	**1976**	5	12:40 am	Pig	**2007**	4	1:14 pm
Dog	**1946**	4	6:05 pm	Snake	**1977**	4	6:34 am	Rat	**2008**	4	7:03 pm
Pig	**1947**	4	11:55 pm	Horse	**1978**	4	12:27 pm	Ox	**2009**	4	12:52 am
Rat	**1948**	5	5:43 am	Goat	**1979**	4	6:13 pm	Tiger	**2010**	4	6:42 am
Ox	**1949**	4	11:23 am	Monkey	**1980**	5	12:10 am	Rabbit	**2011**	4	12:32 pm
Tiger	**1950**	4	5:21 pm	Rooster	**1981**	4	5:56 am	Dragon	**2012**	4	6:40 pm
Rabbit	**1951**	4	11:14 pm	Dog	**1982**	4	11:46 am	Snake	**2013**	4	12:24 am
Dragon	**1952**	5	4:54 am	Pig	**1983**	4	5:40 pm	Horse	**2014**	4	6:21 am
Snake	**1953**	4	10:46 am	Rat	**1984**	4	11:19 pm	Goat	**2015**	4	12:09 pm
Horse	**1954**	4	4:31 pm	Ox	**1985**	4	5:12 am	Monkey	**2016**	4	6:00 pm
Goat	**1955**	4	10:18 pm	Tiger	**1986**	4	11:09 am	Rooster	**2017**	3	11:49 pm
Monkey	**1956**	5	4:13 am	Rabbit	**1987**	4	4:52 pm	Dog	**2018**	4	5:38 am
Rooster	**1957**	4	9:55 am	Dragon	**1988**	4	10:43 pm	Pig	**2019**	4	11:28 am
Dog	**1958**	4	3:50 pm	Snake	**1989**	4	4:27 am	Rat	**2020**	4	5:18 pm
Pig	**1959**	4	9:43 pm	Horse	**1990**	4	10:15 am	Ox	**2021**	3	11:08 pm
Rat	**1960**	5	3:23 am	Goat	**1991**	4	4:08 pm	Tiger	**2022**	4	4:58 am
Ox	**1961**	4	9:23 am	Monkey	**1992**	4	9:48 pm	Rabbit	**2023**	4	10:47 am
Tiger	**1962**	4	3:18 pm	Rooster	**1993**	4	3:38 am	Dragon	**2024**	4	4:37 pm
Rabbit	**1963**	4	9:08 pm	Dog	**1994**	4	9:31 am	Snake	**2025**	3	10:27 pm

Appendix II
How to Take a Compass Direction

Some masters take the door degree from *inside* the building. However, Grandmaster Yap taught his students to take the compass direction—outside, face the door, and at waist level, place the Luo Pan directly on it. This results in a very accurate compass reading. A traditional hiking compass may vary a few degrees from a Luo Pan and a smart phone may vary even more. Purchase a good app that aligns with GPS as phones do not contain a magnet like a regular compass. When using a Luo Pan or hiking compass, place it at waist level and remove all metal belts and jewelry. Take several compass readings to ensure accuracy. Measure all exterior doors and make note the readings.

If using a traditional Luo Pan, stand outside the door and face it. Line up the head of the needle between the two red dots. Look at the 6:00 position near your waist and see the degree.

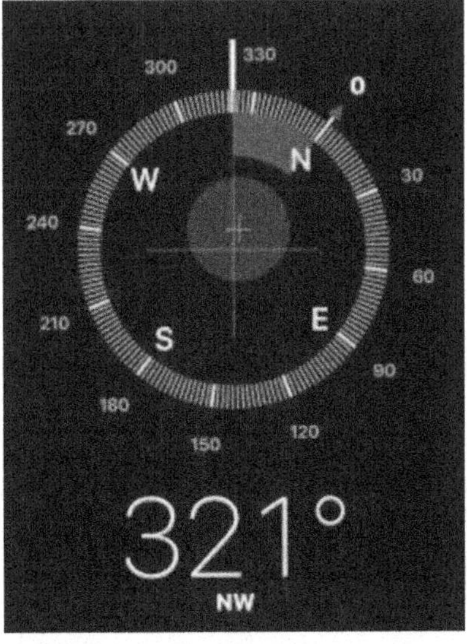

Using your Smartphone to take a compass direction, put your back to the door and it will give you a digital read out similar to this image.

When using a traditional hiking compass, follow the manufacturer's directions.

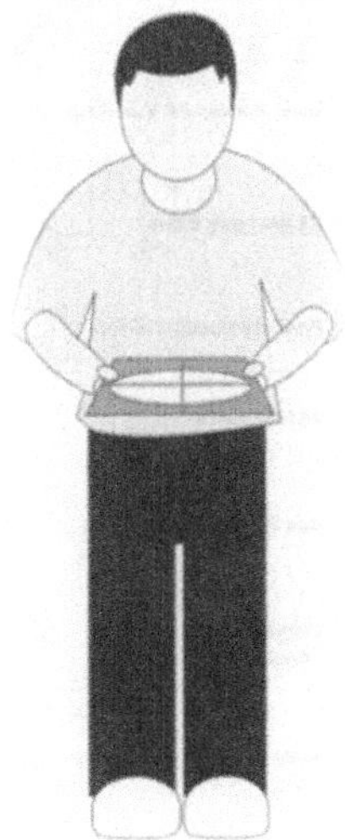

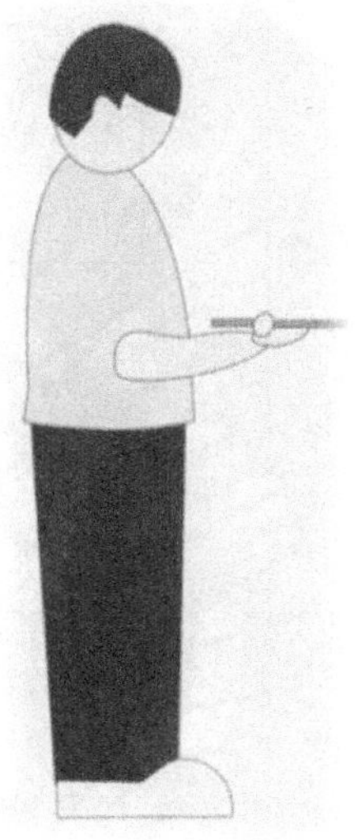

Appendix III

How to Take Allocate the Eight Directions (Cardinals)

SW	W	NW
S		N
SE	E	NE

↓

NW	N	NE
W		E
SW	S	SE

↓

NE	E	SE
N		S
NW	W	SW

↓

SE	S	SW
E		W
NE	N	NW

↓

Appendix III continued

How to Take Allocate the Eight Directions (Intercardinals)

W	NW	N
SW		NE
S	SE	E

↓

N	NE	E
NW		SE
W	SW	S

↓

E	SE	S
NE		SW
N	NW	W

↓

S	SW	W
SE		NW
E	NE	N

↓

Appendix IV
Magic Life-Gua Cards (1 Gua)

Eight Mansions: 1 Gua is EAST LIFE GROUP

SE +90	S +70	SW -90
E +80	1	W -60
NE -70	N +60	NW -80

+90	Sheng Chi: Money Luck	SE
+80	Tien Yi: Health	E
+70	Yen Nien: Relationships	S
+60	Fu Wie: Stable Energy	N
-60	Wo Hai: Troubles/Setbacks	W
-70	Wu Gwei: Lawsuits/Affairs	NE
-80	Liu Sha: Bad Health & Betrayals	NW
-90	Chueh Ming: Divorce/Failures	SW

Dragon Gate Feng Shui • www.dragongatefengshui.com © 2006

Eight Mansions: 1 Gua is EAST LIFE GROUP

SE +90	S +70	SW -90
E +80	1	W -60
NE -70	N +60	NW -80

+90	Sheng Chi: Money Luck	SE
+80	Tien Yi: Health	E
+70	Yen Nien: Relationships	S
+60	Fu Wie: Stable Energy	N
-60	Wo Hai: Troubles/Setbacks	W
-70	Wu Gwei: Lawsuits/Affairs	NE
-80	Liu Sha: Bad Health & Betrayals	NW
-90	Chueh Ming: Divorce/Failures	SW

Dragon Gate Feng Shui • www.dragongatefengshui.com © 2006

Eight Mansions: 1 Gua is EAST LIFE GROUP

SE +90	S +70	SW -90
E +80	1	W -60
NE -70	N +60	NW -80

+90	Sheng Chi: Money Luck	SE
+80	Tien Yi: Health	E
+70	Yen Nien: Relationships	S
+60	Fu Wie: Stable Energy	N
-60	Wo Hai: Troubles/Setbacks	W
-70	Wu Gwei: Lawsuits/Affairs	NE
-80	Liu Sha: Bad Health & Betrayals	NW
-90	Chueh Ming: Divorce/Failures	SW

Dragon Gate Feng Shui • www.dragongatefengshui.com © 2006

Eight Mansions: 1 Gua is EAST LIFE GROUP

SE +90	S +70	SW -90
E +80	1	W -60
NE -70	N +60	NW -80

+90	Sheng Chi: Money Luck	SE
+80	Tien Yi: Health	E
+70	Yen Nien: Relationships	S
+60	Fu Wie: Stable Energy	N
-60	Wo Hai: Troubles/Setbacks	W
-70	Wu Gwei: Lawsuits/Affairs	NE
-80	Liu Sha: Bad Health & Betrayals	NW
-90	Chueh Ming: Divorce/Failures	SW

Dragon Gate Feng Shui • www.dragongatefengshui.com © 2006

Eight Mansions: 1 Gua is EAST LIFE GROUP

SE +90	S +70	SW -90
E +80	1	W -60
NE -70	N +60	NW -80

+90	Sheng Chi: Money Luck	SE
+80	Tien Yi: Health	E
+70	Yen Nien: Relationships	S
+60	Fu Wie: Stable Energy	N
-60	Wo Hai: Troubles/Setbacks	W
-70	Wu Gwei: Lawsuits/Affairs	NE
-80	Liu Sha: Bad Health & Betrayals	NW
-90	Chueh Ming: Divorce/Failures	SW

Dragon Gate Feng Shui • www.dragongatefengshui.com © 2006

Eight Mansions: 1 Gua is EAST LIFE GROUP

SE +90	S +70	SW -90
E +80	1	W -60
NE -70	N +60	NW -80

+90	Sheng Chi: Money Luck	SE
+80	Tien Yi: Health	E
+70	Yen Nien: Relationships	S
+60	Fu Wie: Stable Energy	N
-60	Wo Hai: Troubles/Setbacks	W
-70	Wu Gwei: Lawsuits/Affairs	NE
-80	Liu Sha: Bad Health & Betrayals	NW
-90	Chueh Ming: Divorce/Failures	SW

Dragon Gate Feng Shui • www.dragongatefengshui.com © 2006

Eight Mansions: 1 Gua is EAST LIFE GROUP

SE +90	S +70	SW -90
E +80	1	W -60
NE -70	N +60	NW -80

+90	Sheng Chi: Money Luck	SE
+80	Tien Yi: Health	E
+70	Yen Nien: Relationships	S
+60	Fu Wie: Stable Energy	N
-60	Wo Hai: Troubles/Setbacks	W
-70	Wu Gwei: Lawsuits/Affairs	NE
-80	Liu Sha: Bad Health & Betrayals	NW
-90	Chueh Ming: Divorce/Failures	SW

Dragon Gate Feng Shui • www.dragongatefengshui.com © 2006

Eight Mansions: 1 Gua is EAST LIFE GROUP

SE +90	S +70	SW -90
E +80	1	W -60
NE -70	N +60	NW -80

+90	Sheng Chi: Money Luck	SE
+80	Tien Yi: Health	E
+70	Yen Nien: Relationships	S
+60	Fu Wie: Stable Energy	N
-60	Wo Hai: Troubles/Setbacks	W
-70	Wu Gwei: Lawsuits/Affairs	NE
-80	Liu Sha: Bad Health & Betrayals	NW
-90	Chueh Ming: Divorce/Failures	SW

Dragon Gate Feng Shui • www.dragongatefengshui.com © 2006

Appendix IV *continued*
Magic Life-Gua Cards (2 Gua)

Eight Mansions: 2 Gua is WEST LIFE GROUP

SE -70	S -80	SW +60
E -60	2	W +80
NE +90	N -90	NW +70

+90	Sheng Chi: Money Luck	NE
+80	Tien Yi: Health	W
+70	Yen Nien: Relationships	NW
+60	Fu Wie: Stable Energy	SW
-60	Wo Hai: Troubles/Setbacks	E
-70	Wu Gwei: Lawsuits/Affairs	SE
-80	Liu Sha: Bad Health & Betrayals	S
-90	Chueh Ming: Divorce/Failures	N

Dragon Gate Feng Shui • www.dragongatefengshui.com © 2006

Eight Mansions: 2 Gua is WEST LIFE GROUP

SE -70	S -80	SW +60
E -60	2	W +80
NE +90	N -90	NW +70

+90	Sheng Chi: Money Luck	NE
+80	Tien Yi: Health	W
+70	Yen Nien: Relationships	NW
+60	Fu Wie: Stable Energy	SW
-60	Wo Hai: Troubles/Setbacks	E
-70	Wu Gwei: Lawsuits/Affairs	SE
-80	Liu Sha: Bad Health & Betrayals	S
-90	Chueh Ming: Divorce/Failures	N

Dragon Gate Feng Shui • www.dragongatefengshui.com © 2006

Eight Mansions: 2 Gua is WEST LIFE GROUP

SE -70	S -80	SW +60
E -60	2	W +80
NE +90	N -90	NW +70

+90	Sheng Chi: Money Luck	NE
+80	Tien Yi: Health	W
+70	Yen Nien: Relationships	NW
+60	Fu Wie: Stable Energy	SW
-60	Wo Hai: Troubles/Setbacks	E
-70	Wu Gwei: Lawsuits/Affairs	SE
-80	Liu Sha: Bad Health & Betrayals	S
-90	Chueh Ming: Divorce/Failures	N

Dragon Gate Feng Shui • www.dragongatefengshui.com © 2006

Eight Mansions: 2 Gua is WEST LIFE GROUP

SE -70	S -80	SW +60
E -60	2	W +80
NE +90	N -90	NW +70

+90	Sheng Chi: Money Luck	NE
+80	Tien Yi: Health	W
+70	Yen Nien: Relationships	NW
+60	Fu Wie: Stable Energy	SW
-60	Wo Hai: Troubles/Setbacks	E
-70	Wu Gwei: Lawsuits/Affairs	SE
-80	Liu Sha: Bad Health & Betrayals	S
-90	Chueh Ming: Divorce/Failures	N

Dragon Gate Feng Shui • www.dragongatefengshui.com © 2006

Eight Mansions: 2 Gua is WEST LIFE GROUP

SE -70	S -80	SW +60
E -60	2	W +80
NE +90	N -90	NW +70

+90	Sheng Chi: Money Luck	NE
+80	Tien Yi: Health	W
+70	Yen Nien: Relationships	NW
+60	Fu Wie: Stable Energy	SW
-60	Wo Hai: Troubles/Setbacks	E
-70	Wu Gwei: Lawsuits/Affairs	SE
-80	Liu Sha: Bad Health & Betrayals	S
-90	Chueh Ming: Divorce/Failures	N

Dragon Gate Feng Shui • www.dragongatefengshui.com © 2006

Eight Mansions: 2 Gua is WEST LIFE GROUP

SE -70	S -80	SW +60
E -60	2	W +80
NE +90	N -90	NW +70

+90	Sheng Chi: Money Luck	NE
+80	Tien Yi: Health	W
+70	Yen Nien: Relationships	NW
+60	Fu Wie: Stable Energy	SW
-60	Wo Hai: Troubles/Setbacks	E
-70	Wu Gwei: Lawsuits/Affairs	SE
-80	Liu Sha: Bad Health & Betrayals	S
-90	Chueh Ming: Divorce/Failures	N

Dragon Gate Feng Shui • www.dragongatefengshui.com © 2006

Eight Mansions: 2 Gua is WEST LIFE GROUP

SE -70	S -80	SW +60
E -60	2	W +80
NE +90	N -90	NW +70

+90	Sheng Chi: Money Luck	NE
+80	Tien Yi: Health	W
+70	Yen Nien: Relationships	NW
+60	Fu Wie: Stable Energy	SW
-60	Wo Hai: Troubles/Setbacks	E
-70	Wu Gwei: Lawsuits/Affairs	SE
-80	Liu Sha: Bad Health & Betrayals	S
-90	Chueh Ming: Divorce/Failures	N

Dragon Gate Feng Shui • www.dragongatefengshui.com © 2006

Eight Mansions: 2 Gua is WEST LIFE GROUP

SE -70	S -80	SW +60
E -60	2	W +80
NE +90	N -90	NW +70

+90	Sheng Chi: Money Luck	NE
+80	Tien Yi: Health	W
+70	Yen Nien: Relationships	NW
+60	Fu Wie: Stable Energy	SW
-60	Wo Hai: Troubles/Setbacks	E
-70	Wu Gwei: Lawsuits/Affairs	SE
-80	Liu Sha: Bad Health & Betrayals	S
-90	Chueh Ming: Divorce/Failures	N

Dragon Gate Feng Shui • www.dragongatefengshui.com © 2006

Appendix IV *continued*

Magic Life-Gua Cards (3 Gua)

Eight Mansions: 3 Gua is EAST LIFE GROUP

SE +70	S +90	SW -60
E +60	3	W -90
NE -80	N +80	NW -70

+90	Sheng Chi: Money Luck	S
+80	Tien Yi: Health	N
+70	Yen Nien: Relationships	SE
+60	Fu Wie: Stable Energy	E
-60	Wo Hai: Troubles/Setbacks	SW
-70	Wu Gwei: Lawsuits/Affairs	NW
-80	Liu Sha: Bad Health & Betrayals	NE
-90	Chueh Ming: Divorce/Failures	W

Dragon Gate Feng Shui • www.dragongatefengshui.com © 2008006

Eight Mansions: 3 Gua is EAST LIFE GROUP

SE +70	S +90	SW -60
E +60	3	W -90
NE -80	N +80	NW -70

+90	Sheng Chi: Money Luck	S
+80	Tien Yi: Health	N
+70	Yen Nien: Relationships	SE
+60	Fu Wie: Stable Energy	E
-60	Wo Hai: Troubles/Setbacks	SW
-70	Wu Gwei: Lawsuits/Affairs	NW
-80	Liu Sha: Bad Health & Betrayals	NE
-90	Chueh Ming: Divorce/Failures	W

Dragon Gate Feng Shui • www.dragongatefengshui.com © 2008006

Eight Mansions: 3 Gua is EAST LIFE GROUP

SE +70	S +90	SW -60
E +60	3	W -90
NE -80	N +80	NW -70

+90	Sheng Chi: Money Luck	S
+80	Tien Yi: Health	N
+70	Yen Nien: Relationships	SE
+60	Fu Wie: Stable Energy	E
-60	Wo Hai: Troubles/Setbacks	SW
-70	Wu Gwei: Lawsuits/Affairs	NW
-80	Liu Sha: Bad Health & Betrayals	NE
-90	Chueh Ming: Divorce/Failures	W

Dragon Gate Feng Shui • www.dragongatefengshui.com © 2008006

Eight Mansions: 3 Gua is EAST LIFE GROUP

SE +70	S +90	SW -60
E +60	3	W -90
NE -80	N +80	NW -70

+90	Sheng Chi: Money Luck	S
+80	Tien Yi: Health	N
+70	Yen Nien: Relationships	SE
+60	Fu Wie: Stable Energy	E
-60	Wo Hai: Troubles/Setbacks	SW
-70	Wu Gwei: Lawsuits/Affairs	NW
-80	Liu Sha: Bad Health & Betrayals	NE
-90	Chueh Ming: Divorce/Failures	W

Dragon Gate Feng Shui • www.dragongatefengshui.com © 2008006

Eight Mansions: 3 Gua is EAST LIFE GROUP

SE +70	S +90	SW -60
E +60	3	W -90
NE -80	N +80	NW -70

+90	Sheng Chi: Money Luck	S
+80	Tien Yi: Health	N
+70	Yen Nien: Relationships	SE
+60	Fu Wie: Stable Energy	E
-60	Wo Hai: Troubles/Setbacks	SW
-70	Wu Gwei: Lawsuits/Affairs	NW
-80	Liu Sha: Bad Health & Betrayals	NE
-90	Chueh Ming: Divorce/Failures	W

Dragon Gate Feng Shui • www.dragongatefengshui.com © 2008006

Eight Mansions: 3 Gua is EAST LIFE GROUP

SE +70	S +90	SW -60
E +60	3	W -90
NE -80	N +80	NW -70

+90	Sheng Chi: Money Luck	S
+80	Tien Yi: Health	N
+70	Yen Nien: Relationships	SE
+60	Fu Wie: Stable Energy	E
-60	Wo Hai: Troubles/Setbacks	SW
-70	Wu Gwei: Lawsuits/Affairs	NW
-80	Liu Sha: Bad Health & Betrayals	NE
-90	Chueh Ming: Divorce/Failures	W

Dragon Gate Feng Shui • www.dragongatefengshui.com © 2008006

Eight Mansions: 3 Gua is EAST LIFE GROUP

SE +70	S +90	SW -60
E +60	3	W -90
NE -80	N +80	NW -70

+90	Sheng Chi: Money Luck	S
+80	Tien Yi: Health	N
+70	Yen Nien: Relationships	SE
+60	Fu Wie: Stable Energy	E
-60	Wo Hai: Troubles/Setbacks	SW
-70	Wu Gwei: Lawsuits/Affairs	NW
-80	Liu Sha: Bad Health & Betrayals	NE
-90	Chueh Ming: Divorce/Failures	W

Dragon Gate Feng Shui • www.dragongatefengshui.com © 2008006

Eight Mansions: 3 Gua is EAST LIFE GROUP

SE +70	S +90	SW -60
E +60	3	W -90
NE -80	N +80	NW -70

+90	Sheng Chi: Money Luck	S
+80	Tien Yi: Health	N
+70	Yen Nien: Relationships	SE
+60	Fu Wie: Stable Energy	E
-60	Wo Hai: Troubles/Setbacks	SW
-70	Wu Gwei: Lawsuits/Affairs	NW
-80	Liu Sha: Bad Health & Betrayals	NE
-90	Chueh Ming: Divorce/Failures	W

Dragon Gate Feng Shui • www.dragongatefengshui.com © 2008006

Appendix IV *continued*

Magic Life-Gua Cards (4 Gua)

Eight Mansions: 4 Gua is EAST LIFE GROUP

SE +60	S +80	SW -70
E +70	4	W -80
NE -90	N +90	NW -60

+90	Sheng Chi: Money Luck	N
+80	Tien Yi: Health	S
+70	Yen Nien: Relationships	E
+60	Fu Wie: Stable Energy	SE
-60	Wo Hai: Troubles/Setbacks	NW
-70	Wu Gwei: Lawsuits/Affairs	SW
-80	Liu Sha: Bad Health & Betrayals	W
-90	Chueh Ming: Divorce/Failures	NE

Dragon Gate Feng Shui • www.dragongatefengshui.com © 2006

Eight Mansions: 4 Gua is EAST LIFE GROUP

SE +60	S +80	SW -70
E +70	4	W -80
NE -90	N +90	NW -60

+90	Sheng Chi: Money Luck	N
+80	Tien Yi: Health	S
+70	Yen Nien: Relationships	E
+60	Fu Wie: Stable Energy	SE
-60	Wo Hai: Troubles/Setbacks	NW
-70	Wu Gwei: Lawsuits/Affairs	SW
-80	Liu Sha: Bad Health & Betrayals	W
-90	Chueh Ming: Divorce/Failures	NE

Dragon Gate Feng Shui • www.dragongatefengshui.com © 2006

Eight Mansions: 4 Gua is EAST LIFE GROUP

SE +60	S +80	SW -70
E +70	4	W -80
NE -90	N +90	NW -60

+90	Sheng Chi: Money Luck	N
+80	Tien Yi: Health	S
+70	Yen Nien: Relationships	E
+60	Fu Wie: Stable Energy	SE
-60	Wo Hai: Troubles/Setbacks	NW
-70	Wu Gwei: Lawsuits/Affairs	SW
-80	Liu Sha: Bad Health & Betrayals	W
-90	Chueh Ming: Divorce/Failures	NE

Dragon Gate Feng Shui • www.dragongatefengshui.com © 2006

Eight Mansions: 4 Gua is EAST LIFE GROUP

SE +60	S +80	SW -70
E +70	4	W -80
NE -90	N +90	NW -60

+90	Sheng Chi: Money Luck	N
+80	Tien Yi: Health	S
+70	Yen Nien: Relationships	E
+60	Fu Wie: Stable Energy	SE
-60	Wo Hai: Troubles/Setbacks	NW
-70	Wu Gwei: Lawsuits/Affairs	SW
-80	Liu Sha: Bad Health & Betrayals	W
-90	Chueh Ming: Divorce/Failures	NE

Dragon Gate Feng Shui • www.dragongatefengshui.com © 2006

Eight Mansions: 4 Gua is EAST LIFE GROUP

SE +60	S +80	SW -70
E +70	4	W -80
NE -90	N +90	NW -60

+90	Sheng Chi: Money Luck	N
+80	Tien Yi: Health	S
+70	Yen Nien: Relationships	E
+60	Fu Wie: Stable Energy	SE
-60	Wo Hai: Troubles/Setbacks	NW
-70	Wu Gwei: Lawsuits/Affairs	SW
-80	Liu Sha: Bad Health & Betrayals	W
-90	Chueh Ming: Divorce/Failures	NE

Dragon Gate Feng Shui • www.dragongatefengshui.com © 2006

Eight Mansions: 4 Gua is EAST LIFE GROUP

SE +60	S +80	SW -70
E +70	4	W -80
NE -90	N +90	NW -60

+90	Sheng Chi: Money Luck	N
+80	Tien Yi: Health	S
+70	Yen Nien: Relationships	E
+60	Fu Wie: Stable Energy	SE
-60	Wo Hai: Troubles/Setbacks	NW
-70	Wu Gwei: Lawsuits/Affairs	SW
-80	Liu Sha: Bad Health & Betrayals	W
-90	Chueh Ming: Divorce/Failures	NE

Dragon Gate Feng Shui • www.dragongatefengshui.com © 2006

Eight Mansions: 4 Gua is EAST LIFE GROUP

SE +60	S +80	SW -70
E +70	4	W -80
NE -90	N +90	NW -60

+90	Sheng Chi: Money Luck	N
+80	Tien Yi: Health	S
+70	Yen Nien: Relationships	E
+60	Fu Wie: Stable Energy	SE
-60	Wo Hai: Troubles/Setbacks	NW
-70	Wu Gwei: Lawsuits/Affairs	SW
-80	Liu Sha: Bad Health & Betrayals	W
-90	Chueh Ming: Divorce/Failures	NE

Dragon Gate Feng Shui • www.dragongatefengshui.com © 2006

Eight Mansions: 4 Gua is EAST LIFE GROUP

SE +60	S +80	SW -70
E +70	4	W -80
NE -90	N +90	NW -60

+90	Sheng Chi: Money Luck	N
+80	Tien Yi: Health	S
+70	Yen Nien: Relationships	E
+60	Fu Wie: Stable Energy	SE
-60	Wo Hai: Troubles/Setbacks	NW
-70	Wu Gwei: Lawsuits/Affairs	SW
-80	Liu Sha: Bad Health & Betrayals	W
-90	Chueh Ming: Divorce/Failures	NE

Dragon Gate Feng Shui • www.dragongatefengshui.com © 2006

Appendix IV *continued*

Magic Life-Gua Cards (6 Gua)

Eight Mansions: 6 Gua is WEST LIFE GROUP

SE -60	S -90	SW +70
E -70	6	W +90
NE +80	N -80	NW +60

+90	Sheng Chi: Money Luck	W
+80	Tien Yi: Health	NE
+70	Yen Nien: Relationships	SW
+60	Fu Wie: Stable Energy	NW
-60	Wo Hai: Troubles/Setbacks	SE
-70	Wu Gwei: Lawsuits/Affairs	E
-80	Liu Sha: Bad Health & Betrayals	N
-90	Chueh Ming: Divorce/Failures	S

Dragon Gate Feng Shui • www.dragongatefengshui.com © 2006

Eight Mansions: 6 Gua is WEST LIFE GROUP

SE -60	S -90	SW +70
E -70	6	W +90
NE +80	N -80	NW +60

+90	Sheng Chi: Money Luck	W
+80	Tien Yi: Health	NE
+70	Yen Nien: Relationships	SW
+60	Fu Wie: Stable Energy	NW
-60	Wo Hai: Troubles/Setbacks	SE
-70	Wu Gwei: Lawsuits/Affairs	E
-80	Liu Sha: Bad Health & Betrayals	N
-90	Chueh Ming: Divorce/Failures	S

Dragon Gate Feng Shui • www.dragongatefengshui.com © 2006

Eight Mansions: 6 Gua is WEST LIFE GROUP

SE -60	S -90	SW +70
E -70	6	W +90
NE +80	N -80	NW +60

+90	Sheng Chi: Money Luck	W
+80	Tien Yi: Health	NE
+70	Yen Nien: Relationships	SW
+60	Fu Wie: Stable Energy	NW
-60	Wo Hai: Troubles/Setbacks	SE
-70	Wu Gwei: Lawsuits/Affairs	E
-80	Liu Sha: Bad Health & Betrayals	N
-90	Chueh Ming: Divorce/Failures	S

Dragon Gate Feng Shui • www.dragongatefengshui.com © 2006

Eight Mansions: 6 Gua is WEST LIFE GROUP

SE -60	S -90	SW +70
E -70	6	W +90
NE +80	N -80	NW +60

+90	Sheng Chi: Money Luck	W
+80	Tien Yi: Health	NE
+70	Yen Nien: Relationships	SW
+60	Fu Wie: Stable Energy	NW
-60	Wo Hai: Troubles/Setbacks	SE
-70	Wu Gwei: Lawsuits/Affairs	E
-80	Liu Sha: Bad Health & Betrayals	N
-90	Chueh Ming: Divorce/Failures	S

Dragon Gate Feng Shui • www.dragongatefengshui.com © 2006

Eight Mansions: 6 Gua is WEST LIFE GROUP

SE -60	S -90	SW +70
E -70	6	W +90
NE +80	N -80	NW +60

+90	Sheng Chi: Money Luck	W
+80	Tien Yi: Health	NE
+70	Yen Nien: Relationships	SW
+60	Fu Wie: Stable Energy	NW
-60	Wo Hai: Troubles/Setbacks	SE
-70	Wu Gwei: Lawsuits/Affairs	E
-80	Liu Sha: Bad Health & Betrayals	N
-90	Chueh Ming: Divorce/Failures	S

Dragon Gate Feng Shui • www.dragongatefengshui.com © 2006

Eight Mansions: 6 Gua is WEST LIFE GROUP

SE -60	S -90	SW +70
E -70	6	W +90
NE +80	N -80	NW +60

+90	Sheng Chi: Money Luck	W
+80	Tien Yi: Health	NE
+70	Yen Nien: Relationships	SW
+60	Fu Wie: Stable Energy	NW
-60	Wo Hai: Troubles/Setbacks	SE
-70	Wu Gwei: Lawsuits/Affairs	E
-80	Liu Sha: Bad Health & Betrayals	N
-90	Chueh Ming: Divorce/Failures	S

Dragon Gate Feng Shui • www.dragongatefengshui.com © 2006

Eight Mansions: 6 Gua is WEST LIFE GROUP

SE -60	S -90	SW +70
E -70	6	W +90
NE +80	N -80	NW +60

+90	Sheng Chi: Money Luck	W
+80	Tien Yi: Health	NE
+70	Yen Nien: Relationships	SW
+60	Fu Wie: Stable Energy	NW
-60	Wo Hai: Troubles/Setbacks	SE
-70	Wu Gwei: Lawsuits/Affairs	E
-80	Liu Sha: Bad Health & Betrayals	N
-90	Chueh Ming: Divorce/Failures	S

Dragon Gate Feng Shui • www.dragongatefengshui.com © 2006

Eight Mansions: 6 Gua is WEST LIFE GROUP

SE -60	S -90	SW +70
E -70	6	W +90
NE +80	N -80	NW +60

+90	Sheng Chi: Money Luck	W
+80	Tien Yi: Health	NE
+70	Yen Nien: Relationships	SW
+60	Fu Wie: Stable Energy	NW
-60	Wo Hai: Troubles/Setbacks	SE
-70	Wu Gwei: Lawsuits/Affairs	E
-80	Liu Sha: Bad Health & Betrayals	N
-90	Chueh Ming: Divorce/Failures	S

Dragon Gate Feng Shui • www.dragongatefengshui.com © 2006

Appendix IV *continued*

Magic Life-Gua Cards (7 Gua)

Eight Mansions: 7 Gua is WEST LIFE GROUP

SE -80	S -70	SW +80
E -90	7	W +60
NE +70	N -60	NW +90

+90	Sheng Chi: Money Luck	NW
+80	Tien Yi: Health	SW
+70	Yen Nien: Relationships	NE
+60	Fu Wie: Stable Energy	W
-60	Wo Hai: Troubles/Setbacks	N
-70	Wu Gwei: Lawsuits/Affairs	S
-80	Liu Sha: Bad Health & Betrayals	SE
-90	Chueh Ming: Divorce/Failures	E

Dragon Gate Feng Shui • www.dragongatefengshui.com © 2006

Eight Mansions: 7 Gua is WEST LIFE GROUP

SE -80	S -70	SW +80
E -90	7	W +60
NE +70	N -60	NW +90

+90	Sheng Chi: Money Luck	NW
+80	Tien Yi: Health	SW
+70	Yen Nien: Relationships	NE
+60	Fu Wie: Stable Energy	W
-60	Wo Hai: Troubles/Setbacks	N
-70	Wu Gwei: Lawsuits/Affairs	S
-80	Liu Sha: Bad Health & Betrayals	SE
-90	Chueh Ming: Divorce/Failures	E

Dragon Gate Feng Shui • www.dragongatefengshui.com © 2006

Eight Mansions: 7 Gua is WEST LIFE GROUP

SE -80	S -70	SW +80
E -90	7	W +60
NE +70	N -60	NW +90

+90	Sheng Chi: Money Luck	NW
+80	Tien Yi: Health	SW
+70	Yen Nien: Relationships	NE
+60	Fu Wie: Stable Energy	W
-60	Wo Hai: Troubles/Setbacks	N
-70	Wu Gwei: Lawsuits/Affairs	S
-80	Liu Sha: Bad Health & Betrayals	SE
-90	Chueh Ming: Divorce/Failures	E

Dragon Gate Feng Shui • www.dragongatefengshui.com © 2006

Eight Mansions: 7 Gua is WEST LIFE GROUP

SE -80	S -70	SW +80
E -90	7	W +60
NE +70	N -60	NW +90

+90	Sheng Chi: Money Luck	NW
+80	Tien Yi: Health	SW
+70	Yen Nien: Relationships	NE
+60	Fu Wie: Stable Energy	W
-60	Wo Hai: Troubles/Setbacks	N
-70	Wu Gwei: Lawsuits/Affairs	S
-80	Liu Sha: Bad Health & Betrayals	SE
-90	Chueh Ming: Divorce/Failures	E

Dragon Gate Feng Shui • www.dragongatefengshui.com © 2006

Eight Mansions: 7 Gua is WEST LIFE GROUP

SE -80	S -70	SW +80
E -90	7	W +60
NE +70	N -60	NW +90

+90	Sheng Chi: Money Luck	NW
+80	Tien Yi: Health	SW
+70	Yen Nien: Relationships	NE
+60	Fu Wie: Stable Energy	W
-60	Wo Hai: Troubles/Setbacks	N
-70	Wu Gwei: Lawsuits/Affairs	S
-80	Liu Sha: Bad Health & Betrayals	SE
-90	Chueh Ming: Divorce/Failures	E

Dragon Gate Feng Shui • www.dragongatefengshui.com © 2006

Eight Mansions: 7 Gua is WEST LIFE GROUP

SE -80	S -70	SW +80
E -90	7	W +60
NE +70	N -60	NW +90

+90	Sheng Chi: Money Luck	NW
+80	Tien Yi: Health	SW
+70	Yen Nien: Relationships	NE
+60	Fu Wie: Stable Energy	W
-60	Wo Hai: Troubles/Setbacks	N
-70	Wu Gwei: Lawsuits/Affairs	S
-80	Liu Sha: Bad Health & Betrayals	SE
-90	Chueh Ming: Divorce/Failures	E

Dragon Gate Feng Shui • www.dragongatefengshui.com © 2006

Eight Mansions: 7 Gua is WEST LIFE GROUP

SE -80	S -70	SW +80
E -90	7	W +60
NE +70	N -60	NW +90

+90	Sheng Chi: Money Luck	NW
+80	Tien Yi: Health	SW
+70	Yen Nien: Relationships	NE
+60	Fu Wie: Stable Energy	W
-60	Wo Hai: Troubles/Setbacks	N
-70	Wu Gwei: Lawsuits/Affairs	S
-80	Liu Sha: Bad Health & Betrayals	SE
-90	Chueh Ming: Divorce/Failures	E

Dragon Gate Feng Shui • www.dragongatefengshui.com © 2006

Eight Mansions: 7 Gua is WEST LIFE GROUP

SE -80	S -70	SW +80
E -90	7	W +60
NE +70	N -60	NW +90

+90	Sheng Chi: Money Luck	NW
+80	Tien Yi: Health	SW
+70	Yen Nien: Relationships	NE
+60	Fu Wie: Stable Energy	W
-60	Wo Hai: Troubles/Setbacks	N
-70	Wu Gwei: Lawsuits/Affairs	S
-80	Liu Sha: Bad Health & Betrayals	SE
-90	Chueh Ming: Divorce/Failures	E

Dragon Gate Feng Shui • www.dragongatefengshui.com © 2006

Appendix IV *continued*
Magic Life-Gua Cards (8 Gua)

Eight Mansions: 8 Gua is WEST LIFE GROUP

SE -90	S -60	SW +90
E -80	8	W +70
NE +60	N -70	NW +80

+90	Sheng Chi: Money Luck	SW
+80	Tien Yi: Health	NW
+70	Yen Nien: Relationships	W
+60	Fu Wie: Stable Energy	NE
-60	Wo Hai: Troubles/Setbacks	S
-70	Wu Gwei: Lawsuits/Affairs	SE
-80	Liu Sha: Bad Health & Betrayals	E
-90	Chueh Ming: Divorce/Failures	SE

Dragon Gate Feng Shui • www.dragongatefengshui.com ©2006

Eight Mansions: 8 Gua is WEST LIFE GROUP

SE -90	S -60	SW +90
E -80	8	W +70
NE +60	N -70	NW +80

+90	Sheng Chi: Money Luck	SW
+80	Tien Yi: Health	NW
+70	Yen Nien: Relationships	W
+60	Fu Wie: Stable Energy	NE
-60	Wo Hai: Troubles/Setbacks	S
-70	Wu Gwei: Lawsuits/Affairs	SE
-80	Liu Sha: Bad Health & Betrayals	E
-90	Chueh Ming: Divorce/Failures	SE

Dragon Gate Feng Shui • www.dragongatefengshui.com ©2006

Eight Mansions: 8 Gua is WEST LIFE GROUP

SE -90	S -60	SW +90
E -80	8	W +70
NE +60	N -70	NW +80

+90	Sheng Chi: Money Luck	SW
+80	Tien Yi: Health	NW
+70	Yen Nien: Relationships	W
+60	Fu Wie: Stable Energy	NE
-60	Wo Hai: Troubles/Setbacks	S
-70	Wu Gwei: Lawsuits/Affairs	SE
-80	Liu Sha: Bad Health & Betrayals	E
-90	Chueh Ming: Divorce/Failures	SE

Dragon Gate Feng Shui • www.dragongatefengshui.com ©2006

Eight Mansions: 8 Gua is WEST LIFE GROUP

SE -90	S -60	SW +90
E -80	8	W +70
NE +60	N -70	NW +80

+90	Sheng Chi: Money Luck	SW
+80	Tien Yi: Health	NW
+70	Yen Nien: Relationships	W
+60	Fu Wie: Stable Energy	NE
-60	Wo Hai: Troubles/Setbacks	S
-70	Wu Gwei: Lawsuits/Affairs	SE
-80	Liu Sha: Bad Health & Betrayals	E
-90	Chueh Ming: Divorce/Failures	SE

Dragon Gate Feng Shui • www.dragongatefengshui.com ©2006

Eight Mansions: 8 Gua is WEST LIFE GROUP

SE -90	S -60	SW +90
E -80	8	W +70
NE +60	N -70	NW +80

+90	Sheng Chi: Money Luck	SW
+80	Tien Yi: Health	NW
+70	Yen Nien: Relationships	W
+60	Fu Wie: Stable Energy	NE
-60	Wo Hai: Troubles/Setbacks	S
-70	Wu Gwei: Lawsuits/Affairs	SE
-80	Liu Sha: Bad Health & Betrayals	E
-90	Chueh Ming: Divorce/Failures	SE

Dragon Gate Feng Shui • www.dragongatefengshui.com ©2006

Eight Mansions: 8 Gua is WEST LIFE GROUP

SE -90	S -60	SW +90
E -80	8	W +70
NE +60	N -70	NW +80

+90	Sheng Chi: Money Luck	SW
+80	Tien Yi: Health	NW
+70	Yen Nien: Relationships	W
+60	Fu Wie: Stable Energy	NE
-60	Wo Hai: Troubles/Setbacks	S
-70	Wu Gwei: Lawsuits/Affairs	SE
-80	Liu Sha: Bad Health & Betrayals	E
-90	Chueh Ming: Divorce/Failures	SE

Dragon Gate Feng Shui • www.dragongatefengshui.com ©2006

Eight Mansions: 8 Gua is WEST LIFE GROUP

SE -90	S -60	SW +90
E -80	8	W +70
NE +60	N -70	NW +80

+90	Sheng Chi: Money Luck	SW
+80	Tien Yi: Health	NW
+70	Yen Nien: Relationships	W
+60	Fu Wie: Stable Energy	NE
-60	Wo Hai: Troubles/Setbacks	S
-70	Wu Gwei: Lawsuits/Affairs	SE
-80	Liu Sha: Bad Health & Betrayals	E
-90	Chueh Ming: Divorce/Failures	SE

Dragon Gate Feng Shui • www.dragongatefengshui.com ©2006

Eight Mansions: 8 Gua is WEST LIFE GROUP

SE -90	S -60	SW +90
E -80	8	W +70
NE +60	N -70	NW +80

+90	Sheng Chi: Money Luck	SW
+80	Tien Yi: Health	NW
+70	Yen Nien: Relationships	W
+60	Fu Wie: Stable Energy	NE
-60	Wo Hai: Troubles/Setbacks	S
-70	Wu Gwei: Lawsuits/Affairs	SE
-80	Liu Sha: Bad Health & Betrayals	E
-90	Chueh Ming: Divorce/Failures	SE

Dragon Gate Feng Shui • www.dragongatefengshui.com ©2006

Appendix IV *continued*

Magic Life-Gua Cards to Take to Meetings (9 Gua)

Eight Mansions: 9 Gua is EAST LIFE GROUP

SE +80	S +60	SW -80
E +90	9	W -60
NE -60	N +70	NW -90

+90	Sheng Chi: Money Luck	E
+80	Tien Yi: Health	SE
+70	Yen Nien: Relationships	N
+60	Fu Wie: Stable Energy	S
-60	Wo Hai: Troubles/Setbacks	NE
-70	Wu Gwei: Lawsuits/Affairs	W
-80	Liu Sha: Bad Health & Betrayals	SW
-90	Chueh Ming: Divorce/Failures	NW

Dragon Gate Feng Shui • www.dragongatefengshui.com © 2006

Eight Mansions: 9 Gua is EAST LIFE GROUP

SE +80	S +60	SW -80
E +90	9	W -60
NE -60	N +70	NW -90

+90	Sheng Chi: Money Luck	E
+80	Tien Yi: Health	SE
+70	Yen Nien: Relationships	N
+60	Fu Wie: Stable Energy	S
-60	Wo Hai: Troubles/Setbacks	NE
-70	Wu Gwei: Lawsuits/Affairs	W
-80	Liu Sha: Bad Health & Betrayals	SW
-90	Chueh Ming: Divorce/Failures	NW

Dragon Gate Feng Shui • www.dragongatefengshui.com © 2006

Eight Mansions: 9 Gua is EAST LIFE GROUP

SE +80	S +60	SW -80
E +90	9	W -60
NE -60	N +70	NW -90

+90	Sheng Chi: Money Luck	E
+80	Tien Yi: Health	SE
+70	Yen Nien: Relationships	N
+60	Fu Wie: Stable Energy	S
-60	Wo Hai: Troubles/Setbacks	NE
-70	Wu Gwei: Lawsuits/Affairs	W
-80	Liu Sha: Bad Health & Betrayals	SW
-90	Chueh Ming: Divorce/Failures	NW

Dragon Gate Feng Shui • www.dragongatefengshui.com © 2006

Eight Mansions: 9 Gua is EAST LIFE GROUP

SE +80	S +60	SW -80
E +90	9	W -60
NE -60	N +70	NW -90

+90	Sheng Chi: Money Luck	E
+80	Tien Yi: Health	SE
+70	Yen Nien: Relationships	N
+60	Fu Wie: Stable Energy	S
-60	Wo Hai: Troubles/Setbacks	NE
-70	Wu Gwei: Lawsuits/Affairs	W
-80	Liu Sha: Bad Health & Betrayals	SW
-90	Chueh Ming: Divorce/Failures	NW

Dragon Gate Feng Shui • www.dragongatefengshui.com © 2006

Eight Mansions: 9 Gua is EAST LIFE GROUP

SE +80	S +60	SW -80
E +90	9	W -60
NE -60	N +70	NW -90

+90	Sheng Chi: Money Luck	E
+80	Tien Yi: Health	SE
+70	Yen Nien: Relationships	N
+60	Fu Wie: Stable Energy	S
-60	Wo Hai: Troubles/Setbacks	NE
-70	Wu Gwei: Lawsuits/Affairs	W
-80	Liu Sha: Bad Health & Betrayals	SW
-90	Chueh Ming: Divorce/Failures	NW

Dragon Gate Feng Shui • www.dragongatefengshui.com © 2006

Eight Mansions: 9 Gua is EAST LIFE GROUP

SE +80	S +60	SW -80
E +90	9	W -60
NE -60	N +70	NW -90

+90	Sheng Chi: Money Luck	E
+80	Tien Yi: Health	SE
+70	Yen Nien: Relationships	N
+60	Fu Wie: Stable Energy	S
-60	Wo Hai: Troubles/Setbacks	NE
-70	Wu Gwei: Lawsuits/Affairs	W
-80	Liu Sha: Bad Health & Betrayals	SW
-90	Chueh Ming: Divorce/Failures	NW

Dragon Gate Feng Shui • www.dragongatefengshui.com © 2006

Eight Mansions: 9 Gua is EAST LIFE GROUP

SE +80	S +60	SW -80
E +90	9	W -60
NE -60	N +70	NW -90

+90	Sheng Chi: Money Luck	E
+80	Tien Yi: Health	SE
+70	Yen Nien: Relationships	N
+60	Fu Wie: Stable Energy	S
-60	Wo Hai: Troubles/Setbacks	NE
-70	Wu Gwei: Lawsuits/Affairs	W
-80	Liu Sha: Bad Health & Betrayals	SW
-90	Chueh Ming: Divorce/Failures	NW

Dragon Gate Feng Shui • www.dragongatefengshui.com © 2006

Eight Mansions: 9 Gua is EAST LIFE GROUP

SE +80	S +60	SW -80
E +90	9	W -60
NE -60	N +70	NW -90

+90	Sheng Chi: Money Luck	E
+80	Tien Yi: Health	SE
+70	Yen Nien: Relationships	N
+60	Fu Wie: Stable Energy	S
-60	Wo Hai: Troubles/Setbacks	NE
-70	Wu Gwei: Lawsuits/Affairs	W
-80	Liu Sha: Bad Health & Betrayals	SW
-90	Chueh Ming: Divorce/Failures	NW

Dragon Gate Feng Shui • www.dragongatefengshui.com © 2006

Appendix IV *continued*
Magic Life-Gua Cards (Back)

+90	SHENG CHI: Life giving chi. Generating breath. Great WEALTH. Great Success. Millionaire chi. Best direction for money luck. Good for politics or setting up a high position of power.
+80	TIEN YI: Good for HEALTH. Heavenly doctor protects you. Long life. Brings good friends and social standing out in the world. Unexpected wealth from heaven.
+70	YEN NIEN: RELATIONSHIPS. Family, Love & Networking. Good for longevity and health. Good direction to create harmony in the family.
+60	FU WIE: STABLE in your own energy. Can have the mirror of your own energy in this arrangement. Using this direction can mitigate bad luck.
-60	WO HAI: SET-BACKS, nothing goes smoothly—everything goes wrong. Irritating events that continually bring set backs. Disaster but not the type of disaster that ends everything.
-70	WU GWEI: LAWSUITS, AFFAIRS, bad romance, trouble, hard to have children. Children disobedient and rebellious. Gambling and drug use. Betrayal, bad temper, & gossips.
-80	LIU SHA: BACK-STABBING, thievery, injury, loss of wealth, ill health, bad money luck, bad romance & accidents. Lots of illness, LAWSUITS by the government.
-90	CHUEH MING: Attracts the very worst things to you. BANKRUPTCY. Very bad health. Fatality. DIVORCE. Business failure, loss of wealth, disharmony, & family breakups.

+90	SHENG CHI: Life giving chi. Generating breath. Great WEALTH. Great Success. Millionaire chi. Best direction for money luck. Good for politics or setting up a high position of power.
+80	TIEN YI: Good for HEALTH. Heavenly doctor protects you. Long life. Brings good friends and social standing out in the world. Unexpected wealth from heaven.
+70	YEN NIEN: RELATIONSHIPS. Family, Love & Networking. Good for longevity and health. Good direction to create harmony in the family.
+60	FU WIE: STABLE in your own energy. Can have the mirror of your own energy in this arrangement. Using this direction can mitigate bad luck.
-60	WO HAI: SET-BACKS, nothing goes smoothly—everything goes wrong. Irritating events that continually bring set backs. Disaster but not the type of disaster that ends everything.
-70	WU GWEI: LAWSUITS, AFFAIRS, bad romance, trouble, hard to have children. Children disobedient and rebellious. Gambling and drug use. Betrayal, bad temper, & gossips.
-80	LIU SHA: BACK-STABBING, thievery, injury, loss of wealth, ill health, bad money luck, bad romance & accidents. Lots of illness, LAWSUITS by the government.
-90	CHUEH MING: Attracts the very worst things to you. BANKRUPTCY. Very bad health. Fatality. DIVORCE. Business failure, loss of wealth, disharmony, & family breakups.

+90	SHENG CHI: Life giving chi. Generating breath. Great WEALTH. Great Success. Millionaire chi. Best direction for money luck. Good for politics or setting up a high position of power.
+80	TIEN YI: Good for HEALTH. Heavenly doctor protects you. Long life. Brings good friends and social standing out in the world. Unexpected wealth from heaven.
+70	YEN NIEN: RELATIONSHIPS. Family, Love & Networking. Good for longevity and health. Good direction to create harmony in the family.
+60	FU WIE: STABLE in your own energy. Can have the mirror of your own energy in this arrangement. Using this direction can mitigate bad luck.
-60	WO HAI: SET-BACKS, nothing goes smoothly—everything goes wrong. Irritating events that continually bring set backs. Disaster but not the type of disaster that ends everything.
-70	WU GWEI: LAWSUITS, AFFAIRS, bad romance, trouble, hard to have children. Children disobedient and rebellious. Gambling and drug use. Betrayal, bad temper, & gossips.
-80	LIU SHA: BACK-STABBING, thievery, injury, loss of wealth, ill health, bad money luck, bad romance & accidents. Lots of illness, LAWSUITS by the government.
-90	CHUEH MING: Attracts the very worst things to you. BANKRUPTCY. Very bad health. Fatality. DIVORCE. Business failure, loss of wealth, disharmony, & family breakups.

+90	SHENG CHI: Life giving chi. Generating breath. Great WEALTH. Great Success. Millionaire chi. Best direction for money luck. Good for politics or setting up a high position of power.
+80	TIEN YI: Good for HEALTH. Heavenly doctor protects you. Long life. Brings good friends and social standing out in the world. Unexpected wealth from heaven.
+70	YEN NIEN: RELATIONSHIPS. Family, Love & Networking. Good for longevity and health. Good direction to create harmony in the family.
+60	FU WIE: STABLE in your own energy. Can have the mirror of your own energy in this arrangement. Using this direction can mitigate bad luck.
-60	WO HAI: SET-BACKS, nothing goes smoothly—everything goes wrong. Irritating events that continually bring set backs. Disaster but not the type of disaster that ends everything.
-70	WU GWEI: LAWSUITS, AFFAIRS, bad romance, trouble, hard to have children. Children disobedient and rebellious. Gambling and drug use. Betrayal, bad temper, & gossips.
-80	LIU SHA: BACK-STABBING, thievery, injury, loss of wealth, ill health, bad money luck, bad romance & accidents. Lots of illness, LAWSUITS by the government.
-90	CHUEH MING: Attracts the very worst things to you. BANKRUPTCY. Very bad health. Fatality. DIVORCE. Business failure, loss of wealth, disharmony, & family breakups.

+90	SHENG CHI: Life giving chi. Generating breath. Great WEALTH. Great Success. Millionaire chi. Best direction for money luck. Good for politics or setting up a high position of power.
+80	TIEN YI: Good for HEALTH. Heavenly doctor protects you. Long life. Brings good friends and social standing out in the world. Unexpected wealth from heaven.
+70	YEN NIEN: RELATIONSHIPS. Family, Love & Networking. Good for longevity and health. Good direction to create harmony in the family.
+60	FU WIE: STABLE in your own energy. Can have the mirror of your own energy in this arrangement. Using this direction can mitigate bad luck.
-60	WO HAI: SET-BACKS, nothing goes smoothly—everything goes wrong. Irritating events that continually bring set backs. Disaster but not the type of disaster that ends everything.
-70	WU GWEI: LAWSUITS, AFFAIRS, bad romance, trouble, hard to have children. Children disobedient and rebellious. Gambling and drug use. Betrayal, bad temper, & gossips.
-80	LIU SHA: BACK-STABBING, thievery, injury, loss of wealth, ill health, bad money luck, bad romance & accidents. Lots of illness, LAWSUITS by the government.
-90	CHUEH MING: Attracts the very worst things to you. BANKRUPTCY. Very bad health. Fatality. DIVORCE. Business failure, loss of wealth, disharmony, & family breakups.

+90	SHENG CHI: Life giving chi. Generating breath. Great WEALTH. Great Success. Millionaire chi. Best direction for money luck. Good for politics or setting up a high position of power.
+80	TIEN YI: Good for HEALTH. Heavenly doctor protects you. Long life. Brings good friends and social standing out in the world. Unexpected wealth from heaven.
+70	YEN NIEN: RELATIONSHIPS. Family, Love & Networking. Good for longevity and health. Good direction to create harmony in the family.
+60	FU WIE: STABLE in your own energy. Can have the mirror of your own energy in this arrangement. Using this direction can mitigate bad luck.
-60	WO HAI: SET-BACKS, nothing goes smoothly—everything goes wrong. Irritating events that continually bring set backs. Disaster but not the type of disaster that ends everything.
-70	WU GWEI: LAWSUITS, AFFAIRS, bad romance, trouble, hard to have children. Children disobedient and rebellious. Gambling and drug use. Betrayal, bad temper, & gossips.
-80	LIU SHA: BACK-STABBING, thievery, injury, loss of wealth, ill health, bad money luck, bad romance & accidents. Lots of illness, LAWSUITS by the government.
-90	CHUEH MING: Attracts the very worst things to you. BANKRUPTCY. Very bad health. Fatality. DIVORCE. Business failure, loss of wealth, disharmony, & family breakups.

+90	SHENG CHI: Life giving chi. Generating breath. Great WEALTH. Great Success. Millionaire chi. Best direction for money luck. Good for politics or setting up a high position of power.
+80	TIEN YI: Good for HEALTH. Heavenly doctor protects you. Long life. Brings good friends and social standing out in the world. Unexpected wealth from heaven.
+70	YEN NIEN: RELATIONSHIPS. Family, Love & Networking. Good for longevity and health. Good direction to create harmony in the family.
+60	FU WIE: STABLE in your own energy. Can have the mirror of your own energy in this arrangement. Using this direction can mitigate bad luck.
-60	WO HAI: SET-BACKS, nothing goes smoothly—everything goes wrong. Irritating events that continually bring set backs. Disaster but not the type of disaster that ends everything.
-70	WU GWEI: LAWSUITS, AFFAIRS, bad romance, trouble, hard to have children. Children disobedient and rebellious. Gambling and drug use. Betrayal, bad temper, & gossips.
-80	LIU SHA: BACK-STABBING, thievery, injury, loss of wealth, ill health, bad money luck, bad romance & accidents. Lots of illness, LAWSUITS by the government.
-90	CHUEH MING: Attracts the very worst things to you. BANKRUPTCY. Very bad health. Fatality. DIVORCE. Business failure, loss of wealth, disharmony, & family breakups.

+90	SHENG CHI: Life giving chi. Generating breath. Great WEALTH. Great Success. Millionaire chi. Best direction for money luck. Good for politics or setting up a high position of power.
+80	TIEN YI: Good for HEALTH. Heavenly doctor protects you. Long life. Brings good friends and social standing out in the world. Unexpected wealth from heaven.
+70	YEN NIEN: RELATIONSHIPS. Family, Love & Networking. Good for longevity and health. Good direction to create harmony in the family.
+60	FU WIE: STABLE in your own energy. Can have the mirror of your own energy in this arrangement. Using this direction can mitigate bad luck.
-60	WO HAI: SET-BACKS, nothing goes smoothly—everything goes wrong. Irritating events that continually bring set backs. Disaster but not the type of disaster that ends everything.
-70	WU GWEI: LAWSUITS, AFFAIRS, bad romance, trouble, hard to have children. Children disobedient and rebellious. Gambling and drug use. Betrayal, bad temper, & gossips.
-80	LIU SHA: BACK-STABBING, thievery, injury, loss of wealth, ill health, bad money luck, bad romance & accidents. Lots of illness, LAWSUITS by the government.
-90	CHUEH MING: Attracts the very worst things to you. BANKRUPTCY. Very bad health. Fatality. DIVORCE. Business failure, loss of wealth, disharmony, & family breakups.

Appendix V
Lessons on Location and Direction

Doors: This home faces South and the road. The 'front door' is *located* in the West but faces Southwest which is angled. The interior South-facing garage door is best for those part of the East Life group (1, 3, 4 or 9). The Southwest door is better for the West Life group (2, 6, 7 or 8). However, if the home faces 157° to 172° (South 1) OR 187° to 202° (South 3) either door works well for both groups. This is using Advanced Eight Mansion found on page 25.

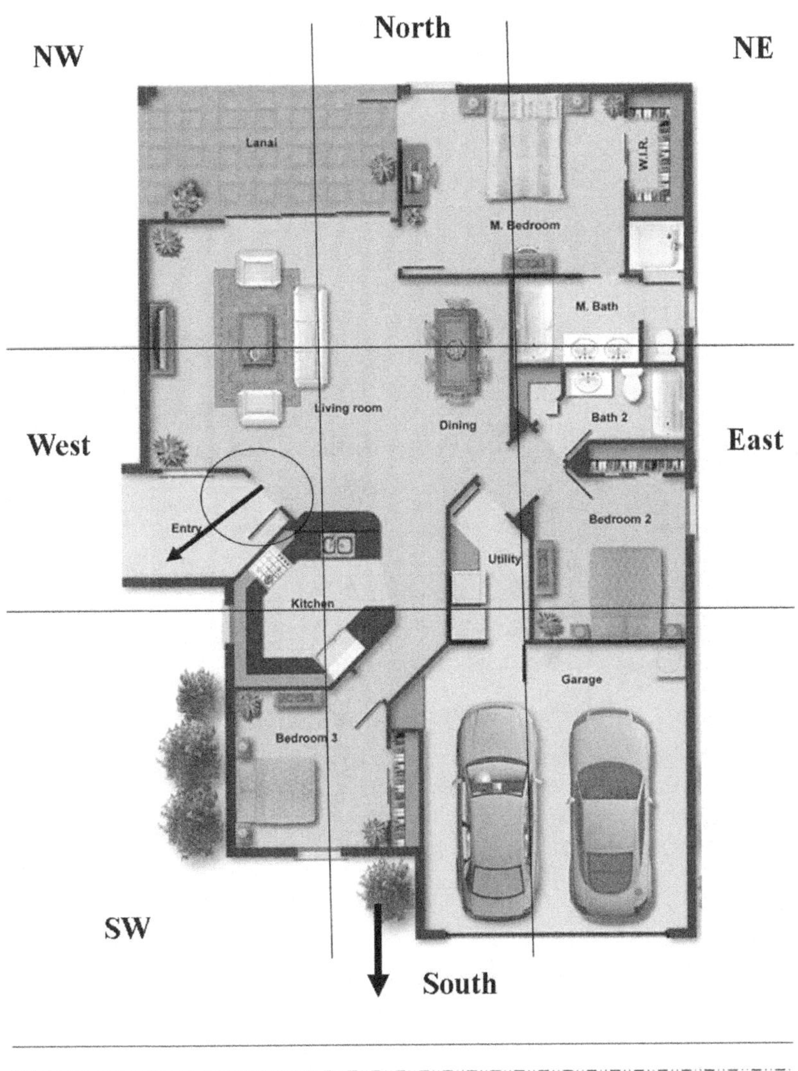

Appendix V

Lessons on Location and Direction *continued*

Doors: This home and the front door, face the Southeast *direction.* It is best used by those part of the East Life group (1, 3, 4 or 9). The interior Northeast-facing garage door is best used by those part of the West Life group (2, 6, 7 or 8). However, if the home faces 142° to 157° (Southeast 3), either door would support both groups. This is using Advanced Eight Mansion found on page 25. Remember using a different door, is a simple yet powerful way to change your luck!

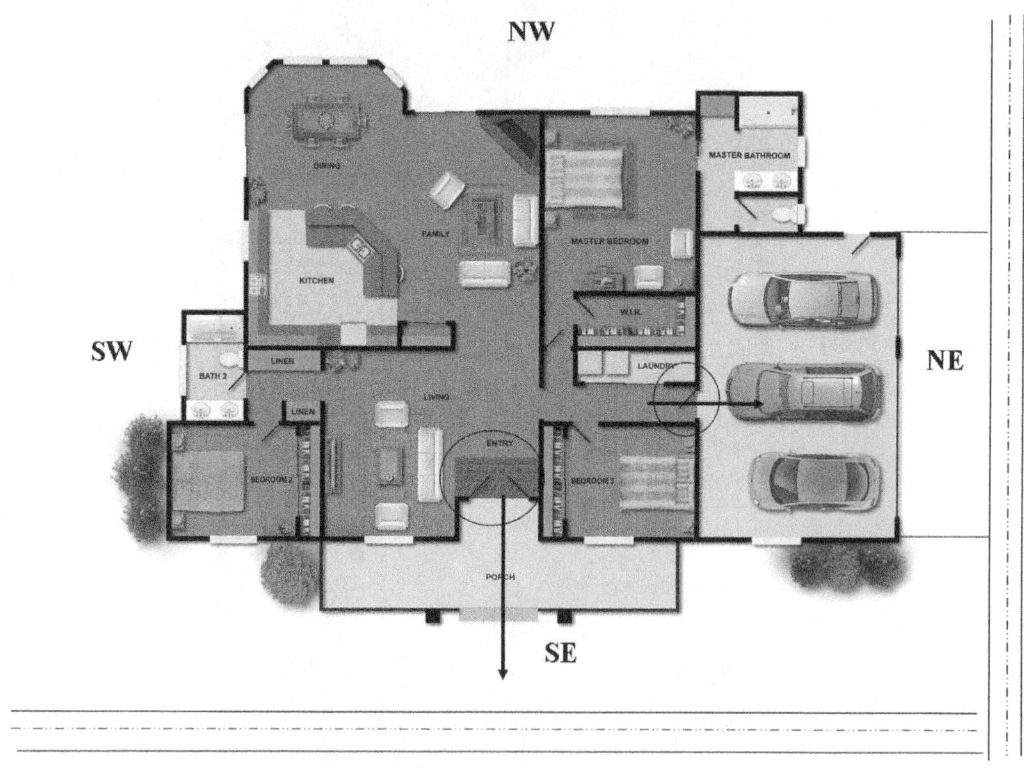

Appendix V

Lessons on Location and Direction *continued*

Beds: In this East-facing home, the master bedroom is *located* in the Northwest area of the house. In the example in the upper left, the bed is placed on the South wall. In upper right, the bed placed on the West-wall activates that *direction*. The lower left, the bed position activates the Southwest direction. In the lower right, the bed placement activates the Northeast direction. If the home faces 67° to 82° (East 1) OR 97° to 112° (East 3), then all the bed placements would work for both Life Groups and all eight Life-Gua numbers.

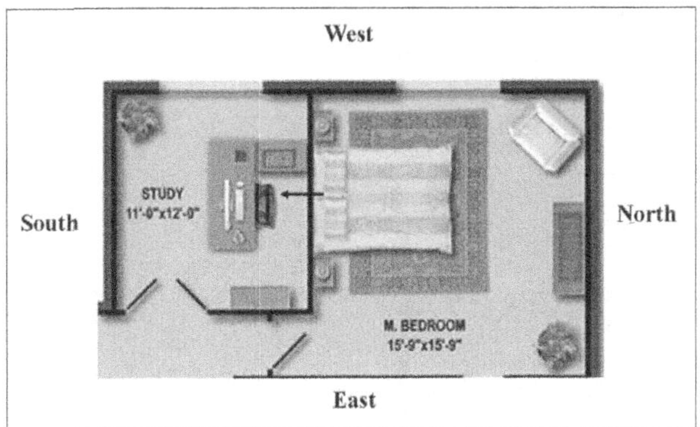

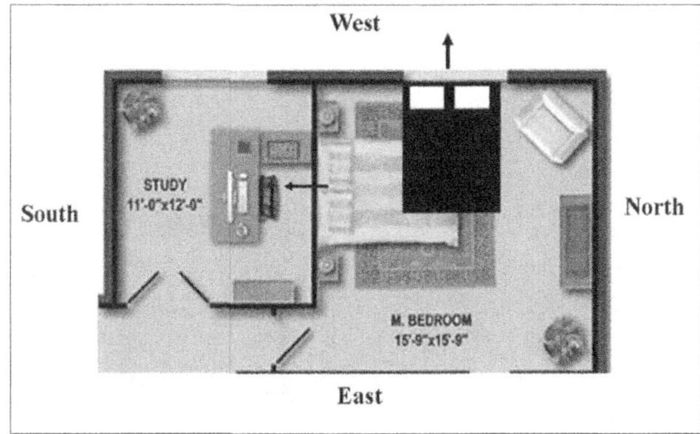

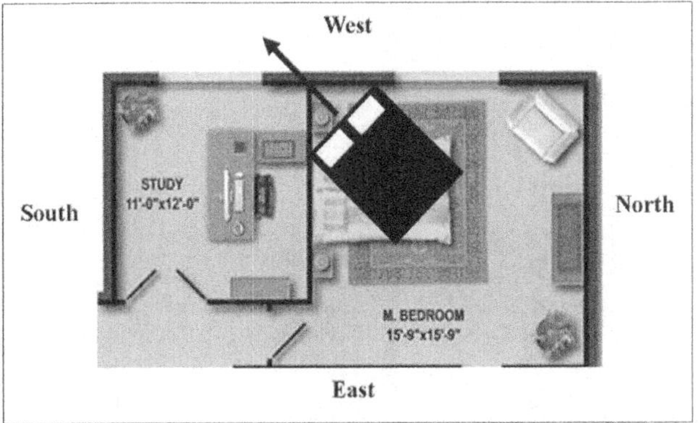

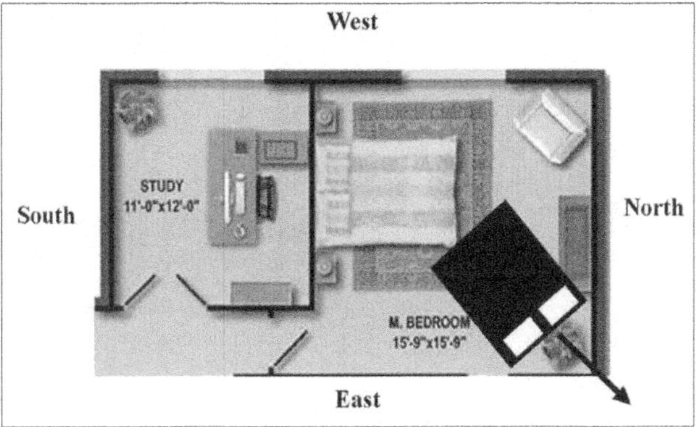

Appendix V

Lessons on Location and Direction *continued*

Stoves and Kitchens: In this East-facing home, the kitchen is *located* in the North. The stove is *located* on the West-wall within the kitchen. The knobs/controls face and activate the North *direction*. If the couple is a mixed Life Group, the stove is set up for the main breadwinner (male or female).

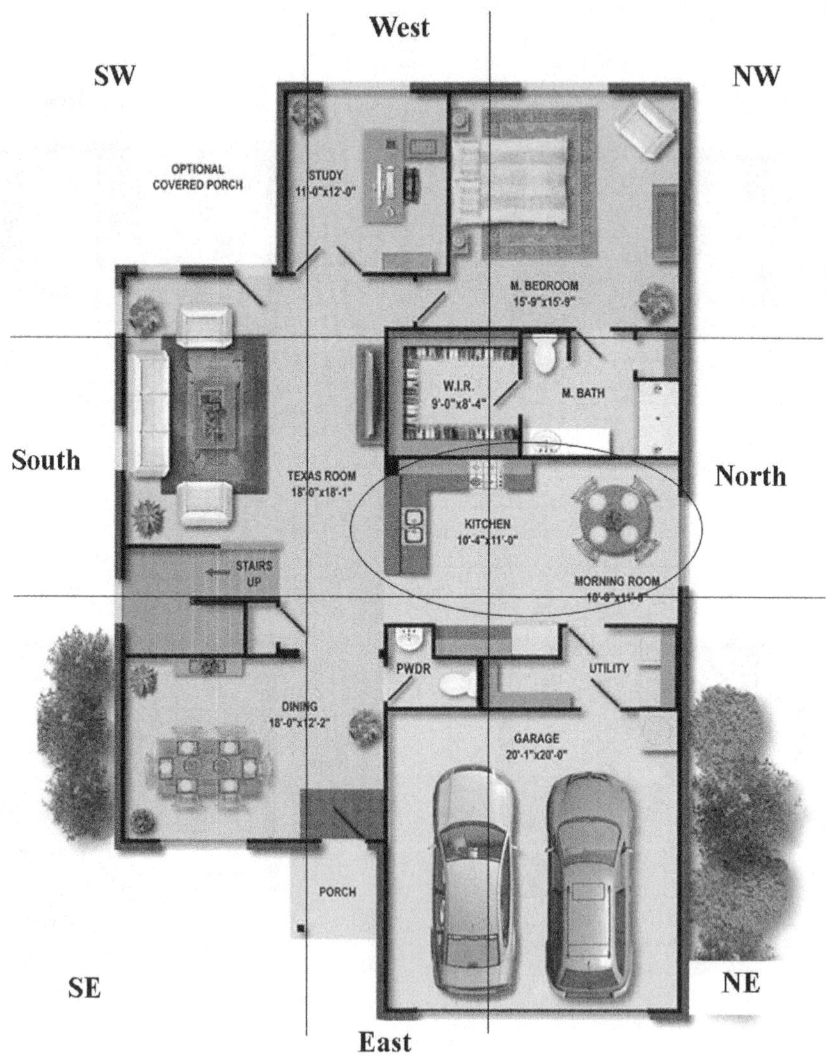

Appendix V

Lessons on Location and Direction *continued*

Stoves and Kitchens: Using the same East-facing home; if this home were occupied by those in the East Life group (1, 3, 4 or 9), the stove placement and knobs are excellent. However, if West Life group people lived here, the stove would burn up their good luck. The solution is to create a new cooking area if you cannot either remodel the kitchen or switch stove and refrigerator. The 'stove' should be placed on the East-wall/countertop and the knobs facing West. See page 42 for ideas on new cooking areas.

West

South

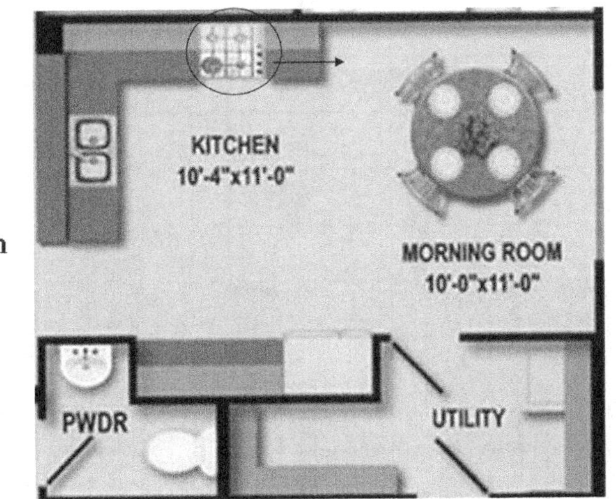

North

East

West

South

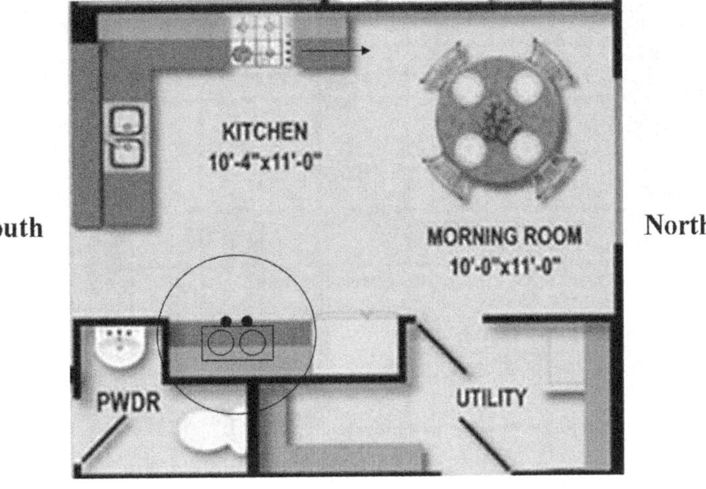

North

East

Appendix V

Lessons on Location and Direction *continued*

The Toilets: In this East-facing home, there are two toilets downstairs. One is located in the North and the other in the East. For those in the East Life group (1, 3, 4 or 9), it is best to frequent another toilet in one of their negative sectors. The toilet placements are excellent for those part of the West Life group (2, 6, 7, or 8). Toilets located too near a front door are considered very bad Feng Shui, no matter your Life-Gua number.

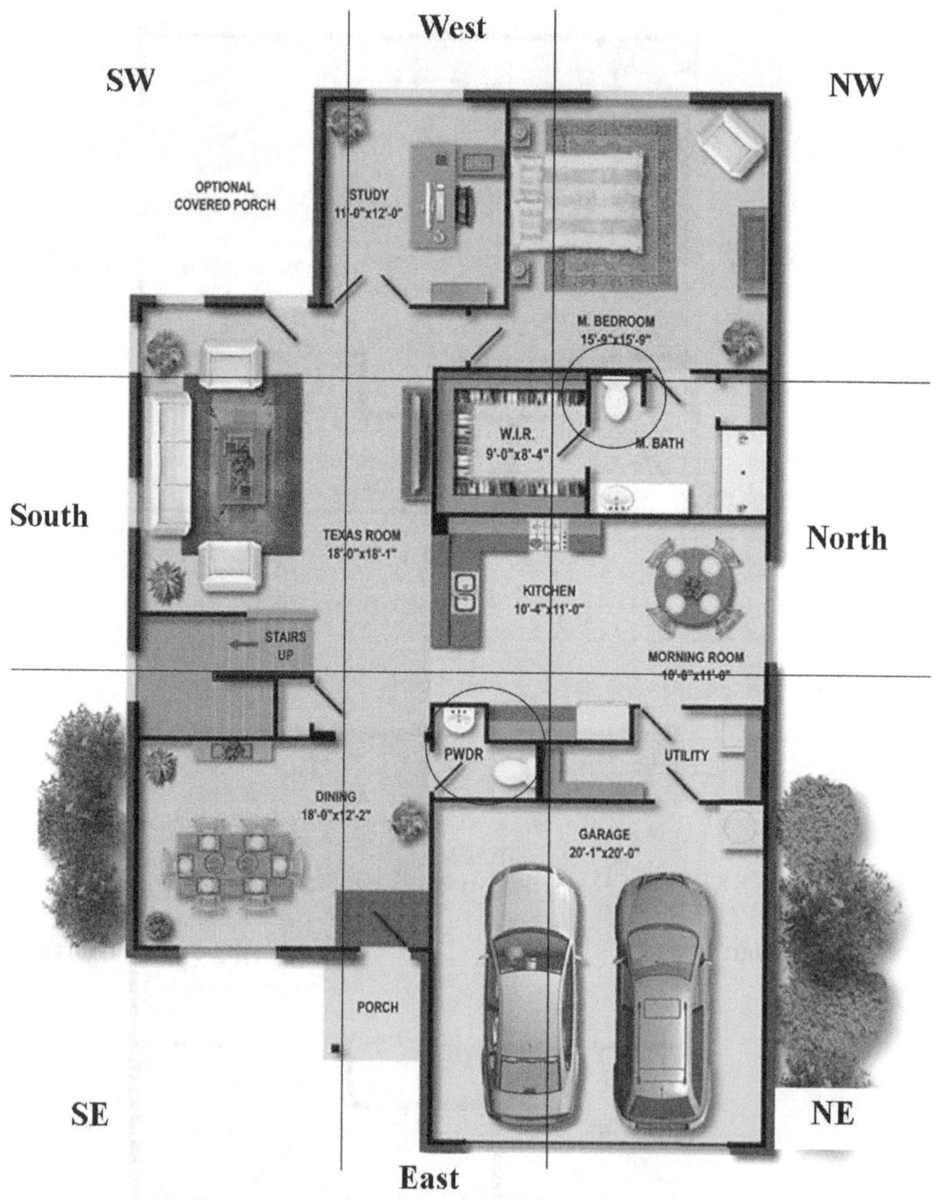

Glossary of Terms

This book includes Feng Shui terms using both Wade-Giles and Pinyin; in several instances the glossary gives both spellings. The Chinese-to-English translations also include some in Mandarin and others in Cantonese; I've chosen the ones most used by my teacher, Grandmaster Yap Cheng Hai and their spellings.

auspicious: The Chinese favor the term *auspicious*, meaning something is lucky, and good events will ensue.

Ba Gua: Also spelled as Pa Kua; an octagonal arrangement of the eight trigrams or Guas.

BaZhai: the Eight Mansion system, also spelled PaChai. This system is also known as the East-West System and Eight House Feng Shui.

Big Dipper Casting Golden Light: Known as *Jin Guang Dou Lin Jing* in Chinese and also spelled as *Kam Kwong Dou Lam King*. This style of Eight Mansions is used in this book; it is also called *Golden Star Classic.*

Black Hat Sect: A new school of Feng Shui invented in the 1980s. It was brought to the Western world by Professor Thomas Lin Yun, a Buddhist monk of the Black Hat Order of Tibetan Buddhism. Although not considered an authentic system of Feng Shui, Black Hat is the most recognized style in the world except in Asian countries, which are most familiar with traditional schools of Feng Shui.

Book of Changes: Also known as the *I Ching*.

Buddhism: is a nontheistic *(not having a belief in a god)* religion that encompasses a variety of traditions, beliefs and practices largely based on teachings attributed to Siddhartha Gautama, who is commonly known as the Buddha, meaning "the awakened one". According to Buddhist tradition, the Buddha lived and taught in the eastern part of the Indian subcontinent sometime between the 6th and 4th centuries BCE.

cardinal directions: Points of geographic orientation—North, South, East and West. The specific and exact points of these directions are 0/360, North; 90 degrees, East; 180 degrees, South; and 270 degrees, West.

Chai: House, also spelled Zhai.

Chen: One of the eight trigrams of the Ba Gua. It represents the eldest son, thunder and spring. In the Later Heaven arrangement of the Ba Gua, the Chen trigram is located in the East.

Chueh Ming: In the Eight Mansions system, this represents total loss, divorce and bankruptcy. According to Master Yap's numeric representation, it is the -90.

Chi: The vital life-force energy of the universe and everything in it; sometimes chi is referred to as *cosmic breath*. It is also spelled *ch'i* or *qi* and is pronounced *chee*.

Chien: One of the eight trigrams of the Ba Gua also spelled as *Qian*. It represents the father, the heavens, and late autumn. In the Later Heaven arrangement of the Ba Gua, the Chien trigram is located in the Northwest.

Chinese Lunar and Solar Calendars: All Feng Shui experts worth their salt use the Chinese Solar Calendar as the basis of their practice as its formulas are very time sensitive and this calendar is very accurate. This is not to say they don't celebrate the Lunar New Year, in fact, they do; the *Chinese New Year*, as well as other holidays, is extremely important. The ancient Chinese used the Solstices and Equinoxes to fix their calendar. 15º Aquarius is exactly half way between the Winter Solstice and the Spring Equinox (on the Northern Hemisphere). In the past, Chinese Lunar New Year started around the Winter Solstice.

In 104 BC Emperor Han Wu Di moved the beginning of the year so that the Winter Solstice occurs in the eleventh month. Winter Solstice falls on the 15th day of Zi/Rat month, the middle of the winter, 15° Aquarius is the Sun's position. Whenever the sun reaches that position that is the Chinese Solar New Year. This could be February 3, 4, 5. The Chinese chose the 15º Aquarius as the starting point of the Spring season and the New Year. The Spring Equinox falls exactly in the middle of the Spring season; this is always on the 15th day of Mao/Rabbit month. Lunar calendar defines the lunar month on the first day of the appearance of the New Moon. A Lunar New Year begins on the 1st day of this new "moon".

A lunar month is from the new moon to the next new moon. The ecliptic was divided into 12 equal divisions by the ancients. The Chinese Solar year is based on these 24 divisions called 24 solar terms. The year is divided into 24 periods of 15 days. Li Chun is the first of the 24 terms. The names of these divisions date back to the late Chou Dynasty (10450—221BC). The most important of the 24 terms is the New Year.

Chinese Zodiac: is a system that relates each year to an animal and its reputed attributes, according to a 12-year mathematical cycle. It remains popular in several East Asian countries, such as China, Vietnam, Korea and Japan.

Classical Feng Shui: Also known as Traditional Feng Shui. It is the authentic, genuine Feng Shui that has been developed and applied for hundreds, even thousands, of years in Asia. Sophisticated forms are practiced in Hong Kong, Taiwan, Malaysia, and Singapore. Classical Feng Shui is just being introduced and practiced in Western countries, and has not reached main stream status. The traditional systems of Feng Shui are the *San He*, meaning three combinations, and *San Yuan* or three cycles. All techniques, methods, and formulas will be under one or the other. Feng Shui masters and practitioners will use both systems as one comprehensive body of knowledge.

compass, Chinese: See Luo Pan.

Cosmic Trinity: Known in Chinese as *Tien-Di-Ren*. Three categories of luck, specifically heaven-luck, man-luck, and earth-luck. The Chinese believe heaven-luck is fixed, however, humans have control over Feng Shui (earth-luck) and personal effort (man-luck).

Dao: also spelled *Tao*, is a Chinese concept signifying the way, path, route, or sometimes known as the doctrine or principle. Within the context of traditional Chinese philosophy and religion, Tao is a metaphysical concept originating with Lao Tzu that gave rise to a religion and philosophy (Taoism). The concept of Tao was shared with Confucianism and Zen Buddhism. Within these contexts Tao signifies the primordial essence or fundamental nature of the universe. In Taoism, Chinese Buddhism and Confucianism, the object of spiritual practice is to *become one with the Tao* or to harmonize one's will with Nature in order to achieve effortless action; this involves meditative and moral practices.

direction: One of the most important aspects of determining the energy of a site or structure is

dragon: In Feng Shui a dragon is a mountain. Dragon is a term also used for something powerful or curving, as in the mythical body of a dragon. It can apply to land and water. The Chinese so revere the dragon that it is used in multiple applications and meanings.

Early Heaven Ba Gua: This is the first arrangement of the eight trigrams; known as the *Ho Tien* or *Fu Xi* Ba Gua in Chinese. It can be easily recognized as the Chien trigram (three solid lines) and is always placed on the top. This is the arrangement used in Ba Gua mirrors to deter sha Chi.

Earth Luck: One of the three categories of luck that humans can experience; your luck will increase by using Feng Shui, also known as Earth Luck. The Chinese word for earth is *Di.*

East Life Group: In the Eight Mansions system, people are divided into the East or West group. The 1, 3, 4 and 9 Life Guas are part of the East Life Group.

Eight House: This is another name for the Eight Mansions; in Chinese it is *Pa Chai* or *BaZhai.*

Eight House Bright Mirror: In Chinese *Pa Chai Ming Jing*, is one of the eight different styles of the Eight Mansions system. This style uses the sitting direction of the house instead of the facing.

Eight Life Aspirations: Also known as the *Eight Life Stations*, these stations correspond to a point on the Ba Gua and an aspect of life—South, fame; Southwest, marriage; Southeast, wealth; North, career; and so forth. This is the work of Black Hat Sect founder Lin Yun. Eight Life Stations is not found in classic texts or part of the genuine Feng Shui of ancient practice and principles. It is neither an aspect of the Eight Mansions system nor even a derivative of that system. Some popular Feng Shui books that promote Classical Feng Shui also include the Eight Life Aspirations, which only adds to the confusion.

Eight Mansions: also known as *Eight House Feng Shui*, the *East-West System*, *BaZhai* which is also spelled *PaChai;* this system, based on your personal Gua/Kua Number, gives you the four good and four bad directions to use and mitigate in your living space or wherever you happen to be such as at a meeting, your offices, a seminar and so forth to bring good fortune.

Eight Wandering Stars: also known as the *Big Wandering Sky*, these stars are matched with the nine stars of the Big Dipper, they are as follows: Tan Lang (*Greedy Wolf* aka *Ravenous Wolf*) is matched with **Sheng Chi**; Jue Men *(Huge Door* aka *Great Door)* is matched with **Tien Yi**; Wu Chu *(Military Arts)* is matched with **Yen Nien**; Tso Fu & Fu Pi *(Left/Right Assistant* aka the *Big Dipper's Handle*) is matched with **Fu Wei**; Lu Chun *(Rewards/Salary)* is matched with **Wo Hai;** Lien Zheng *(Five Ghosts aka Chastity)* is matched with **Wu Gwei**; Wen Qu *(Literary Arts* aka *The Scholar)* is matched with **Lui Sha**; Tien Kong *(Broken Soldier* aka *Destructive Army)* is matched with **Cheuh Ming**. These nine stars and their unique energy are very important in many Feng Shui systems. More on the nine stars in Chapter Five; the Chinese names above are also the 'secret names' of the nine stars.

energy: The Chinese call energy chi (also spelled ***qi***) and pronounced ***chee***. Our entire universe is energy; there are many types of chi—human, environmental, and heaven (the solar system).

esoteric: Knowledge that is available only to a narrow circle of enlightened or initiated people or a specially educated group. Feng Shui is part of Chinese metaphysics and is considered esoteric.

external environment: This covers the terrain and topography, including mountains, water, and other natural formations. It also encompasses man-made features, such as roads, pools, retaining walls, highways, poles, drains, washes, tall buildings, stop signs, fire hydrants, and other structures.

facing direction: The front side of the home or building, generally where the front or main door is located and faces the street.

Feng: The Chinese word for ***wind;*** pronounced *fung,* although *foong* is a more accurate sound.

Feng Shui: Known as *Kan Yu* (translated as *the way of heaven and earth*) until about a hundred years ago, the Chinese system of maximizing the accumulation of beneficial chi improves the quality of life and luck of the occupants of a particular building or location. The literal translation is wind and water; however, in Classical Feng Shui wind means *direction* and water means *energy*. Pronounced *foong shway.*

Feng Shui master: One who has mastered the skills of Classical Feng Shui and/or has been declared as such by his or her teacher, or both. Most Feng Shui masters from classic traditions will belong to a lineage of their teachers. This is also known as *a lineage carrier,* meaning the master carries on the teachings and practices of his or her education. A Feng Shui master generally oversees his or her own school and students, too.

Feng Shui schools: There are two major schools or branches (not physical locations, rather they are systems) of Classical Feng Shui, San He and San Yuan; hundreds of formulas, techniques, and systems serve as sub sets of either school. If you practice Classical Feng Shui, you use the

San He and the San Yuan systems as one extensive body of knowledge. See the article in the compendium for details on each school.

Flying Stars: Known as *Xuan Kong Fei Xing* in Chinese, which means *mysterious void* or the *subtle mysteries of time and space.* It is a popular Feng Shui system that is superior in addressing the time aspect of energy. Refer to Chapter Four for additional information on this vast system.

Fu Wie: The direction and location for stability as it applies to the Eight Mansions system. According to Master Yap's numeric representation, it is the +60.

Fu Xi: A sage, king and shaman who was responsible for discovering and arranging the Early Heaven Ba Gua.

Gen: One of the eight trigrams of the Ba Gua also spelled as *Ken.* It represents the youngest son, the mountain and early spring. In the Later Heaven arrangement of the Ba Gua, the Gen trigram is located in the Northeast.

grandmaster of Feng Shui: This person has been practicing and teaching for many years, belongs to a respected lineage of masters, and has at least one master among his or her pupils.

Grandmaster Yap Cheng Hai (GMY): Master Yap was born and raised in Singapore; although he did live briefly in Xiamen, China for four years. He moved to Kuala Lumpur, Malaysia in 1963 to manage his uncle's business and soon became a citizen. Although his life was full, he pursued two passions, that of Feng Shui and Martial Arts. He began practicing Feng Shui professionally in the early 60's. He has consulted with prominent figures such as members of royalty, ministers, corporations, banks, and developers. His loyal client since the sixties, Paramount Garden consulted him to plan their townships that included SEA Park, Damansara Utama and Bandar Utama. GMY is quite famous in Southeast Asia for his *Water Dragon* techniques. He learned this specialized method from Grandmaster Chan Chuan Huai in Taiwan who created several billionaires there. GMY began teaching in the late 1990's to those wishing to learn authentic, Classical Feng Shui. I graduated from his 2001 class as a Master right after 9/11.

Gua: Alternatively spelled *Kua* and also known as a trigram. It represents one of eight Guas of the Ba Gua, defined by a combination of three solid or broken lines.

Gua Number: Also referred to as *Ming Gua* (nothing to do with the Ming Dynasty). To determine your personal Life Gua number, use your birthday. See Chapter Three for specific instructions.

GYM Code: this is a code devised by Grandmaster Yap to easily identify your good and bad directions in the Eight Mansions system; the +90, +80, +70, +60 are your *good* directions representing wealth, health, relationships/longevity and stability respectively. The code of -90, -80, -70, and -60 represent your *bad* directions that if activated, will cause divorce/bankruptcy, bad health/betrayals, affairs/lawsuits and setbacks respectively.

Heaven Luck: One of the three categories of luck that humans can experience. The Chinese believe every human has a destiny and a fate determined by the heavens (tien). This category cannot be changed and is considered *fixed.* See also Tien-Di-Ren.

high-rise building: In the external environment, high-rise buildings and skyscrapers function as *virtual* or *urban mountains*.

Ho: The Chinese word for fire.

Ho Hai: Also known as *Wo Hai.* Part of the Eight Mansions system and can bring mishaps—nothing goes smoothly. According to Master Yap's numeric representation, this is the -60.

Hsia: pronounced *she-ah*; this is the name for the Chinese Solar Calendar based on the cycles of the Sun. The Solar Calendar regulates agriculture because the *Sun* determines the seasons; also used in all Feng Shui techniques for its accuracy. The solar year begins on February 4th or 5th , there are two possible dates is not because an uncertainly, but due to the fact that the Western calendar 'wobbles' because of the insertion of the extra day during 'leap years'.

Inauspicious: means very unlucky and in Feng Shui could indicate negative events.

I Ching: A philosophical and divinatory book based on the sixty-four hexagrams of Taoist mysticism. It is also known as the *Classic of Changes* or *Book of Changes*.

interior environment: The interior environment encompasses anything that falls within the walls of a structure, including kitchen, staircase, Master Bedroom + Family, fireplaces, bathrooms, hallways, dining room, bedrooms, appliances, furniture, and so on.

intercardinal directions: Northwest, Southwest, Northeast and Southeast.

Kan: One of the eight trigrams. It represents the middle son, the moon and mid-winter. In the Later Heaven Arrangement of the Ba Gua, it is located in the North.

Kun: One of the eight trigrams. It represents the mother, the earth and late summer. In the Later Heaven Arrangement of the Ba Gua, it is located in the Southwest.

Later Heaven Ba Gua: The second arrangement of the trigrams known as the *Wen Wang* or *Xien Tien* Ba Gua. This is used extensively in the application of Classical Feng Shui.

Li: One of the eight trigrams. It represents the middle daughter, fire and full summer. In the Later Heaven Arrangement of the Ba Gua, it is located in the South.

Life Gua Number: a number assigned to people, based on birthday and gender, in the Eight Mansions system (BaZhai also spelled Pa Chai).

Life-Gua Personalities™: a description of personality types based on the Life Gua number in the Eight Mansion system expanded on and trademarked by the author and first seen in *Classical Feng Shui for Wealth and Abundance.*

Life-Gua Zodiac Personalities™: this is an expanded version of the *Life Gua Personalities* which include the Zodiac animal year of birth.

Liu Sha: In the Eight Mansions system, it also known as the *Six Killings* direction and can bring backstabbing, affairs, and lawsuits. According to Master Yap's numeric representation, it is the -80.

location: A particular place or position, differing from the concept of *direction.* For example, your living room might be located on the South side of your home (location), but your desk faces North (direction).

lunar calendar: A calendar based on the cycles of the moon.

Lung: The Chinese word for dragon.

Luo Pan: The Luo Pan is the quintessential tool of a Feng Shui practitioner. It is a compass that contains four to forty concentric rings of information. The most popular model is approximately ten inches across, square, and often constructed of fine woods. The circle part of the Luo Pan is made of brass and rotates to align with the compass itself, which is located in the center. There are three major types of Luo Pans—the *San Yuan* Luo Pan, the *San He* Luo Pan, and the *Chung He* Luo Pan (also known as *Zong He* or *Zhung He*), which is a combination of the first two. Though Luo Pans have similar basic components, Feng Shui masters do customize their own with secret information for them and their students.

Luo Shu: A square that contains nine palaces or cells with a number in each; it adds to fifteen in any direction. The Luo Shu is also known as the *Magic Square of 15.*

Magic Life-Gua: some masters call your personal Gua number by many names—Magic Life-Gua, Ming Gua, or Life Gua.

main door: This is usually the front door of the home or business. If the occupants always enter the residence from the garage, this may also be considered a main door.

Man Luck: One of the three categories of luck that a human can experience. This area of fortune is mutable and defined by individual effort, such as hard work, study, education, experience, and good deeds. The Chinese word for man is *Ren.* See Tien-Di-Ren.

Ming Dynasty: A ruling dynasty of China, which lasted from 1368 to 1644.

Ming Gua: another name for Life-Gua.

Nien Yen: This is the incorrect spelling of the *Yen Nien* (+70) in the Eight Mansions system; you will see this mistake in many Feng Shui books.

Pa Chai: the Eight Mansions system, also spelled BaZhai.

road: A route, path, or open way for vehicles. In Feng Shui, roads are *rivers* of energy, or chi and play a huge part in analyzing a site because energy is powerful. These virtual, or urban, rivers are calculated when assessing, designing, enhancing, or implementing counter measures or enhancements for a site.

San He: Also known as *San Hup*. One of the two major schools of study in Classical Feng Shui—the other is San Yuan. The San He system, excellent for tapping natural landforms, primarily addresses large-scale projects, land plots, urban developments, city planning, and master-planned communities. The system is extensive and has several practical techniques for new and existing residential spaces as well. When assessing and altering a site or a structure, San He and San Yuan can be blended for maximum results.

San Yuan: One of the two major schools of Classical Feng Shui. The Flying Stars is part of this system; it excels in techniques of timing. See the *Schools of Feng Shui* in the compendium for more details.

sector: An area inside or outside a building: South sector, North sector, and so on.

sha chi: Also known as *shar chi*. Extremely negative energy, or killing chi.

Shan: The Chinese word for *mountain*.

Sheng Chi: Part of the Eight Mansions system. It can bring life-generating energy, wealth, and opportunities. Using Master Yap's numeric representation, this is the +90.

Shui: The Chinese word for *water;* pronounced *shway*.

sitting: In Feng Shui it refers to the back of the house, as if the structure is sitting in a chair on the land or property. It is the heavy part of the house; also consider a mountain.

Sitting Star: Also known as the Mountain Star in the Flying Star system. It influences people luck, such as fertility, employees, and health.

solar calendar: A calendar based on the movements of the sun.

Southeast Asia: Countries South of China and East of India, including Thailand, Vietnam, Cambodia, Laos, Myanmar, the Philippines, and Singapore.

Tao: also known as *The Way*, and is core of Taoism (pronounced with a D sound).

tapping the energy or chi: A technique that invites the available energy from the external environment to support the occupants of a structure.

Tien Yi: Part of the Eight Mansion system. It can bring excellent health and wealth. In Chinese it means *heavenly doctor* or *the doctor from heaven watches over you*. Using Master Yap's numeric representation, it is the +80.

tilting a door: A time-honored tradition used by Feng Shui masters and practitioners to change the degree of a door and the energy of a space. The doorframe and threshold are re-angled toward the desired degree. When the door is re-hung, it is tilted on a different degree.

T-juncture: When two roads meet perpendicularly to create a *T*. The formation is toxic when a home or business sits at the top and center of that *T*.

Traditional Feng Shui: Another term for Classical Chinese Feng Shui.

Tui: Also spelled *Dui*. One of the eight trigrams that represents the youngest daughter, the lake, and mid-fall. In the Later Heaven Ba Gua it is located in the West.

Twelve Animals: Rat, Ox, Tiger, Rabbit, Dragon, Snake, Horse, Goat, Monkey, Rooster, Dog and Pig; part of the Chinese Zodiac and used extensively in Classical Feng Shui and Chinese Astrology.

water: In Feng Shui, water is the secret to enhancing wealth, prosperity, longevity, nobility, and relationships. The Chinese word is *Shui,* and it represents energy and life force. Water, according to Feng Shui, is the most powerful element on the planet.

West Life Group: In the Eight Mansions system, people are divided into the East or West group. The 2, 6, 7, and 8 Life Guas are part of the West Life Group.

Western Feng Shui: In addition to the Black Hat Sect, other schools cropped up that incorporated the principles, but not the rituals, associated with Lin-Yun's followers. As the masters of Classical Feng Shui started to teach around the world, some of the most well-acclaimed instructors and authors of Western Feng Shui began to learn Classical Feng Shui. Unwilling to give up the Western-style Feng Shui that made them famous, they mixed the old with the new, thereby adding to the confusion over authentic Feng Shui. More than half of the Feng Shui books written about the subject include a hodgepodge of both theories.

Wu Gwei: Part of the Eight Mansions system that can attract lawsuits, bad romance, and betrayals. Using Master Yap's numeric representation, it is the -70. This is also known as the *Five Ghosts* direction.

Wu Xing: Also known as the five elements of Feng Shui: wood, fire, earth, metal, and water.

Yang: Alive, active and moving energy; considered the male energy of the Yin-Yang symbol.

Yang Feng Shui: Feng Shui was first practiced for the selection of a perfect gravesite, or what is commonly known by the Chinese as Yin Feng Shui—Feng Shui for the dead. Later, techniques were developed to increase luck and opportunities for houses of the living.

Yen Nien: Part of the Eight Mansions system that can bring longevity, good relationships, and love. Using Master Yap's numeric representation, it is the +70. It is a common mistake to spell this term as Nen Yien.

Yin: Female energy, passive, and dead; the perfect complement is yang energy.

Xing Fa: An approach to assessing form and shape in the environment.

Xun: One of the eight trigrams of the Ba Gua, also spelled as *Sun*. It represents the eldest daughter, the wind and early summer. In the Later Heaven arrangement of the Ba Gua, the Xun trigram is located in the Southeast.

Worldwide Classical Feng Shui Schools and Consultants

The following is a list of Classical Feng Shui teachers around the world who, in addition to Feng Shui training, also offer consulting services, books, and other products. Most non-Asian Masters will generate a written/electronic report as well; this is not the custom in Southeast Asia.

There are a number of excellent Feng Shui masters around the world that offer classes on one or more of the Five Chinese Metaphysical Arts. You can receive training on Classical Feng Shui (*San He* and *San Yuan),* Face Reading (*Mian Xiang*), Chinese Astrology (*BaZi* also known as *Four Pillars of Destiny* and *Zi Wei Dou Shu*), Xuan Kong Da Gua Date Selection, Qi Men Dun Jia, and Oriental medicine (acupuncture, herbology).

Matriculating from a respected lineage is desirable, but this alone should not determine the master you choose to study with. Select one with whom you resonate. I do not personally know every teacher/consultant I have listed, and you will need to do your own due diligence in selecting a qualified professional teacher or consultant. The list is by no means exhaustive, and I have not listed anyone who mixes Classical Feng Shui with Western. Needless to say, I have not listed anyone practicing Western styles or Tibetan Black Hat Tantric Feng Shui (TBHT) at all.

The American College of Classical Feng Shui (ACCFS)
Dragon Gate Feng Shui International Consultants
Master Denise Liotta Dennis
Houston, Texas USA
Phone: 713-897-1719
Email: denise@dragongatefengshui.com
Website: www.dragongatefengshui.com

Offers consulting services, books, free seminars, and training classes. There are several ways to learn more about Feng Shui. The following programs are suitable for real estate agents, architects, Feng Shui enthusiasts, interior designers, self-taught Feng Shui practitioners, builders and Feng Shui professionals seeking to deepen their knowledge, and those aspiring to a career in Feng Shui.

3-Day Intensive: Professional Certification
In this course you will learn sophisticated techniques to accurately analyze a home or business that will prepare you to be a sought-after consultant. You will learn how to simultaneously use Eight Mansions and Flying Stars, the two most important systems for interiors. Our classes are amazing, exciting and very effective, in just three days you'll know how to apply your new or years of knowledge to create impressive results.

3-Day Intensive: Master Certification
The demand for skilled consultants who can produce results has far outstripped the supply. Here you will learn the most advanced techniques of Classical Feng Shui. Experienced practitioners are often hired for large projects for the development of master-planned communities, office buildings, shopping centers, hotels, and casinos.

Private Mentoring: FENG SHUI MASTER Program
This is the traditional method of learning Feng Shui mastery and not for everyone. It is a 1-year program (36 Modules) taught twice a month via Skype; Saturday or Sunday is an option if needed. The mentoring program is taught monthly and provides the most personalized, comprehensive program we offer. Contact Denise Liotta-Dennis at denise@dragongatefengshui.com or call 713-897-1719.

Coming Fall of 2020
Master the Art of Feng Shui ONLINE Series
Feng Shui That Rocks the House: The Eight Mansions System 14 Modules)
Flying Stars for Modern Spaces (14 Modules)
Dynamic Duo: Flying Stars + Eight Mansions (6 Modules)

Certifications are offered for all the above classes through *The American College of Classical Feng Shui (ACCFS).*

Yap Cheng Hai Academy Sdn. Bhd.
(This school was formerly ***Yap Cheng Hai Feng Shui Center for Excellence***, started by Grandmaster Yap Cheng Hai now ran by his youngest son)
Master Yap Boh Chu
Suite 11-01, 11th Floor
Wisma Hangsam
1 Jalan Hang Lekir
50000 Kuala Lumpur, Malaysia
Phone: +603 2070 8009
e-mail: info@ychacademy.com
Website: www.ychacademy.com
Offers products, consulting and training on Classical Feng Shui, primarily in Kuala Lumpur.

Lillian Too's World of Feng Shui
Lillian Too, Feng Shui Master
Kuala Lumpur, Malaysia
Phone: 603-2080 3488
e-mail: courses@wofs.com
Website: www.lillian-too.com
Offers books, magazines, products, Luo Pans, and live classes on Classical Feng Shui in Kuala Lumpur

Feng Shui Research Center
Grandmaster Joseph Yu
26 Betty Roman Blvd.
Markham, Ontario L6C 0A4
Canada
Phone: 905-604-0998
Phone: 416-721-7094
e-mail: josephyu@astro-fengshui.com
Website: www.astro-fengshui.com

Offers books, Luo Pans, live classes worldwide and correspondence courses on Chinese Astrology and Classical Feng Shui

The America Feng Shui Institute
Grandmaster Larry Sang
111 N. Atlantic Blvd., Ste. 352
Monterey Park, CA 91754
Phone: 626-571-2757
e-mail: fsinfo@amfengshui.com
Website: www.amfengshui.com
Offers books, Luo Pans, live classes in California, and online courses on Classical Feng Shui, Chinese Astrology, and Face Reading

Mastery Academy of Chinese Metaphysics Sdn. Bhd.
Master Joey Yap
19-3, The Boulevard, Mid Valley City
59200 Kuala Lumpur, Malaysia
Phone: +603-2284-8080
e-mail: enquiry@masteryacademy.com
Website: www.masteryacademy.com
Offers books, all traditional style Luo Pans, videos, live classes worldwide, and online training on Classical Feng Shui, Chinese Astrology, and Face Reading.

Raymond Lo Feng Shui Research
Grandmaster Raymond Lo
Rm. 1233A, Star House
Tsimshatsui, Kowloon, Hong Kong
Phone: + (852) 2736 9568
Phone: + (852) 9024 9438
e-mail: raymond@fengshui-lo.com
Website: www.raymond-lo.com
Offers books, Luo Pans, and live classes worldwide on Classical Feng Shui and Chinese Astrology

Feng Shui Dragon Enterprises
Master Gayle Atherton
PO Box 886
Double Bay, NSW 1360
2028, Australia
Phone: 02 9362 8089
e-mail: inquiries@fengshui.com
Website: www.fengshui.com.au
Offers consulting services, Chinese Astrology, books, free mini-seminars on her website and a Feng Shui Kit

The Imperial School of Feng Shui and Chinese Horoscopes
Grandmaster Chan Kun Wah
59 Pettycur Road
Kinghorn, Fife, KY3 9RN, Scotland
Phone: + 44 (0) 159 289 1682
e-mail: pam@masterkwchan.com
Website: www.masterkwchan.com
Offers correspondence and live training worldwide on Classical Feng Shui and Chinese Astrology

The International School of Feng Shui
Master Ken Lai
PO Box 2124
Maple Grove, MN 55311
Phone: 763-218-1484
e-mail: kenlai93@yahoo
Website: www.kenlaifengshui.com
Offers live training courses world-wide on Classical Feng Shui and Chinese Astrology

Feng Shui masters who teach through books but may also consult with clients are: **Grandmaster Dr. Stephen Skinner** (www.sskinner.com); **Master Val Biktashev,** and **Master Elizabeth Moran** (www.aafengshui.com).

Healing Qi
David Twicken, Feng Shui Master
e-mail: david@healingqi.com
Website: www.healingqi.com
Offers books, e-books, correspondence and live courses internationally on Classical Feng Shui, Qi Gong, Oriental Medicine, and Chinese Astrology

Singapore Feng Shui Centre
Master Vincent Koh
10 Ubi Crescent #04-66 Ubi Techpark
Singapore 408564
Phone: (65) 6747 8226
e-mail: singfc@fengshui.com.sg
Website: www.fengshui.com.sg
Offers books, software, and live training courses on Feng Shui and Chinese Astrology

Pak Hok Ming Metaphysic Institute
Master Pak Hok Ming
8/F, Bangkok Bank Building
490-492 Nathan Road, Kowloon, Hong Kong
Phone: (852) 2388 6878
e-mail: fengshui@hongkong.com
Website: www.hokming.com

Offers books, products, compass/Luo Pan tools, and courses on Feng Shui and Chinese Astrology.

Feng Shui College
Howard Choy, AIA, Feng Shui Master
Sydney, Australia
Phone: 49 30 2838 5855
e-mail: info@fengshuicollege.ac
Website: www.arqitektur.com
Offers books and training course internationally on Classical Feng Shui.

The School of Chinese Metaphysics (SCM)
Master Peter Leung
102 Allanford Road
Toronto, ON M1T 2N5
Phone: (416) 288-9238
e-mail: info@fengshuisos.com
Website: www.fengshuisos.com
SCM offers books, software, live training courses on Classical Feng Shui.

Central Academy Of Feng Shui (CAFS)
Master Francis Leyau
169-1, Jalan Sarjana, Taman Connaught,
Cheras, 56000
Kuala Lumpur, Malaysia
Phone: 60 3-91320199
e-mail: enquiry@fengshuimastery.com
Website: www.fengshuimastery.com
CAFS offers books, products, and live training courses on Feng Shui and Chinese Astrology.

Thomas Coxon Associates
Thomas Coxon, Feng Shui Master
20 Lutterworth Road, Aylestone
Leicester, England LE2 8PE
Phone: 44 116 2836777
e-mail: fengshui@webleicester.co.uk
Website: www.fengshui-consultants.co.uk
Offers live training classes, consulting services, and seminars.

Feng Shui 100
Master Mas Kehardthum
31st Floor of the State Tower, Silom Road
Bangkok, Thailand
Phone: 668-1431-4011
email: info@fengshui100.com
Website: www.fengshui100.com

Offers live Feng Shui training classes in Thailand, correspondence courses, books, and software.

Feng Shui That Works
Alan Stirling, Feng Shui Master
16 Ash Road, ME2 2JL UK
Phone: 44 (0)203 0114938
e-mail: alan888@btinternet.com
Website: www.fengshuithatworks.co.uk
Offers live and correspondence courses on Feng Shui, 9 Star Ki (Japanese Astrology), Dowsing, and Chinese Astrology

These Feng Shui Masters also offer consulting services: Jennifer Bonetto, Newport Beach, California; Katherine McClerkin, Little Rock, Arkansas; Nathalie Ekobo, Barbara Harwell, Kristy Coup, Marianne Kulekowskis, Peggy Lanese, Kristie Yeckel, and Jillian Rothschild-Scholar, of Phoenix, Arizona; Peg Burton, Chicago, Illinois; Sudarika Mitchell of Texas; (*all master graduates of ACCFS*); Jennifer Bartle-Smith, Australia; Maria Santilario, Spain; Bridgette O'Sullivan, Ireland; Cynthia Murray, Colorado; Jayne Goodrick; England; Di Grobler and Christine McNair, South Africa; Nathalie Mourier and Helen Weber, France; and Birgit Fischer, Petra Coll-Exposito, Nicole Zoremba, and Eva-Maria Spöetta, Germany.

Author's Bio

Denise A. Liotta-Dennis,
Feng Shui Master, Speaker, Teacher, International Author

She's known as the "fast-talkin' Texan"—an interesting and delightful oxymoron—Denise A. Liotta-Dennis is the founder and president of Dragon-Gate Feng Shui (DGFS), LLC an international consulting and development firm, specializing in authentic Feng Shui site selection, planning, design, audits, and assessments for commercial and residential real estate and construction projects. In 2006, Denise founded The American College of Classical Feng Shui, the training arm of Dragon-Gate, a premier platform to learn Classical Feng Shui.

Born to a Houston entrepreneurial family, Denise, who possesses a quarter century of business ownership experience, is among a rare breed of Feng Shui consultants. Denise not only resonates with all things spiritual, she talks the language and walks in the shoes of business people. Growing up in the shadow of her father's construction and real estate development companies, Denise discovered early in life an innate love of business lifestyles and entrepreneurship. Her work with Feng Shui is also an outgrowth of a natural affinity for interior design. In fact, Denise has more than twenty-five years experience working in interior design, including residential and commercial projects.

With a rapid-fire delivery that keeps audiences spellbound, wide-eyed, and on the edge of their seats, Denise—a gifted educator and speaker on Feng Shui and business topics—offers high-energy, content-rich presentations. Peppering her talks with a quaint Southwestern humor, Denise's stories are couched in the real-life foibles of entrepreneurs and those seeking a spiritual path. She shares the spiritual side of life with a practical commercial bent not found among the more esoteric practitioners common to Feng Shui.

Classical Feng Shui for Health, Beauty & Longevity
is now translated into Czech and Estonian!

Denise has studied with four noted Feng Shui Masters from China, Malaysia and Australia, including Grand Master Yap Cheng Hai and belongs to his 400- year Wu Chang Feng Shui Mastery lineage.

Ms Liotta-Dennis' first book was released in major national and international bookstores March 8, 2013 entitled *Classical Feng Shui for Wealth and Abundance,* her second book was released January 8, 2015 entitled *Feng Shui for Romance, Sex & Relationships,* and her third book will be released in the fall of 2016 entitled *Classical Feng Shui for Health, Beauty & Longevity* (endorsed by Grandmaster Dr. Stephen Skinner). This book has been translated into the native languages of Czechoslovakia and Estonia. She has a total of nine Feng Shui books in print.

Denise's books are sold in fine book stores in the United States, Canada, the United Kingdom, Australia, New Zealand, and Singapore. They are offered online at Walmart, Target, Barnes & Noble, Amazon, and are housed in several American libraries. International online-booksellers in Sweden, Germany, France, Poland, Japan, Italy and Denmark sell her books in English.

Classical Feng Shui for Wealth & Abundance
ISBN 978-0-7387-3353-1
$17.99

Unlock the full wealth potential of your home or office using the potent formulas and wisdom of Classical Feng Shui. Written by a Feng Shui master, *Classical Feng Shui for Wealth & Abundance* reveals authentic techniques for success with money, business, and career. In this book, beginners and advanced students will learn:

- The two most popular Feng Shui systems: Eight Mansions and Flying Stars
- Easy-to-use Get Rich Keys and your personal Life Gua number for money luck
- Wealth building formulas such as Five Ghosts Carry Treasure, Dragon Gate, and Water Dragons
- How to identify and eliminate killing chi like Eight Roads of Destruction, Robbery Mountain Sha, and Eight Killing Forces

Whether you're buying a house, creating a home, or managing a business, these ancient and powerful techniques are exactly what you need to capture prosperity and success.

Purchase this book at Barnes&Noble.com, Amazon.com and Llewellyn.com. It is also available at Barnes & Noble brick and mortar locations.

Classical Feng Shui for Romance, Sex & Relationships
ISBN 978-0-7387-4188-8
$19.99

Harness the ancient power and wisdom of Classical Feng Shui to enhance all of your relationships, from romantic pursuits to day-to-day interactions with friends, family, and coworkers. Explore real-life stories of men and women's struggles with love and relationships and how Feng Shui enabled them to overcome their obstacles. Whether you are a beginner or advanced student, Master Denise Liotta Dennis provides you with step-by-step instructions on:

- The two most popular Feng Shui systems: Eight Mansions and Flying Stars
- How to heal your house of detrimental formations that will repel romance and cause negative relationships
- Never-before-seen insights on the Life-Gua Zodiac, which helps you assess personality matches
- Other closely held secrets used by Feng Shui masters, including a variety of period charts

Classical Feng Shui for Romance, Sex & Relationships is filled with effective methods for attracting love, prosperity, and even your soul mate. Use this comprehensive guide to improve not just the energy of your living space today, but also your happiness for many years to come.

Purchase this book at Barnes&Noble.com, Amazon.com and Llewellyn.com. It is also available at Barnes & Noble brick and mortar locations.

Classical Feng Shui for Health, Beauty & Longevity
ISBN 978-0-7387-4900-6
$21.99

Improve your wellness, extend your longevity, and secure a healthy environment with the ancient power and wisdom of Classical Feng Shui. This comprehensive guide reveals ancient and modern techniques for lasting health and beauty that both beginners and advanced students can use. Providing step-by-step instruction, Feng Shui Master Denise Liotta Dennis teaches you:

- The two most popular Classical Feng Shui systems: Flying Stars and Eight Mansions
- Feng Shui's Taoist roots and a variety of health modalities from ancient and modern times
- Profound secrets of the "Heavenly Doctor" position and its importance in enhancing health
- Ways to protect your body and mind from detrimental formations, devices, and environments

With well-researched information, period charts, astoundingly accurate health predictions, and much more, *Classical Feng Shui for Health, Beauty & Longevity* will help you be happier and healthier. P*raise:* "Denise Liotta Dennis has done a great job of clearly expressing [the application of feng shui to health], going into great detail."—Grand Master Dr. Stephen Skinner

Purchase this book at Barnes&Noble.com, Amazon.com and Llewellyn.com. It is also available at Barnes & Noble brick and mortar locations.

The Secrets to Mastering Flying Stars Feng Shui
ISBN-13: 978-1985760127
$38.95

Flying Stars is the most popular, intriguing and misunderstood Feng Shui system in the world. Whether you're a practitioner or a novice, you'll be able to master and deepen your understanding of a method used for 'superior living'. This book delivers a detailed explanation of how *time* and *space* will affect all categories of Feng Shui—prosperity, relationships and health.

A fully illustrated, comprehensive and systematic home-study course that is designed for anyone who wants to put Flying Stars Feng Shui to personal, professional or practical use. With over 20 years experience, Master Liotta Dennis reveals the best tricks-of-the-trade. Step by step you are guided to shake up the energy and make-over your home or office while simultaneously learning the profound secrets of Flying Stars.

Purchase this book on amazon.com and BarnesandNoble.com

Hollywood's Fatal Feng Shui
By **Master Denise Liotta Dennis & Master Jennifer Bonetto**
ISBN-13:978-1986981965
$29.95

This is the first book to do a critical assessment of the tragic homes of Marilyn Monroe, Michael Jackson, O.J. Simpson, Nicole Brown Simpson, Phil Hartman, Anna Nicole Smith, Sharon Tate, Phil Spector, Lyle and Erik Menendez, and Brittany Murphy using Feng Shui. These famous Hollywood stories still haunt us today. These celebrities' homes attracted illicit affairs, drug abuse, lawsuits, murder, sexual scandals, greed, bankruptcy, cult-driven murders, loss of reputation, and fatal illness.

Feng Shui can explain why the energy of these gorgeous properties created the perfect storm and turned their lives upside down! The book took over a year of digging through public records locating accurate floor plans and land surveys. Along with other research, this allowed for a comprehensive assessment of each property.

Classical Feng Shui systems, formulas and methods are explained so the reader may appreciate how it *all* went so wrong. You'll learn about disastrous formations such as the **Peach Blossom Sha** (illicit affairs, fatal attractions), **Eight Roads of Destruction/Hell** (bankruptcy, divorce), **Eight Mountain Killing Forces** (murder and crimes of passion), **Robbery Mountain Sha** (being hurt by knives), deadly **Flying Star** combinations and much, much more.

Purchase this book on amazon.com and BarnesandNoble.com

How to Start and Grow a Feng Shui Business
By Master Denise Liotta Dennis
ISBN 13: 978-1726468718
$19.95

How to Start and Grow a Feng Shui Business is for Classical Feng Shui practitioners and professionals who desire to begin their studies, near completing or have completed. The first book of its type to guide you in every aspect of creating a successful consulting business. Some topics discussed:

- How to conduct an assessment step-by-step
- Generating a professional report and delivering results
- Classical Feng Shui cures and enhancements
- Fees, checklist, charts, and more
- How to generate a constant flow of clients
- Lecturing to realtors, interior designers and other groups
- Sample Feng Shui reports
- Creating a brand and marketing materials
- Going public—TV, Radio Talk Shows, Vloging and YouTube videos
- Writing books and blogging
- Organizing a professional consulting book
- Adjunct services you could offer—home staging, BaZi, date selection, interior design, real estate, architecture, or remodeling
- 100+ photos of Denise's studies with Grandmaster Yap in Germany, Malaysia, South Africa and Sedona

Purchase this book at Amazon.com

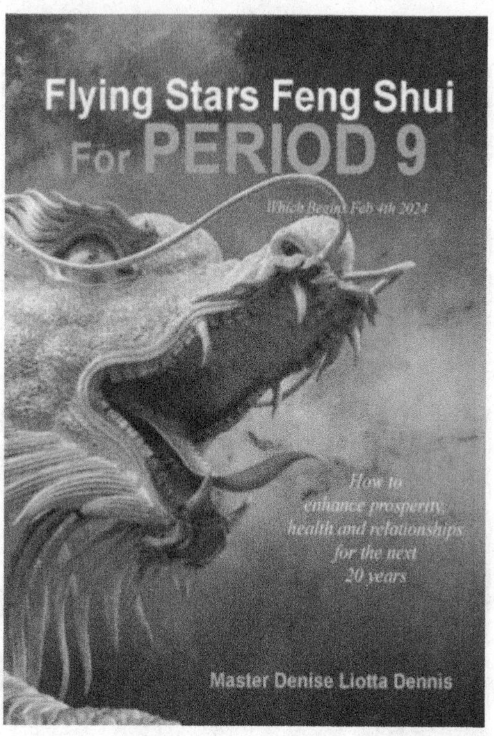

Flying Stars Feng Shui for Period 9
By **Master Denise Liotta Dennis**
ISBN-9781983872242
$29.99

Period 9, the *Age of Fire,* will begin on Feb 4, 2024. This is a capital change for all structures worldwide. It will be a time of great intellectual leaps, accomplishments, technology, and a future filled with bright prosperity! It is an 'age' for women.

Flying Stars Feng Shui for Period 9 reveals all you need to know in order to prepare for this incredible and auspicious time. Flying Stars is a potent method of Feng Shui that addresses the time transformation of chi. This changing flow of energy is expressed as numbers in a Flying Star Chart. Worldwide, this capital change happens every 20 years. Therefore, slight adjustments to your home or office need to take place. This exciting, subtle, and important aspect of Feng Shui is the focus of the book.

Flying Stars is the most popular Classical Feng Shui system used by practitioners today. This is because it has a potent effect on properties where it is used. Feb 4, 2024 marks the date when Period 8 ends and Period 9 begins. This book will explain the significant implications of a Period change.

Purchase this book at Amazon.com

The Real Estate Feng Shui Series

Feng Shui for High-Rise Living (release date Jan 2021)
Feng Shui for Commerical Real Estate (release date Jan 2021)

Feng Shui Handbook for Real Estate Agents
By **Master Denise Liotta Dennis and Master Barbara Harwell**
ISBN: 9781704068367
$19.99

Finally, a Feng Shui book that a REALTOR® can use! *Feng Shui Handbook for Real Estate Agents* reveals practical solutions for selling a property quickly. Moreover, it explains the difference between Western and Classical Feng Shui. Today it's more important than ever to be informed about how Feng Shui works, and why builders and developers are incorporating it into their projects. While there are savvy Asian buyers investing in America and other countries, non-Asian buyers also use the Ancient Chinese principles of Feng Shui.

After reading this book, you will understand how to identify good homes, recognize why some homes sit on the market, how to cure issues and how to help your buyers and sellers in meaningful ways. You will learn how to use lucky numbers to price homes to sell faster and successfully negotiate counter offers. As a real estate agent you may have read several books and taken CE classes and are still confused as what Feng Shui is and how to apply it—until now.

Agents who want to use 'out of the box' thinking to sell properties will find this book a must-read. It has been written by two Feng Shui masters, including one who is a licensed agent. More scientific and sophisticated Feng Shui methods will be revealed to you. It will become your secret weapon and go-to handbook for exceptional service to your clients!

Purchase this book at Amazon.com

Made in the USA
Las Vegas, NV
21 August 2023